HOUDINI'S FINAL INCREDIBLE SECRET

HOUDINI'S FINAL INCREDIBLE SECRET

How Houdini Mystified Sherlock Holmes' Creator

by

Bob Loomis

Magic Circle Librarian
Editor of The Magical Spectator
Author of The Quest For The Ultimate Secret
One of only three Honorary Associates of the Inner Magic Circle
Order of Merlin Excalibur of International Brotherhood of Magicians

Attempting to discover the origin of a particular trick has always
been an interesting way for magicians to get out of the dirty job
of trying to get more bookings.
- John Mulholland, Jinx No. 108

Cover Design by Matthew Loomis

PROLOGUE

By psychologist, best-selling author, magician, and noted television and YouTube personality Professor Richard Wiseman.

In the 1930s a good friend of Harry Houdini described how he had once seen the legendary magician perform an amazing trick for Arthur Conan Doyle. The trick took place at Houdini's house in New York, and involved a slate, a small white ball and a saucer of white paint. Over the years magicians across the world have proposed a range of elaborate hypotheses in an attempt to explain the mystery of Houdini's mind-blowing trick. Bob Loomis has dug deeper than any other investigator. He has searched for hidden documents in private libraries, uncovered clues in Houdini's copious correspondence, and attempted to understand the mind of one of the world's greatest magicians. Piece by piece, Bob has slowly constructed the most detailed and plausible solution to date.

But this book is not just about the secret of a great trick. It is also about the very fabric of magic itself, including the complex relationships between each generation of performers, the way in which tricks evolve over time, and ultimately, the surprising truth about the fundamental nature of mystery. Throughout it all Bob acts as the perfect guide. Knowledgeable, quirky and thorough, he documents his thinking at each point in his journey, presents every twist and turn in fascinating detail, and describes both his lucky finds and dead ends with enthusiasm and energy.

Take your seat because the show is about to start. The house lights are fading to black and the band begins to play. Ladies and gentlemen, please welcome to the stage a brilliant historian, stunning raconteur, and all-round good egg - the remarkable Mr. Bob Loomis.

1

THE LEGEND

Houdini "The Escape King" is mentioned somewhere in the world every minute. His legend continues to grow. It's the classic tale of the poor immigrant child who became an entertainment superstar. Harry Houdini has been venerated in every art medium from painting to film. He is a magic icon. Many of today's magicians are so captivated by him they live and breathe "Handcuff Harry" in a lifelong devotion of hero worship. [No, your author is not one of those Houdini nuts. Okay, I admit it, but only a wee bit!]

The problem is that Houdini's legend is full of exaggerations. Many people are convinced his extraordinary secrets died with him. Others are certain his methods are locked away until a specific date when they will be revealed to an eagerly awaiting world. Those notions make excellent copy for would-be escapologist's press kits; but, as most novice magicians can tell you, there are no unsolved Houdini mysteries. Knowledgeable conjurers know Houdini took revenge on his copyists by publishing his escape secrets when he moved to other magic areas.

Magic historians say there is no myth of 'the big secret' because Houdini's wife and brother ignored his instructions to destroy his notes and equipment when he died. Houdini experts confirm it. There are no unsolved Houdini mysteries…. There is just one small catch with that last sentence. IT'S WRONG! There is still one major Houdini mystery that the best minds in magic have not adequately explained. You are about to discover what that unsolved enigma is, and the amazing secret behind it.

It involves the creator of the great fictional detective Sherlock Holmes. Houdini showed his friend Sir Arthur Conan Doyle something that made him insist Harry had used supernatural assistance to accomplish it. What was the baffling performance, and did Houdini actually use occult powers? You are about to learn the incredible answer to Houdini's last great riddle.

Chapter 1: INTRODUCTION

"Magic is a childhood disease for which there appears to be no cure as you grow up"
- Alan Shaxon.

"CHILD: Mommy I want to be a magician when I grow up.
MOTHER: Sorry dear you can't do both!"
-Jay Marshall.

THE MAGIC BUG

Houdini, the legendary escapologist and mystery man, performed a unique piece of magic for Sherlock Holmes' creator that completely baffled him. Now, for the first time, I'm going to reveal precisely how Houdini fooled Sir Arthur Conan Doyle. BUT, if before I had begun my investigation I had known how much work, effort, stress, and lack of sleep it would involve, you wouldn't be reading this book. Okay, okay, I admit it! I love a good quest, and enjoyed every minute of it. So, join me as I describe my magical exploration, and along the way you will learn some of the surprising psychology behind magicians' illusions, as well as discover the fascinating history of mystery.

But, before we commence, just a few words from our sponsor.....only kidding. First let me tell you how I got involved in this mystery, AND, more importantly, get you up to speed on the world of magic....

I can still remember the first time I heard about Juan Ponce de Leon. More than 60 years ago, our history teacher explained that he was the Spaniard who opened up Florida in 1513. He had braved the inhospitable swamps because the Indians told him the fountain of youth was located there. I clearly remember thinking he must have been the biggest fool of all time. As I approached the age of 50 I began to understand exactly how he had felt, as well as what he was looking for. No, I wasn't going to find a fountain of rejuvenation, but perhaps if I rediscovered some of the things I had lost along the way, I could recapture a small piece of my youth.

My main obsession as a lad had been magic. I had spent many hours practicing complicated sleight of hand. I'd even performed at kids' parties to help earn my way through university. As I neared my half-century, in 1990, the quest for my lost youth, reactivated the magic malady, which had been fairly dormant for several years. Now, it returned stronger than ever. This time around I was much older and slightly wiser. Instead of wasting precious hours manipulating the mandatory magical items - playing cards and coins - I did the manipulations with what was left of my mind.

I analysed the interaction between the magician and the spectator [willing victim], and eventually concluded that magic was probably the only performing art that could not be accomplished without an audience of at least one. I reasoned that a magician was incapable of fooling himself. He knew the secret and could not forget it. For the magic to happen the wonder-worker needed an observer. A magician without a spectator was just 'practicing', not 'practising', magic.

Based on that insight I set up the Association of International Magical Spectators (AIMS). Initially it was more of a prank than a serious organisation, but with the help of several well-known, generous, and very kind conjurors, as well as magic collectors and magic magazine editors, I was able to firmly establish it in the secretive world of conjuring. In addition to assuming the President's post of the society, I became the editor and publisher of its journal, The World's Greatest [and only] Magical Spectators' Newsletter, 'The Magical Spectator'. The newsletter's aim was to advance Professional Magical Spectating in a hopefully humorous manner. As well as a very small, select band of non-performers, several magicians who had attained the peak of their profession joined us as members. After all, when you reach the top in your magic career, where else can you go but cross over and become a "born again" spectator?

If you are not yet ready for a lesson in magic theory this early in the book, skip the next three paragraphs....Still here? Right, how do Professional Spectators differ from other spectators? Applauding a performance to show appreciation is a learned reaction. We seldom clap or boo when sitting alone in front of a television. When responding to an entertainment in the company of others, we tend to follow the actions of those around us. In the past, this reaction was exploited by the unscrupulous use of the claque, or paid audience. Traditional audience reactions are often suspended when watching a magicians' act. Although the observers enjoy themselves, they frequently are so baffled, or amazed, they forget to applaud. Then neither the person hiring the magician, nor the wonder-worker himself, knows if the act has accomplished its paid objective. This is where the Professional Magical Spectator comes to the rescue. As well as audibly gasping at all the appropriate points, he or she initiates the applause in the traditional manner. So, having a Professional Magical Spectator in the audience is a tremendous asset to any working magician.

It is even more essential to have a Professional Spectator in an audience of mainly fellow magicians. When magicians watch other magi perform, they also don't react in the normal manner. They are usually too busy speculating on how the trick was done, thinking they could do better, or appreciating the technical skill involved. Additionally, magicians' reactions often occur at points that a normal person would not understand, such as applauding a hidden move, or laughing if something goes wrong. Once again, a Professional Spectator comes to the rescue of the performing magus by providing all the right reactions.

Are there advantages to being a Professional Spectator? Yes. The spectator is the customer, and as such is always right. If he/she has not enjoyed him/herself the magician has failed. Even if the spectator has had a diabolical day and is in an extremely nasty mood, the magician must make him/her forget all about it and enjoy him/herself. Magicians do not believe in magic. Magical spectators do! The magician is a benevolent con man specializing in deception by means of gimmicks, ruses, stratagems and fakes. The magical spectator is a completely normal person who can temporarily leave his real world problems behind to wonder at the amazing sights that appear before his very eyes. A magician has to tell lies - the bigger the liar the better the magician. Spectators have the option of telling the truth. Being a Professional Spectator is a winning situation with no downside, other than the addiction caused by the dreaded magic bug's virus. Okay, your first lesson is over.

Whether the world was ready for it or not, by 1995 the time had come to further advance the cause of Professional Magical Spectating. The decision to take the next step came from reading that the place to be magically was in cyberspace, on a new playground called the Internet. What better way to promote the cause of magical spectating than being at the cutting edge of the magic kingdom, surfing the new information superhighway known as The Web.

Connecting to "the net" today is relatively painless - not so back in 1995. It was the era of "steam-driven" modems and "clock-work" computers. Okay, okay, it wasn't quite that bad, but you needed several programs to get onto the Internet. Those items of software were all available, but there was a catch 22. You had to get onto the Internet to download them. The main program you required was called a browser. The speeds available then were extremely slow. It took over an hour and a half for your computer, and your external modem, to download the browser from the Internet. At about the hour and twenty minute point you were forced to leave the room because the worry of the computer crashing, yet again, became too much to handle. I won't go on about it, but when the "old-timers" tell you how hard it was, believe most of what they say.

After what seemed like months of shouting at the computer and pounding my fist on the desk [in lieu of bouncing the computer off the wall], I graduated from the "Newbie" stage. I managed to create a World Wide Web presence complete with my own magical spectating home page and a registered domain name to show I had really arrived. Although the computer bug took over for a short time, the magic virus proved to be made of stronger stuff. Many magicians, once they have a business card printed, proclaim themselves to be the World's Greatest Conjuror. Following this precedent, on the Internet, I declared myself the undisputed World's Greatest Magical Spectator - Professional Category. I became the champion of those poor demented victims of the magic bug who were not necessarily driven to perform magic. Fortunately, no one was daft enough to challenge me for the title.

Many happy hours passed as I surfed the magic related Web sites, posting replies to messages appearing in magic 'usenet' newsgroups and bulletin boards. Typical of the many knowledgeable conjurors I humorously crossed swords [wands?] with in cyberspace was magic historian Gary Brown. Gary's greatest desire was to start an Internet Newsgroup devoted to his first love, magical history. After many struggles with bureaucratic red tape, he finally created the alt.magic.history newsgroup. The perversity of information superhighway access providers led to me, in the U.K., posting the first messages to the group, while Gary, in the U.S.A., could not see his own creation. Initially I relayed the happenings on Gary's own newsgroup to him via e-mail! In the wee small hours of the morning, I enjoying jousting with magicians in magical virtual reality, or I did until I received Michael Edward's e-mail.

THE CONTEST

Michael Edwards, another Internet magic historian, in a moment of magical madness, came up with an idea for a magic contest in cyberspace. Instead of lying down quietly until it had passed, he sent e-mails to Gary Brown, Charles Greene, and myself asking us to judge his competition. Foolishly, without giving the idea proper consideration, I volunteered, and unknowingly began a quest that would take up a large percentage of my time for nearly two decades.

What had overly activated Michael's imagination was a section in William Hjortsberg's 1994 novel 'Nevermore'. The plot of the fictional thriller involved Harry Houdini and Sir Arthur Conan Doyle tracking down a serial killer whose crimes mirrored the stories written by Edgar Allen Poe. The scene that had beguiled Michael was the one where Houdini performed a remarkable trick for Conan Doyle. In Michael's words, the effect went like this:

"Houdini hands Sir Arthur a schoolboy's slate which he examines and suspends in the middle of the room. Four cork balls are then shown to Conan Doyle. He freely chooses one of them, which is then sliced in two in order to demonstrate that the balls are nothing but solid cork. The remaining three balls are placed in a bowl of white ink.

Houdini then asks Sir Arthur to leave the house, walk as far as he likes in any direction, and then -- when he is absolutely certain he is alone and unobserved -- to write down some phrase or quote in his own notebook using his own pen. Conan Doyle does this, jotting down some words from the Old Testament that randomly pop into his head. He returns to the house where Houdini has him select one of the remaining three balls now covered with ink. Conan Doyle -- following Houdini's instructions -- carries the ball to the hanging slate where it inexplicable adheres to the black stone surface. It then begins to roll across the vertical face of the slate, leaving words in its path...the words are exactly what Conan Doyle had written in his notebook."

After reading the book, Michael had thought about it as a magic problem and tried to find a solution to it. Eventually he decided to hold a contest in cyberspace for the most interesting, original, and convincing method for accomplishing the effect. Gary Brown volunteered to supply the prize. A friend of Gary's was a friend of the author, so Gary was able to provide the winner with of a copy of the book appropriately signed by the author. Although the incident in the book was fictitious, the contest asked the question: "Could such an effect really have been performed in 1920's New York?" and if so "how?"

Michael preferred to think of it as "The Nevermore Problem", although he admitted that Sir Arthur's most famous character might well have called it "The Case of Corks and Slate." Several creative solutions were submitted for judging. Magicians prefer not to criticise their fellow magi. They instead use terms like "interesting", "challenging" and "different." So, I'll do likewise and say no more than that there were several interesting submissions. Those suggestions would have possibly fooled Conan Doyle, but not a magician. I submitted my judgement to Michael Edwards thinking I was finished with the episode. Then I received the fatal e-mail from Gary Brown.

Gary wrote that he had contacted the author of 'Nevermore' and told him about the contest. Gary had asked where the idea for the cork ball incident had come from and discovered that it was NOT an entirely fictitious incident! William Hjortsberg said he remembered reading it in the book "Houdini and Conan Doyle". The incident was true, but the book did not suggest how it was done. Hjortsberg had inserted the true facts of Houdini and Doyle's friendship into his fictional setting to describe their clash of beliefs about Spiritualism. The title of the book that he got the story from seemed familiar. I vaguely recalled glancing through a copy of it some thirty years earlier. During that early stage of my magical development, I was searching for tricks, tricks, and more tricks. The book seemed to be merely an analysis of major historical figures. It was definitely not the sort of thing a trick happy magic nut would have wanted to study.

Now, being a bit more grown up magically, I recalled that one of the authors of the book Hjortsberg had read was Houdini's best friend, while the other was one of his greatest enemies. Instead of completely ignoring the subject, like I should have, I was intrigued. I managed to locate a copy of the book, Bernard M. L. Ernst and Hereward Carrington's 1932 tome, 'Houdini and Conan Doyle'. It dealt with the letters between two of the most interesting men of their generation. A review of the book in the leading magic magazine of the day, ('The Sphinx' Apr. 1932), stated that it only dealt with their correspondence, and "contains no tricks in description or explanation." That was totally WRONG! It contained the description of that one specific, amazing trick. An advertisement for the book, in the same issue of 'The Sphinx', asked, "Do you know about Houdini's cork ball and slate trick which NOBODY has ever been able to explain and which Doyle insisted was supernatural?"

I also discovered that, as well as Conan Doyle, an extremely knowledgeable magician had actually been present at the performance. Conan Doyle was dumb-founded by the presentation and attributed Houdini's methods to possible psychic intervention. The magician observer, who had stayed with Houdini while Conan Doyle left the house, couldn't fathom out Houdini's method either. This inexplicable piece of legerdemain, possibly done by supernatural means, grabbed me and I set off on the quest of a lifetime. I had to discover its secret.

NOTE TO NON-MAGICIANS: The information in curved brackets (....) is for magic nuts who wish to do further research on my findings. So, ignore any you see. BUT, do read the messages in square brackets [....] as they are usually additional information, and [often facetious] comments.

(NOTE TO MAGICIANS: My aim here is to be completely ethical, and not gratuitously expose any secrets of magic that are not directly involved in Houdini's feat. I hope to give the reader an appreciation and admiration of the painstaking effort involved in the creation and correct presentation of your astonishing theatrical art.)

[NOTE TO HOUDINI ADDICTS: You have my full sympathy. You don't need any notes. If I wrote the word "Houdini" on a scrap of paper you'd have to read it. So, here's an extra one for you....HOUDINI.]

GETTING STARTED

Everybody should have an equal chance-
but they shouldn't have a flying start.
-Harold Wilson

The novelist, afraid his ideas may be foolish,
slyly puts them in the mouth of some other fool
and reserves the right to disavow them.
-Diane Johnson.

I once asked a marathon runner what the hardest part was when running his 26 miles. I expected him to describe the "brick wall" you hit at about the 13th mile. He completely fooled me by replying that the hardest part was putting on his shoes! Procrastination is the enemy. It was attacking me on this project. My subconscious was aware of the hard work I was about to undertake. It is amazing what the mind can produce when it doesn't wants to put in the effort to do something. I could think of every reason in the world for not starting on this quest. The answer was action.

So to fight procrastination, I asked the first question: "How do you begin to solve an 'inexplicable' mystery?" Pondering over how Sherlock Holmes' creator was involved in it, I imagined what the great detective would have done:

BOB: How would you begin to solve Houdini's enigma?
HOLMES: Sorry, old boy, but if my creator couldn't unravel it neither can I!

BOB: Can't you at least give me a suggestion?

HOLMES: Try Kipling.

BOB: I'm afraid I haven't Kipled in years.

HOLMES: No, Watson, the author! That's a category you have aspirations of one day joining, although on your present output....

BOB: [I didn't want to put him off by telling him I wasn't Watson.] Oh, you mean the 'Jungle Book' - Boy Scouts, Walt Disney and all that.

HOLMES: Right church, wrong pew.

BOB: Hmm, let's see. I think you mean I'm close, but I haven't got it yet. Ahh...yes, I know! You are referring to Kipling's poem 'If'. It's something about: "If you can keep your head when all about you are losing theirs...."

HOLMES: You are already losing yours, you're talking to an imaginary person!

BOB: Very funny.

HOLMES: You were close, but no cigar. Try again.

BOB: Okay, you are saying I still haven't won. Let's see... I've got it! You mean Kipling's poem about his helpful men. I remember reading it years ago.

HOLMES: Congratulations. I knew you'd get there eventually. Three final words of advice - "Investigate everything thoroughly!" Good bye and good luck.

Well, now I had my starting point. So, I set off to investigate Rudyard Kipling's poem. After many trials and tribulations I at last managed to track it down. Okay, Okay, I just went to the public library. But paying overdue fines can be somewhat traumatic. Kipling's men turned out to be in his poem "The Elephant's Child":

> I keep six honest serving men
> (They taught me all I knew)
> Their names are WHAT and WHY and WHEN
> and HOW and WHERE and WHO....

Could Kipling's six men really help solve an unsolvable mystery? I thought it was a pity I couldn't ask Kipling....

KIPLING: Why not? If you can interrogate an imaginary character like Holmes, why can't you converse with someone who actually existed?

BOB: Okay, you win. I'll ask you. How can I best use your poem to solve the mystery?

KIPLING: "...start again at your beginnings".

BOB: All very cryptic. It sounds like you've been reading "Alice in Wonderland". Now, where did that appear? Yes I remember, that phrase definitely did come from your celebrated poem, "If".

KIPLING: All right, flattery will get you everywhere.

BOB: But if I were to "start again at your beginnings" it would have been helpful if you had known Houdini as Holmes' creator had. [Yes, I was procrastinating!]

KIPLING: What was the last thing Holmes said?

BOB: "Good bye and good luck."

KIPLING: [Audible sigh] No, before that!

BOB: "Investigate everything thoroughly!"

KIPLING: Well, what are you waiting for? Put your shoes on and get running!

So, although I couldn't quite see what it had to do with Houdini's mystery, I got on with it. It would at least get me into the research mode. I turned to the historical section of my magic working library and there I made an intriguing discovery. On page 298 of Kenneth Silverman's book 'Houdini!!!'. It said: "He [Houdini] exchanged letters with Thomas Edison, Upton Sinclair, and Rudyard Kipling..."

BOB: Well I'll be! You did know Houdini. What did you write about?

KIPLING: What do you think?

BOB: Surely it couldn't be magic. I know, I know, "Investigate everything thoroughly!"

I still couldn't quite see what it had to do with the problem in hand, but if the 'Nevermore' book could have Edgar Alan Poe, why couldn't I have Rudyard Kipling! As any competent investigator will tell you, the fastest way to locate facts about someone deceased is to read his or her obituary. Hopefully, both your obituary, dear reader, and mine, will not be published for some time to come. My trusty desk top encyclopaedia told me that Kipling had passed away in 1936. He was famous enough that, if he had been involved in the world of magic, the magic magazines of the time would have noted his death. So, all I had to do was find a Kipling obituary in a 1936 magic magazine.

I had developed my magic working library to the point where it was more than adequate in answering most day-to-day questions concerning the mysteries of magicians [for full details refer to my out of print book 'The Quest For The Ultimate Secret'. - Don't you just hate it when authors plug their own books?] When it came to detailed historical questions though, like this one, it was time to move up to the big collections. So, I visited the late Alan Wesencraft, the curator of the Harry Price Library, at the University of London. In 1936, Harry Price, the famed "Ghost Hunter" and magic nut, had given his extensive magic and occult book collection to the University. For more years than either of us cared to remember, Alan Wesencraft, the spry octogenarian, had helped me locate answers to questions on the weird and wonderful world of wizards. It didn't take us long to triumph yet again.

The February 1936 issue of 'The Magic Circular' had the Obituary of Rudyard Kipling, O.M., M.M.C. The last three letters stood for Member of the Magic Circle. [I would later become an honorary Associate of the Inner Magic Circle – AIMC.] Yes, Kipling had been a member of the World's Most Prestigious Magic Society. As the Circular said: "...The MAGIC CIRCLE has lost an honoured member, the World is poorer by the passing of a Great Man."

BOB: So, you too were a magic nut. Is that a detailed enough investigation for you?
KIPLING: Not bad. [Even if you do say so yourself!]
BOB: It's a pity that you didn't know Conan Doyle as well. That would have made you an authority on both of the major celebrities in this investigation.

KIPLING: Do I have to tell you again?
BOB: Okay, Okay, I'll check it out.

I didn't have the nerve to tell him, but I was going to take the easy way out and ask an expert. One of my early keen spectators and a contributor to my clubs' newsletter, was the author Daniel Stashower. At that time, Daniel was doing research for a book on the life of Sir Arthur. I couldn't think of a better person to ask if Conan Doyle and Kipling had known each other. I sent an e-mail to Daniel telling him that I knew both had been reporters in South Africa during the Boer War and both were celebrated authors. Did he know if they had ever met or corresponded? Daniel replied that Conan Doyle had spent two days of Thanksgiving 1894, visiting Kipling when he lived in the American state of Vermont. After that they corresponded for years. (For further information on their meeting refer to page 185 of Daniel Stashower's "Teller of Tales.")

BOB: So, you knew both of the central characters involved in Houdini's mystery and you were a magic nut. I can't think of anyone better to ask. Can you give me a clue on where to start?
KIPLING: What?
BOB: Give me a clue!
KIPLING: [Another audible sigh] No, "What?"!
BOB: Ohhh....your first category. [Kipling was telling me to stop stalling and get on with it!]

Kipling's categories would help fight procrastination by splitting the subject down into discrete portions, and viewing each in isolation. They would also help maintain an impartial view. I needed to avoid preconceptions. Many researchers in the past came unstuck by only looking for evidence to support their existing theories. Having a magic background would tend to make me believe Houdini was tricking Conan Doyle, and not using unconscious mediumistic powers as Sir Arthur thought. My mission was to be as un-biased as possible. So, 'WHAT' actually happened?

17

Chapter 2: WHAT?

"The case has, in some respects, been not entirely devoid of interest."
- Sherlock Holmes [Sir Arthur Conan Doyle]

Magic consists in creating, by misdirection of the senses,
the mental impression of supernatural agency at work.
- Maskelyne and Devant.

WHAT precisely is the Houdini mystery that has puzzled some of magic's best thinkers, and what has it to do with the great fictional detective Sherlock Holmes? I decided that summarizing the answer, in a few words, would give an overview and help set my research parameters. Here is my initial attempt: Holmes' creator, Sir Arthur Conan Doyle, wrote down a phrase, while on his own, several blocks from Houdini's home. On his return, Houdini caused those same words to visibly appear on a slate Doyle himself had hung in the middle of Houdini's library. Doyle was completely baffled.

That concise description was enough for a general impression, but to begin answering the mystery, I needed as much information as possible on what had actually happened all those years ago. Fortunately, a written, detailed, eyewitness account existed in Bernard M. L. Ernst & Hereward Carrington's 1932 book, Houdini and Conan Doyle. Here is exactly what Ernst said he had seen:

"Houdini sometimes had a provoking way of performing seemingly "impossible" feats, and refusing to disclose afterwards how he had accomplished them. Mr. Ernst vividly remembers how Houdini once produced a series of extra-ordinary table levitations, in good light, which puzzled him exceedingly, and for which he could never find an adequate explanation. Houdini refused to tell how he had succeeded in producing them. He was constantly doing things of that sort. One of the most striking cases of this character was a "test" which Houdini gave to Sir Arthur and Mr. Ernst - for the former's especial benefit - in his own home, some years before his death. It was certainly a most extraordinary and inexplicable feat, and Houdini positively refused to tell how he had accomplished it. It was as follows:

Houdini produced what appeared to be an ordinary slate, some eighteen inches long by fifteen inches high. In two corners of this slate, holes had been bored, and through these holes wires had been passed. These wires were several feet in length, and hooks had been fastened to the other ends of the wires. The only other accessories were four small cork balls (about three-quarters of an inch in diameter), a large inkwell filled with white ink, and a tablespoon.

Houdini passed the slate to Sir Arthur for examination. He was then requested to suspend the slate in the middle of the room, by means of the wires and hooks, leaving it free to swing in space, several feet distant from anything. In order to eliminate the possibility of electrical connections of any kind, Sir Arthur was asked to fasten the hooks over anything in the room which would hold them. He hooked one over the edge of a picture-frame, and the other on a large book, on a shelf in Houdini's library. The slate thus swung free in space, in the centre of the room, being supported by the two wires passing through the holes in its upper corners. The slate was inspected and cleaned.

Houdini now invited Sir Arthur to examine the four cork balls in the saucer. He was told to select any one he liked, and, to show that they were free from preparation, to cut it in two with his knife, thus verifying the fact that they were merely solid cork balls. This was accordingly done. Another ball was then selected, and, by means of the spoon, was placed in the white ink, where it was thoroughly stirred round and round, until its surface was equally coated with the liquid. It was then left in the ink to soak up as much liquid as possible. The remaining balls Sir Arthur took away with him for examination, at Houdini's request.

At this point, Houdini turned to Sir Arthur, and said: "Have you a piece of paper in your pocket upon which you can write something?" The latter stated that he had, also a pencil. Houdini then said to him: "Sir Arthur, I want you to go out of the house, walk anywhere you like, as far as you like in any direction; then write a question or sentence on that piece of paper; put it back in your pocket and return to the house." Sir Arthur walked three blocks and turned a corner before he wrote upon the paper - doing so in the palm of his hand. He then folded the paper, placed it in an inside pocket, and returned to Houdini's home. Meanwhile, Houdini had kept Mr. Ernst with him in order to see that he did not leave the house.

Upon Sir Arthur's return, Houdini requested him to stir up the cork ball once more in the white ink, and then to lift it, by means of the spoon, and hold it up against the suspended slate. He did so, and the cork ball stuck there, seemingly of its own volition! It then proceeded to roll across the surface of the slate, leaving a white track as it did so. As the ball rolled, it was seen to be spelling words. The words written on the slate were: "Mene, mene, tekel, upharsin." The cork ball then dropped to the floor, and Houdini invited Sir Arthur to take it home with him, if he so desired. Sir Arthur extracted the piece of paper from his pocket, and upon it he had written, "Mene, mene, tekel, upharsin." The message written upon the slate was therefore an exact copy of the message which Sir Arthur had written upon the paper.

Both witnesses were completely nonplussed and unable to explain what they had seen. Houdini then turned to Conan Doyle and said to him: "Sir Arthur, I have devoted a lot of time and thought to this illusion; I have been working at it, on and off, all winter. I won't tell you how it was done, but I can assure you it was pure trickery. I did it by perfectly normal means. I devised it to show you what can be done along those lines. Now, I beg of you, Sir Arthur, do not jump to the conclusion that certain things you see are necessarily 'supernatural,' or the work of 'spirits,' just because you cannot explain them. This is as marvellous a demonstration as you have ever witnessed, given you under test conditions, and I can assure you that it was accomplished by trickery and by nothing else. Do, therefore, be careful in future, in endorsing phenomena just because you cannot explain them. I have given you this test to impress upon you the necessity of caution, and I sincerely hope that you will profit by it."

Sir Arthur, certainly, was completely baffled by what he had seen, and Mr. Ernst was also quite unable to explain it. The miracle of the writing was one thing; how Houdini had managed to obtain a knowledge of the contents of the written message was another. The conditions seemed fraud-proof. Sir Arthur came to the conclusion that Houdini really accomplished the feat by psychic aid, and could not be persuaded otherwise. Mr. Ernst made a suggestion; he said, "Well, Houdini, you could settle the matter very definitely, one way or the other, by disclosing either to Sir Arthur or to me just how the feat was accomplished." This, however, Houdini refused to do, and there the matter rested. What is one to think of this extraordinary occurrence? Bearing in mind all the details of the illusion, it seems indeed incredible that it could have been accomplished by means of simple trickery; and yet few people, we imagine, would seriously consider the possibility of its being anything else! Houdini was constantly doing things of this sort, and his refusal to disclose the secret of his methods must have been thoroughly tantalizing to those who were half-inclined to believe that what he did was really genuine, and that he merely refused to admit the fact. There are many, doubtless, who will feel as Sir Arthur felt, while sceptics will see in all this nothing more than an ingenious illusion. All this happened years ago, and the mystery of that slate-test remains as great a mystery as ever!"

So, there it is, a seemingly impossible riddle to solve. Did Houdini really accomplish the feat by psychic means, as Sir Arthur concluded, or, was it all pure trickery as Houdini himself stated?

21

Conan Doyle wrote these words for his famous detective Sherlock Holmes: "...when you have eliminated the impossible, whatever remains, however improbable, must be the truth." That is what Doyle seems to have done; BUT, as Doyle was not a knowledgeable conjuror, he could not have eliminated all the possible tricks a magician can get up to. I decided that as Houdini had declared it was all trickery, I would do likewise until I had eliminated all the 'possible' magic illusion modus operandi. Once I'd done that, I could then start considering psychic powers.

So, having decided Houdini's test was an "ingenious illusion", before I wasted too much time seeking a solution, I quickly looked to see if anyone else had managed to adequately solve it.

ATTEMPTS TO SOLVE HOUDINI'S MYSTERY

As soon as Ernst and Carrington published the above description, magicians began puzzling over how Houdini had accomplished it. Many speculations were put forward. Most appeared to be acceptable in theory, BUT proof of their validity was to actually do what the conjectures suggested. I did this in many cases, and found they all failed to produce the miracle performance exactly as Ernst had described. Often Ernst's eyewitness testimony was modified to suit someone's idea. [Yes, the old ploy of altering the facts to fit your theory.] Here are just a few examples of suggested methods.

Early efforts at explaining Houdini's test appeared in the "About Magicians" column of 'The World's Fair'. They were in response to a prize the paper offered for the best solution. The paper's correspondent, "B.W." [magician Brunel White], gave "a short account of the effect" in the July 9, 1938 issue to set up the contest. Unfortunately, his version contained several 'funnies'. One was that it occurred "in a room in which the blinds were partially drawn", which in a later issue of the paper was used to justify a theory that would not work in full daylight. Another blunder was that the cork which Doyle cut in half was used to write on the slate. The paper received several replies but admitted that they did "not measure up to the requirements" of what Houdini was said to have presented. B.W.'s conclusion was that although "the trick as described is a rather tall order", it was "the kind of mystery that magicians love to ponder over." After nearly two decades of doing exactly that, I can tell you categorically that he got the last part of the last sentence completely correct.

Three quarters of a century after Ernst first described it, magicians were still "pondering over" how Houdini had accomplished his trick. A reproduction of Ernst's report appeared in William Kalush and Larry Sloman's 2006 book (The Secret Life of Houdini). Unfortunately, they omitted two sentences: a) "The slate thus swung free in space, in the centre of the room,..."; and b) "Meanwhile, Houdini had kept Mr. Ernst with him in order to see that he did not leave the house." The fact that the slate was hanging in the middle of the room was possibly ignored because a few pages later they gave their answer to Houdini's 'test'. It was very similar to a version you'll find all over the internet. The supposed secret is reverse writing on the back of the slate, done by a hidden assistant, through a secret panel in the wall. A magnetized pointer is used to move a substituted magnetized ball.

The problem with that conjecture is that because the slate was actually in the middle of the room a pointer would be too unwieldy and could also be seen by at least one of the spectators. So, what did the authors do? They wrote: "Houdini (or Ernst) had forced Doyle into putting the blackboard into a corner..." I don't like spoiling their fun [especially after Bill Kalush very kindly printed an article of mine in his Conjuring Arts Bulletin (Spring 2009) and his Ask Alexander data base was extremely helpful in solving this problem], BUT, TWICE Ernst's eyewitness account says it was in "the middle/centre of the room". In addition lawyer Ernst would also appear to be an accomplice who is deceiving his client Conan Doyle. What happened to attorney/client privileges? [I'll touch on this subject again.]

In 2006, Massimo Polidoro attempted to solve "Houdini's Impossible Demonstration". In the 'Skeptical Inquirer' (July 2006) he too went for the magnet on a rod operated by a hidden assistant through a secret panel. Polidoro gets full marks for crediting the idea to Melbourne Christopher, and even leaves the slate in the centre of the room; BUT, again, sorry – it is too angle dependent. [Yes, I managed to find a photo of the room – see the WHERE section for details.] For an extremely long, awkward to handle pole to remain unseen would have needed the spectators' noses to be within inches of the slate!

To his credit, Polidoro also attempted to explain how Houdini discovered the message Doyle had written outside [presumably using Christopher's speculation]. Many authors have just ignored that part of the problem. It seems "Ernst had not remembered" that Houdini had looked at Doyle's paper to make sure Sir Arthur had folded it, and while doing so switched it for a blank one! Then afterward, to check the message was correct, had switched it back again. Terribly sorry, but according to Ernst, Doyle provided the original piece of paper. To exchange someone's piece of paper for another, without being detected, you need to substitute one that is as near as possible to the original. Doyle could have provided a paper of any size or colour, let alone one that had printing on the outside, such as using the back of a bill or a receipt. Unless Houdini had immediate access to every conceivable piece of paper in the world, there is no way a switch would have gone undetected. Also, it's very funny how Ernst even remembered in great detail which pocket the paper was in ["in an inside pocket"] but didn't recall the paper coming out and going back in again.

In addition, Massimo Polidoro states that once Houdini knew the contents of the paper, he apparently "cued his hidden assistant" with his conversation. I spent almost half a lifetime studying the major verbal coding systems, in several of the foremost magic libraries of the world, so I can tell you that to code a non-English sentence, like the one Doyle wrote, would need a code word for each single letter. Even allowing for a cue word meaning repeat the previous word, it would still be too awkward to manage without a knowledgeable magician like Ernst spotting it. And besides, how could Houdini be sure his 'hidden assistant' heard every single word. Stage acts have a responding cue, sent by the receiver of the signal, meaning 'repeat the last bit because I missed it'. No, a code would be far too uncertain.

The above accounts are typical of the many unworkable solutions, and text alterations, I came across. Unhappily, they then began to make me wonder about the accuracy of Ernst's report.

ERNST'S ACCURACY

Most of those trying to solve Houdini's test had altered Ernst's description in some way. By doing so, they seemed to be saying they didn't believe what he had written. That forced me into deciding on the validity of Ernst's report before I spent too much time attempting to solve something that may not have been accurately reported.

The question of accuracy also arose when I came across an article (The Linking Ring, Oct. 1947) about Sid Radner's wonderful collection of Houdini items. Sid owned the copy of Harold Kellock's Houdini biography (Houdini: His Life Story, 1928) that had belonged to Houdini's brother Hardeen. The title page contains the statement that the book was taken from the recollections and documents of Houdini's widow, Bess, and as well, it is dedicated to Ernst [who witnessed our test]. So you'd think the book could be trusted. Well, on the inner cover of Hardeen's copy he scrawled his opinion that it was "a pack of lies!" I discovered confirmation of that in a letter from Houdini's eccentric friend and undercover man, Bob Gysel [see the "WHO" section] who wrote, "The story book by Kellock of The Life of Houdini is just jammed full of nonsense."

There is another side to the question of accuracy of observation. Houdini's friend, magician Joseph Dunninger, mentioned it in his book (Inside The Medium's Cabinet, 1935). Joe described the human tendency to exaggerate a marvel, and said that everyone versed in the art of deception could testify to that fact. You can easily confirm this by asking any magician to tell you some of the 'funnies' spectators have told them when recalling the tricks they did. Most magi have heard descriptions of their impossible miracles that, unfortunately, they cannot duplicate. The bottom line is that although we think we have a reasonably good memory, most of us have ones that are surprisingly flawed. The magician, of course, takes advantage of this by using misdirection and psychology to confuse the unsuspecting spectator. [More on this in the 'HOW' section.]

As our sole evidence for the validity of Houdini's amazing slate presentation is a single eyewitness testimony, it could severally limit the conclusions we can reach. In the 'WHO' section, you will see that the two witnesses to the event had completely different mind-sets about what transpired. We have only the report of one of them written from his viewpoint. There is also the fact that we cannot be completely sure whether the report has been edited. The final copy was obviously produced by Carrington, based on Ernst's description, because he uses the words "Mr. Ernst vividly remembers".

Often the information needed to fully assess a magic trick is not included in a report because natural human bias purges it. As Uriah Fuller put it (Confessions of a Psychic, 1975), nobody can remember exactly what happened during a magic trick. Only a magician knows what to look for, and he too can miss a crucial detail if it's a trick he doesn't know. On the plus side there is the fact that Ernst was a competent magician who would have been looking for tricky techniques.

Joseph Jastrow's 1935 book (Error And Eccentricity In Human Belief) pointed out that wish diverts wisdom. Jastrow stated that man tends to fashion his beliefs out of his desires, not out of objective, rational thought. [As many of the supposed answers to how Houdini did it reveal.] He stressed that the prepossessed mind finds what it looks for. He explained that we are primed to think of ourselves as rational and forget about the vast areas of emotional and imaginative thinking to which we are prone.

So, what have Jastrow's views got to do with this matter? Well, it means that all humans are fallible and biased. To confirm it, just ask any policeman, trial lawyer, or insurance investigator about eyewitness testimony. Multiple witnesses to the same event often give contradictory accounts of what happened. We don't all notice the same things. What we consider important can be unimportant to others. As well, we do not always remember correctly what we thought was important. Our expectations determine what we see and how we interpret it. This means that Ernst's report could be subject to human error and misperception. We have to question how accurate it is. Was vital information omitted or distorted or emotionally coloured by personal bias?

Sherlock Holmes would surely have ruled out all natural possibilities before embracing the supernatural explanation, unfortunately his creator didn't. Conan Doyle was convinced Houdini had employed paranormal assistance in carrying out the test. Ernst, although he could not explain it, appears to have just recorded what he saw. William James' book (The Will To Believe...., 1896) talks of passionate versus intellectual considerations. He says that as a rule we disbelieve all facts and theories for which we have no use. Conan Doyle seems to have abandoned the intellectual side of his creation Sherlock Holmes and gone over completely to his passionate side. [We'll look at his possible reason when we get to the "WHY" section.] One thing I tried to resist was making the snap judgement that Conan Doyle was wrong. Keeping an open mind was the only logical route to take. At this point I remembered a situation from my past that helped keep me on the path of not prejudging.

I discovered that I too was driven by my opinions several years ago. While on a lunch break from work, I noticed an older colleague walking along the street arm in arm with a lovely girl, who looked to be half his age. I instantly concluded that he was a dirty, [lucky], old man. Later that day he came over to my desk. I was sure it was to boast about his lunch time escapade. With a large grin on his face, he delighted in telling me that he had had lunch with a beautiful young girl - his daughter! I was forced to revise my opinion, and attempt in future to avoid emotional based instant judgements until I was in possession of all the relevant facts. Yes, beauty is in the eye of the beholder.

The plus side of Ernst's account is that he seems to have presented the facts as he saw them, without prejudging what happened. He does not appear to give us his beliefs and opinions of the events. Ernst would appear, as a lawyer, to have been a trained observer and a competent eyewitness. I decided that his description would be a reasonable base from which to judge how it had been done, but there was still a downside.

The downside was that the description was based on his memory, which was open to influence by effects of bias and decay with time. The only written information available on Houdini's test was published many years after the event. We can only read the report. We cannot see Houdini do it. There is no collaborating report of the event. The observers cannot be interviewed. We are dependent solely on the veracity of our single informant. We have to make do with a second hand report by Ernst. We don't have Conan Doyle's description of his part in the event. It is a pity that Doyle did not put his thoughts on paper, because he might have given us a clue to exactly what happened out on the street.

At this point in the search, I recalled another incident from my past that had shown me just how little we actually see of what is around us. Once again it was from a work situation. A colleague's desk faced mine, so that every day for several months, each time he looked up he saw my face. [Please, no comments about how unfortunate for him!] On awaking one morning, I decided to shave off the full beard that I had worn for several years. At work, my colleague kept looking at me quizzically. Finally his expression changed, and he said he knew what was bothering him - I had had my hair cut! That morning, no other workmate noticed anything out of the ordinary until someone from another department came to my desk. That person had a beard. The first thing he said was: "You've shaved off your beard!" My colleague instantly agreed. The conclusion seems to be that we only see what we are interested in - everything else gets ignored.

Shortly after writing the last paragraph, I was talking to a lady friend who my wife and I meet each week. She was telling us how all of her men friends had thought there was something different about her, but could not tell what it was. She said that all the women knew it was her new hairdo. At that point, I realised that I too had not noticed it. The even more fascinating thing was that she was totally unaware that I was wearing a new, completely different style of glasses! A day or so later, I told two people we meet every few days that story. Those two had not noticed my new glasses either, until I told that story! We look, but we don't see!

With all of that in mind, I decided to see if any research had been done on spectator's views of magic presented as a séance. If so, could it affirm Ernst's recollections? If we don't always see what's under our noses, what chance do we have when someone is deliberately trying to mislead us? Fortunately there was a study done at the height of public enthusiasm for spiritualism. In 1887, researchers R. Hodgson and S.J. Davey faked a séance by using magic tricks. Then they asked the observers to write down what they had seen. In their detailed 114 page report (Proceedings of the Society for Psychical Research Vol. 4, 1887), Hodgson and Davey revealed there had been a great amount of mal-observation and lapse of memory. Those attending invented events that did not happen, omitted others that did, and many of the things that actually took place were remembered in the wrong order. Richard Wiseman's book (Deception and Self-Deception, 1997) mentions several more recent experiments along similar lines. All Professor Wiseman's experiments, more than a century later, obtained the same results as Hodgson and Davey, including underestimating the number of people present in the séance room!

But, fortunately, there is one major finding of those experiments that will help here. It seems that people who did not have a strong belief in the paranormal made more accurate observations. Your belief biases your ability to recall events because your brain interprets what it receives from the eye. You often see what you expect to see. Although Doyle was a believer in the occult, Ernst, a magician, was more interested in what trick methods Houdini was employing. This is more in line with what I was after. As information that is relevant to the viewer's expectancy is more accurately recalled, the strength of a memory is directly related to the importance you give it. Magicians know this to be part of human nature and deliberately take advantage of the fact. If they can make something seem unimportant then their audience will not recall it.

Houdini was manipulating Conan Doyle's expectations by presenting his mystery in a way that matched as near as possible a medium's normal offering. Doyle thus subconsciously looked for confirmation of his strongly held beliefs. But, on the other hand, Ernst was scrutinizing Houdini from a magician's far more analytical viewpoint, i.e. looking for trickery. While one viewer took Houdini's illusion to be the real thing, the other tried to understand what was actually going on behind the false reality. So, although Ernst's description was better for uncovering deception than a non-magician's would have been, my problem was to guess what Ernst thought was unimportant and subsequently forgot. If Houdini was really doing a magic trick he certainly made a few things vanish from Ernst's report, as no magician so far has adequately explained the mystery based on Ernst's account.

In addition to initial observation bias, there was yet another factor to allow for. It was the recall and reconstruction period. How long was it before Ernst actually wrote down his opinion of what he saw? Are all the details complete, or has memory decay made it ambiguous in important areas? It had taken place a decade before the book describing it was published. Ernst was in his fifties then. As I can verify from sad experience, he was entering the time of life when you have trouble remembering what you had for breakfast, let alone what you did ten years earlier. I eventually decided that the great amount of small details, such as exactly where Doyle went, and into which pocket he placed the paper, answered the question. I assumed that he had remembered all those subtle points because he had puzzled over Houdini's marvellous presentation every day for ten years. Ernst was now finally writing it down in the hope that others might be able to solve the riddle. After all, the book was really about the letters between the two great men. There was no letter involved here.

Finally, after much exploring in the field of eyewitness accuracy, I began to realize there was still one more area to consider. I had to weigh up whether the title of Kipling's poem, 'If', should have been one of his "six honest serving men". Yes, I started to wonder if the event had actually happened. Could it have been the product of a hallucination or a dream, or perhaps the ingesting of too much alcohol or other stimulants? Might it have been an outright hoax to promote the book? If it hadn't actually occurred I was going to waste a considerable amount of my valuable time. I finally decided that if others in the past had accepted it as a true historical fact, then I would lemming-like join them. [More on this area in the "WHEN" section... I have to admit that the thought did cross my mind to use the possibility that it might not have happened as an excuse if I could not find a solution.]

If you look long enough and hard enough for something, the chances are that you will eventually succeed. The trouble is that we often stop looking too soon. I had to continually remind myself not to give up searching, because often serendipity produces an answer when you least expect it. In this case it happened while I was hunting for something completely different. By chance I came across evidence of how accurately Ernst recalled past events. It was an incident involving Houdini that was described in a book written by Ernst's legal partner Melville Cane (The First Firefly, 1974). Ernst had also described the event in a magic magazine

(The Sphinx, Oct. 1936). The incident had occurred at least ten years before the time Ernst wrote it up for the magazine. By comparing the two versions I was able to get a very good idea of Ernst's ability to recall a situation that was at least a decade old.

Cane wrote: "We stepped off the elevator at the Liberty Street floor onto a deserted corridor, its main electric lighting already turned off. Ernst ran ahead, while we lingered in the semi-darkness, only to report that we were locked in. As I started toward the other way out, Houdini called: 'Hold it! First let me check.' In less than a minute of fiddling with a gimmick he had with him, he managed to hit on Open Sesame, and led us into the street...."

Ernst wrote: "I had forgotten for the moment that it was customary to lock the Liberty Street entrance at six o'clock. As we approached the doors, I found that they were locked. I turned and began walking toward the other entrance. As Houdini did not follow me, I looked around and found him operating on the door lock. 'Come on,' he said, 'it's open.'"

By comparing the two reports, you can see that, although they are nearly 40 years apart, they are basically the same. The only major omission was that Ernst did not mention Cane. I made a mental note to remember, when I got to the 'WHO' section, that Ernst was liable to exclude others who were present. Otherwise he was reasonably accurate with his description. I decided to carry on.

HOUDINI'S PRESENTATION STYLE

Based on all of the above contemplation, I decided to take it that Ernst's account gave an acceptable, general, unbiased description of Houdini's slate 'test'; but, NOT the specific details of Houdini's presentation technique. What do I mean by that? Well, for example, what was his general attitude? How did he relate to his friends? How would you have seen him act if you had been there? Is it still possible at this late date to get an idea of what Harry's actual approach to the presentation would have been? It sounds impossible, but the answer is yes!

Magicians employ various presentational styles depending on their natural personalities, and whether they choose to portray a character. Those dramatic approaches can range from the profound to the comical. So, what was Houdini's attitude during his slate 'test'? Well, in 1906, he wrote in his 'Conjurers Monthly' magazine: "In addressing your audience do not become bombastic or overbearing in demeanour but speak as you would to critical friends, thereby gaining their confidence and sympathy, and no matter what may worry or trouble you, never let your audience detect any irritability or ill temper, but always display a bright and pleasing manner." [Yes, a long rambling sentence like your author has been known to occasionally produce.] Houdini added.... "Nothing is more offensive to an audience than a performer to appear surly and bad tempered. He is to please the public and to do so he must be on the best of terms with himself and I may add – the best of humour."

Was Houdini still of that opinion two decades later [at the time of our experiment]? In 'M-U-M', for Jan. 1923, Harry wrote on the subject of "Addressing An Audience". He stressed, "The experiment and apparatus are both of secondary consideration." He said, "Work with determination that you intend to make them 'believe' what you say. Say it as if you mean it and believe it yourself. If you 'believe' your own claim to miracle doing and are sincere in your work, you are bound to succeed."

Other writers give clues to Houdini's performance technique that seem to back up Harry's above statements. American writer and literary critic, Edmund Wilson, revealed (The Shores of Light, 1952) that when Houdini performed his tricks he did so with the directness and simplicity of an expert giving a demonstration. It seems that Harry talked straightforwardly, in plain speech, with a German accent, and was thoroughgoing, earnest, and enthusiastic. Magician and Magical M.C. Dorny is quoted as saying (Magicol, Aug. 2003): "Houdini always presented his show in a serious manner, without trying for humour or comedy." Walter B. Gibson confirmed this (The Original Houdini Scrapbook, 1977) when he said Houdini's stage manner was slow and deliberate. Gibson added that even in the lightest moments, Houdini had a way of adopting a serious air.

So, combining all the above, I'm reasonably certain he presented his slate 'test' in a lecture type style. When Ernst and Doyle were invited to examine the props, they would have been more like co-workers sharing an adventure, than taking on the challenge of solving a puzzle. I feel that Houdini would have begun his 'test' by understating his position. By not making a specific claim, he was following most psychics, and also playing down his efforts to make the final result even more amazing. So it would be presented as an experiment that might or might not work.

That 'experiment' probably began much earlier than Houdini's guests realized. Ernst does not tell us how Houdini actually brought up the subject of doing 'something' for his guests. It would certainly not be the reason why they visited him that day. He would most likely have employed his understanding of human reactions and people persuasion skills to plant an idea into a conversation, which caused one of the guests to later suggest a 'test'. This 'sleight of tongue' [emotional engineering] technique could have been carried out days ahead of time. Then the observers would think it was just a spur of the moment idea they themselves suggested. If all else failed, Houdini could still have 'set the scene' by offering to do 'a little something' to amplify the discussion they were having. He would attempt an impromptu, minor demonstration of an untried experiment that might, or might not, work. In other words, he would 'undersell' his 'test'. The last thing he wanted them to grasp was what he later admitted: "I have devoted a lot of time and thought to this illusion.... working at it, on and off, all winter."

Max Maven is quoted, in Eugene Burger's 1986 book, 'Spirit Theater', as saying, "The hard part is not getting that writing to appear on the slate; the hard work is getting the audience to get the

most out of that experience...and that's very, very hard to do."
Houdini was unquestionably an accomplished actor at playing the
part of a magician. Like all top thespians, Harry's imagination
allowed him to suspend his critical faculty and fully believe that
he was really doing what he purported to do. [That is why it is said
that to be a magician you have to be a child at heart. You must
have a child's wonderful imagination.] There would have seemed
to be no pretending involved – at that moment he actually was a
magician. Each of his actions would spontaneously give off the
subconscious signal that he was sincerely doing what he appeared
to be, and the thought of any trickery was the last thing on his mind.
His guests would then feel the same emotions in sympathy with
him. What Kenneth Silverman calls (in Houdini!!!, 1996) Harry's
"contagious smile", would have strengthen their response.

When I said Harry used a lecture style of presentation, I didn't
mean that it was the dull academic torture many of us slept through
during our school days. In fact, it was imperative that it wasn't
boring. So, what did Houdini do? His approach would be like the
ones he'd watched over and over again in his early days while
working in the side shows and dime museums. He would have
observed the showmen lecturers shepherding the punters around
the performers and freaks, and learned their technique of holding
and building up interest. The communication here would be two
way. You can't force people to do anything, but you can motivate
them. So Harry, like all top-notch performers, would have used his
naturally humorous style to liven up the proceedings without
losing the mystery. How can I be sure? Well, Silverman gives us a
typical quip of Houdini's as he was about to be locked into a chest.
He pointed out that if he succeeded it would be a fine trick, but if
he didn't it was still a good chest! I like to think that he told his
guests that if his experiment didn't work he would leave the slate
hanging there to 'chalk up' his losing score.

It's been said many times that Houdini was a super showman.
Showmanship is the ability to effectively 'sell' an 'effect'. Harry
had the knack of taking a commonplace magic trick and making it
into a miracle by appealing directly to the spectators' emotions. He

was able to judge the ambience [pick up the vibes] of an audience and then exaggerate the ordinary just enough to make it interesting. Why am I sure of that? Well, John Booth tells us (Forging Ahead In Magic, 1939), "Houdini had a gift for showmanship equalled by few men." So, his flair for the dramatic would have turned his experiment into a drama that held his guests attention throughout. Booth also quotes Houdini as saying that effective magic required suspense. So, he would definitely have built up the suspense of the grand finale by appealing to their curiosity of what was about to happen.

So, we can be reasonably sure Houdini's presentation was aimed at Conan Doyle and would have been in a similar style to that of a 'genuine' spirit medium. Like the presentation of his escapes on stage, Houdini would have dramatized the conditions involved in the experience. If he had presented it as a pseudopsychic trick then Conan Doyle would not have jumped to the conclusion that he was taking part in an authentic supernormal experience. He would have been looking to see if he could fathom out how it was done, and merely put it down to a clever deception.

So, what did Houdini do during the concluding phase of the experiment? I think his complete mastery of showmanship would have helped him create the maximum moment of magic. He would have dramatically held up his hand to request complete stillness, and then focused their total attention on the slate as Doyle offered the ball up to it. That final profound impact of the ball inexplicably writing the words known only to Sir Arthur would have occurred in complete, stunned silence. There was a powerful force at work here that was beyond the observers' understanding – no words could describe it. Houdini would have left it to their imaginations to attempt to understand what they had seen. Then when the impact began to wane, he would bring his astonished guests back to reality with his usual trick ending proclamation (per Edmund Wilson's The Shores of Light, 1952), "Will wonders never cease?"

CONCLUSIONS

'What' was happening was that Houdini was 'attempting' a once-in-a-lifetime experiment. He always advertised that he would 'attempt' to do his escapes. By doing so he emphasized the fact that failure was a definite option, so it couldn't possibly be a trick. His aim was to remind Doyle to not always trust his senses. Although he suggested that it might not work, he was about to demonstrate that Doyle's senses most certainly could be deceived.

Houdini was performing for two completely different spectators. Doyle was what magicians call "a layperson". Ernst was a fellow magician. Because Houdini was presenting it as a pseudo-scientific lecture experiment, Doyle was prepared to suspend his disbelief and go along with the experiment as if it was actually real. Ernst on the other hand was not concentrating on the theatrical aspect of the presentation. He was looking at it as a puzzle he wanted to solve. Afterward Ernst must have spent many hours trying to reconstruct exactly how Houdini had accomplished his miracle. So, Houdini's presentation had to be faultless because he was being observed from two completely different viewpoints.

If it were indeed a marvellous illusion, then there were two completely different realities happening at the same time - the false reality of the two spectators and the real one of the magician. As well as the 'test condition' details Ernst wrote about, there were the unseen actual secret actions necessary to create the false illusion. My job was to uncover those concealed activities and reveal the completely different alternate reality [i.e. what actually happened as against what was perceived]. Houdini was a Master Magician, who was exceptionally skilled at making people believe one thing was happening while another actually took place, so it was not going to be easy.

An interesting fact is that no two audiences are the same. A magician must be able to improvise if things don't go as planned. This is especially true for the case we are considering. Houdini would have allowed for deviations from the prepared script. If something unplanned occurred then he would have improvised until being able to get back on track. So, it's quite possible that what Doyle and Ernst saw was not quite what had been initially planned, but we'll never know if it was.

Finally, when Sir Arthur insisted that Houdini explain his trick, or admit he was an unconscious medium, Doyle obviously forgot what he had written 30 years earlier, in his 1892 'Study In Scarlet'. There he has Sherlock Holmes say this to Dr. Watson:

"I'm not going to tell you much more of the case, Doctor. You know a conjurer gets no credit when once he has explained his trick; and if I show you too much of my method of working, you will come to the conclusion that I am a very ordinary individual after all."

It seems that Doyle had changed his attitude in the intervening three decades. Talking of attitudes, let's move on to look at 'WHY' the mystery was presented.

Chapter 3: WHY?

Medium (at séance) – "Spirit, are you there? If so,
rap once; if not, twice."
- 'The Sphinx', Feb. 1926.

Denial ain't just a river in Egypt!
- Mark Twain.

After a bit of thought, I decided there were several 'WHYS' that could help solve this mystery, so I began with the obvious one.

One of the first things Sherlock Holmes would have looked for was a motive. In our case, we needed to ask: "WHY did Houdini perform the puzzling 'experiment' for his guests?" Ernst and Carrington's book asserted that Houdini undertook his "test" specifically for Sir Arthur's benefit. Both Houdini and Doyle were intriguing personalities, famous, and strong willed. Both were committed to studying the "psychic world"; but they seemed to be approaching it from different directions. Ernst stated that "each tried to persuade the other of the correctness of his standpoint." What better way for the not so well educated, street-wise Master Magician to get his view across to the cultured author than by performing an inexplicable mystery?

Sadly, in the end, their friendship could not survive the fact that they were each trying to defend conflicting views on the subject. So, I had to look into the history of Spiritualism. Here is a very brief summary of an extremely complex subject:

SPIRITUALISM HISTORY

Harry performed his slate mystery specifically because of Sir Arthur's ardent belief in Spiritualism. Fortunately, I spent over forty-five years, off and on, exploring the magic section of a vast, wonderful library, containing a significant segment devoted to Spiritualism. This assembly of unusual books, devoted to frauds of all kinds, is the delightfully unique Harry Price Library, housed in the University of London Library. Psychic researcher, and ghost hunter, Price had assembled the curious collection to aid his investigations of psychic impostors, which also included the testing of spirit mediums. So, beginning with Harry Price's collection, I began delving into Spiritualism.

I found that around the time we are investigating, Price and Eric J. Dingwall, a fellow magician and member of the Society of Psychic Research, reprinted one of the first major books exposing fraudulent mediumship (Revelations of a Spirit Medium, 1922). The book, written by an anonymous, reformed, dishonest medium, caused quite a stir when it initially appeared in 1891. As the two Harrys, Price and Houdini, had corresponded on the subject of Spiritualism quite frequently [Price's library includes over 40 letters from Houdini], I decided to begin with Price's reprinted book. Using the new glossary Price and Dingwall had added, along with additional information from a small hardback on mediums Dingwall wrote not long afterward (How to go to a Medium, 1927), I was able to define a spiritualist. A spiritualist was a supporter of the spiritual philosophy, who believed that departed spirits communicated with us through mediums. That gave me my starting point - the deceased are not gone forever but can get in touch with us through mediums.

Next I needed to define a medium. Price and Dingwall called a medium: "A person professing to be possessed, or controlled, by the personality of some person who has died, so as to speak or act from the intelligence of that person." Often when a medium was being possessed things mysteriously appeared, so the medium also supplied the 'force' used by spirits in 'materialisation'. How this interaction and phenomena occurs is still not understood, but the medium seems to be the channel for it [hence the modern term for it of 'channelling']. But my favourite definition of 'mediums' was that of J. Barton Bowyer [Bart Whaley] (Cheating, 1982), who called them: "those who claim that they are capable of tapping into the supernatural on call".

Eventually, I constructed a mini-outline of mediumship, and the world of spiritualism, as it existed at the time of Houdini's slate performance. The key element was the medium, who claimed super-normal faculties. There were two main types, the mental medium and the physical medium. Mental mediums could be called the straightforward basic variety. They communicated on behalf of the dead by either speaking, or writing messages. They saw, heard or sensed the deceased person.

The second type, materialising or physical mediums, were far more complex. They additionally produced physical phenomena by making forms appear, or moved objects without contact. Materialising mediums are not very common today [apparently their numbers decreased greatly with the invention of devices allowing investigators to secretly see and film in the dark]; but they were very much in evidence during Houdini and Doyle's day. They specialised in creating:

a) spirits who rapped out messages,
b) spirits who wrote out messages through the mediums [automatic writing],
c) spirits, or entities, in the form of human shape,
d) spirits who moved, tipped or levitated tables,
e) disembodied voices from trumpets,
f) ectoplasm [a whitish 'substance' extruded from the medium's body],
g) apports [the perplexing appearance of small objects],
h) music from trumpets, tambourines, etc.,

i) spirit forms developed on photographs and paintings, and

j) messages on slates [as in Houdini's 'test' that we are analysing].

Some mediums were also called 'test mediums' when they focused on working in conditions where it was apparently impossible for them to commit fraud. That is why authors have referred to Houdini's slate mystery as a 'test' [which I will do from time to time to keep you on your toes]. Often these test mediums worked for 'top-heavy investigators'. They were scientific men 'overloaded' with degrees who failed to detect the simplest of tricks. 'Helping out the spirits' was a polite term for doing the phenomena yourself.

In addition to the investigators of mediums, and the spiritualists [or believers] they investigated, there were also the 'backslider spiritualists'. They were believers who, having investigated the claims and phenomena of Spiritualism, became disgusted and renounced their faith. Finally there were the non-believers or 'skeptics' who thought all mediums were frauds and all phenomena fraudulent. Although Houdini is usually said to be a skeptic, he usually claimed to be still willing to be a believer if convincing proof of survival emerged. [At my advanced age, I too would like to believe there is some survival after death.]

Séances were public or private meetings held to study or produce psychic phenomena. Many séances were dark séances, where the phenomena took place in the absence of light, while the medium and attendees, or 'sitters', held hands. In a cabinet séance most phenomena were produced inside an enclosed structure or behind a sheet hung across a corner of the room. The medium inside the cabinet would often be tied with ropes to ensure that only the spirits were doing the manifestations. [Yes, this is quite likely where Houdini got his idea for the challenge escape act.] The guide or control was a particular spirit that attached itself to a medium. Often the medium would be in a trance or hypnotic state while being controlled by that spirit.

The phenomenon Houdini produced for Sir Arthur was known as Independent Slate Writing. It was usually the direct writing by spirits upon ordinary school slates, that had been supplied by either the medium or the sitter. Often the message was to answer questions written upon papers that had been placed between closed and sealed slates. William Robinson wrote (Spirit Slate Writing and Kindred Phenomena, 1898) that the supposed writing on school slates by spirits converted more people to spiritualism than any other phenomenon. It had been very common in both England and America, but although still popular in America at the time we are looking at, by then it was almost extinct in England. A medium specialising in slate-writing effects was known as a Slate Writing Medium. So, Conan Doyle accused Houdini of being an unconscious Slate Writing Medium.

Now that I had the background of how Spiritualism was functioning around the time in question, I looked to see how it had begun. Although communication with spirits goes back to ancient times, most writers will tell you that "modern" Spiritualism was "unleashed" on the world in 1848. Sir Arthur Conan Doyle (The History of Spiritualism, 1926) called March 31, 1848, "One of the great points in psychic evolution." [Yes, he seems to have missed the obvious fact that it was the eve of April Fools' Day - the day you pull pranks on people!] Its rapid world-wide growth started that date in a little cottage in Hydesville, New York. There two young sisters, Margaret and Katie Fox, claimed the loud, eerie rappings, or knockings, occurring in their vicinity, were messages from dead people's spirits.

Soon the girls learned that by using a code they could communicate with the apparently supernatural agency producing the raps. People were unable to suggest a plausible solution. The editor of 'The New York Tribune', Horace Greeley, encouraged the fad, and Spiritualism swiftly swept around the world. It has been estimated that within five years of the Fox sisters beginning modern Spiritualism, there were 30,000 practicing mediums in America alone.

The reason for Spiritualism's rapid spread was that it was well before the advent of those two killers of verbal communication in the home, radio and television [not to mention mobile phones]. Families would gather in their parlours on a Saturday night and entertain each other. Common amusement skills ranged from playing the piano to reciting poetry, with the odd magician thrown in [and today some of them are still pretty odd]. Holding a séance in your home to communicate with deceased relatives and friends became the latest thrilling craze. Stories of wonders happening at these exciting séances rapidly spread, acquiring the usual embellishments as they grew. Believers vehemently supported spiritualism while others, equally passionately, opposed it. Just plain raps soon became boring, so the spirits expanded their repertoire. Manifestations such as table tipping and automatic writing rapidly became the norm, along with apports, ectoplasm and spirit forms. Spirit guides or controls soon graduated from mere friends and relatives to famous deceased individuals.

Due to their charismatic personalities, some mediums acquired celebrity status, along with accompanying wealth. Mediums like the American Davenport Brothers, Englishman D.D. Home, and Italian Eusapia Paladino became world famous. So too did the scientists investigating them like Sir Oliver Lodge, and as well two fellows I've already mentioned, Harry Price and Hereward Carrington. It is said that even Queen Victoria, in England, and President Abraham Lincoln, in the U.S., attended séances.

To aid scientific investigation, The Society for Psychical Research was founded in London in 1882, and three years later the American Society for Psychical Research was established. Spiritualism grew and receded over the years. Its progress was greatest during times of turmoil, especially after wars. Thanks mainly to Conan Doyle, it peaked in the era we are looking at.

Sadly not all mediums were honest. Some charlatans employed magic trickery to deceive observers, but unlike magicians who freely admitted they were fooling you, the fraudsters denied any fabrication of phenomena. Total darkness and hidden assistants led to many apparent miracles. They also had an advantage over magicians because of time being no objective. Before stooping to their trickery, wrongdoers could wait hours until the observers began to tire. Bogus mediums played on the longing in many people's hearts to confirm that their loved ones still existed on some higher plane, and weren't just a memory. Although many mediums were exposed as deceitful, the will to believe still brought people back to them. Many celebrities such as the novelists Thackery and Victor Hugo boosted the Spiritualist movement. So, you might say that Conan Doyle was merely following their lead.

Ultimately, there are two main ways to account for Spiritualism. The first is that it is the direct result of spirit power. There have been many books written to boost that concept. The main ingredient required is faith and a willingness to believe. No, I'm not going to discuss here the pros and cons of whether death ends it all. [As I said, now that I've reached more than my Biblical span of three score and ten years on earth, I'd very much like to think that something does carry on]. The so-called 'rational' second answer is that the 'tests' are all purely, and simply, the result of fraud and trickery.

Because my initial theory was that Houdini did not employ supernatural methods, I will concentrate now on the latter aspect of the question to help bolster my case that Houdini was using magic tricks. To provide the "skeptic" approach to Spiritualism, I'll begin with H. L. Mencken's comment on spiritualists (American Mercury, June 1932): "the essential thing is that they believe it as an act of pure faith, and without any regard for the apparent facts." Oscar S. Teale pointed out (The Sphinx, Oct. 1925) that Horace Greeley, the great supporter of Spiritualism, after 5 years, apparently had a "change of heart." It seems that editor Greeley printed in 'The New York Tribune': "We look upon the spirit rapping question as a most detestable swindle. While we believe that many of the mediums are poor, deluded creatures, we are convinced that the projectors and promoters of the affair are knaves as infamous as ever served out a life sentence in a state prison." Yes, heavy stuff from a former enthusiast [a backslider spiritualist]!

Margaret & Kate Fox, who had started it all in the first place, gave a series of public lectures in 1888 confessing to their lifelong fraud of merely snapping their finger and toe joints to produce the raps. This revelation did little to stop the growth of Spiritualism. Supporters said that because both sisters were alcoholics their confessions should be dismissed, and furthermore they returned to the fold again when the tours revealing their misdemeanours were not financially successful. [Did a lifetime of fraud drive them to drink?] The tour manager for their exposing talks, magician Elmer P. Ransom, described (The Sphinx, Sept. 1932) how believers caused riots at their meetings and claimed the unmasking was all a fake.

Eugene Burger (Spirit Theater, 1986) asserted that by the mid-1880s nearly every American and English medium of reputation had been convicted, or caught in the act of fraud. Magician and researcher for Houdini's books, Oscar S. Teale listed a few of the famous mediums that had been exposed up to 1925 (in The Sphinx, Dec. 1925) as: Slade, Diss, Debar, Palladino, Slater, Bessinet, Margery, Argamassilla, "and many more too numerous to name." In an effort to enlighten the public [and no doubt to also gain at the box office] many magicians exposed the tricks of fake spiritualists as part of their shows. With the notable exception of a few leading magi, like Will Goldston, in the main magicians agreed with the Occult Committee of the U.K.'s prestigious Magic Circle. It reported (The Magic Circular, Aug-Sept. 1925): "So far the committee has not been satisfied that any medium working in this country has produced anything in the shape of supernormal phenomena."

In the 1850s, John Henry Anderson, The Great Wizard of the North, was one of the leaders of the attack by magicians on the pseudo-occult. During his world travels, Professor Anderson sold booklets at his performances containing explanations of fraudulent mediums' methods. Another magical Great, famous English magician John Nevil Maskelyne, began his career by exposing the top mediums of his day, The Davenport Brothers, in 1865. Maskelyne also performed slate-writing feats during the trial of the notorious medium Slade. Leading magician of the 1880s and 90s, Alexander Herrmann, exposed fake mediums' methods during his New York shows. And during the era we are investigating, Houdini's special investigators [see the 'WHO' Section] exposed many of the day's leading mediums. As Houdini's magician friend Joseph Dunninger put it (Inside The Medium's Cabinet, 1935), "Houdini, in his war on fake psychics, was simply carrying to an extreme, demonstrations that many others had attempted before him." So, like Conan Doyle, Houdini was merely following the lead of others.

There is another aspect of pseudo-mediumship that I must touch on to complete the picture. It is those mediums who deceived themselves. To understand what I mean, think in terms of a sleep walker. As Dingwall's book (How to go to a Medium, 1927) explained, somnambulists can perform very complicated actions yet are not aware they are doing so. The subconscious is a very tricky thing and in some cases can trick the mediums themselves. Those who actually go into a trance, or a form of self-hypnosis, can often not be communicating with departed spirits, as they think they are, but with their own internal phantoms through mental dissociation.

As well as delusional belief systems, paranoia and mental instability, there is a further area of self-deception involved in the séance room. It is that of the eyewitnesses. High expectations, anxiety, dark conditions and dramatic atmosphere, along with suggestion can stimulate sitter's imaginations. They often suffer illusionary experiences when caught up in the excitement of reaching across an unknown void. This can make their testimony unreliable and frequently is the source of falsely spread stories of marvellous phenomena that in turn get exaggerated. E. H. Jones, who acted as a false medium while attempting to escape from capture during World War I, confirmed this mal-observation of sitters in his book (The Road To En-Dor, 1920). Jones explained that what is ridiculous in daylight can be intensely eerie in the dark. The faithful believer is often stirred by his emotions. The feeling that he is dealing with an unknown force will not only blind his powers of observation, but can often distort it.

There is another question that has often been asked – "What about the mediums who did not charge for their services, surely they weren't in it for financial gain?" Well, sadly, in addition to the hunger for fame and fortune, there can be other rewards for fraudulent mediums. As Eugene Burger says (Spirit Theater, 1986), many people erroneously confuse charging a fee with personal integrity. Other motivators to deception can be raised self-esteem, as well as the benefit from increased attention and personal power. It may be as simple as just plain ego massaging and having a bit of fun fooling people. This latter reason comes under the heading of hoaxes, which are often thought to be less unscrupulous. As 'Mahatma' (Feb. 1899) stated: "A craving for notoriety impels some people as powerfully as want of money."

There is also the dilemma of the justification for 'someone assisting the spirits when they refuse to show up,' i.e. faking it. What is the excuse? It's that they are being socially helpful. People often think, "What's wrong with someone helping confirm a person's cherished desire to believe in a life after death, and as well comforting them in bereavement by providing some solace in their hour of need, even if the medium wasn't being exactly genuine?" Well, as Maurice Wright, in the introduction to Dingwall's book (How to go to a Medium, 1927) says about this pseudo-psychic bereavement counselling, "It is (very) harmful when beliefs, which may in themselves be perfectly valid and based upon truth, are shattered by the exposure of fraud." So, the question seems to be, are they actually consoling individuals in troubled times, or are they spreading false hopes and exploiting vulnerable people? Some skeptics say it harms the grieving process by making it difficult to leave the deceased behind.

Eugene Burger warns that in addition to mediums bringing smooth reinforcing messages, notoriously they often impart stinging ones as well. Houdini's boyhood friend and fellow magician, Joseph Rinn (Sixty Years of Psychic Research, 1950) listed some of the horrors. A typical one was that of Mrs. Lindsauer who amputated her arm when told to do so by spirits. You only have to read Richard Wiseman's book (Deception & Self-Deception, 1997) to see that the trickery and deceit rampant in Houdini's day still goes on. Wiseman gives examples of scams that bilk a great amount of money from the trusting, by exploiting their emotional needs. Wiseman's worst case was of a young man who, having been told by a medium that he'd be dead by the time he was 28, went home and committed suicide.

If, after reading the above, you're thinking, "What kind of person could do such a thing?", you only have to look through reformed, dishonest medium M. Lamar Keene's book (The Psychic Mafia, 1997). There he talks of the "true-believer syndrome", and says that it needs study by science. He could not understand how when he, and his former trickster 'friends', would be exposed people would still cling to them even harder. Maurice Wright, in the introduction of Dingwall's book (How to go to a Medium, 1927), talks of a public willing and anxious to be gulled, and resenting bitterly any imputations against their favourite mediums. Keene says that the average person is exceedingly easy to fool, and asserts that the need to believe in phoney wonders exceeds not only logic, but also often sanity. So, it seems that Keene, and his kind, look on susceptible, trusting people as fools ripe for the picking.

Maurice Wright also says, "One of the saddest things I know is the way in which men and women of the highest integrity, with well-balanced judgement, good critical faculties for all the ordinary affairs of life, will bring to a séance room the gullible mind of a child, to accept any marvel, any so-called evidence for survival." In the introduction to Keene's book, Ray Hyman suggests that it is the deep sense of loss from the death of an important person in their lives that makes people susceptible to the wiles of the charlatans. So, both Houdini and Conan Doyle's losses of loved ones made them vulnerable, but when it came to trickery Houdini was not the "average person". Conan Doyle would seem to fit

Dingwall's statement: "It is only when investigating spiritualism that ordinary people think the business requires no training and no knowledge. It is on such people that the fraudulent medium preys."

To balance the above, I must now stress that no one can make a sweeping statement about the subject. A 'skeptic' who asserts that all Spiritualism is fraudulent is most definitely wrong - it cannot be proved! At the same time a believer who says that the fraud must be a copy of something that did exist is equally incorrect. It could be just a copy of something from someone's imagination. Instead I'll just refer to magical Great, J. N. Maskelyne's stance on the matter. [As I said, he got his start in magic by exposing The Davenport Brothers, who were considered to be the top mediums of his day.] J. N. wrote (The Magic Circular, Feb. 1914) on the subject of 'detecting fraud in spiritual intercourse' almost a decade before Houdini's slate performance for Doyle. He asserted: "However eminent, however talented, or however sincere a man may be, he has no right even to form a conclusion without expert guidance." This, of course, could be said to apply to Sir Arthur.

As Richard Wiseman & Robert Morris wrote (Guidelines For Testing Psychic Claimants, 1995) some of the easiest individuals to fool are those who are very confident of their ability to detect deception. Uriah Fuller [Martin Gardner] adds (Confessions of a Psychic, 1975) that most scientists, engineers, reporters, etc. are trained in the straight-line approach of deductive reasoning. This won't work here; magic principles aren't like any other principles. You need a magician's double or lateral thinking in misdirection and psychology to be able to realize where human frailty and weakness are being exploited. BUT, M. Lamar Keene's book (The Psychic Mafia, 1997) calls this an exaggerated claim. Perhaps Dunninger is more to Keene's way of thinking when he says (Inside the Medium's Cabinet, 1935) that the knowledge of trickery is insufficient. He insists that a real investigator must study mediums as personalities and have an understanding of the psychological factors involved. Uriah Fuller's [Martin Gardner's] second book (Further Confessions of a Psychic, 1980) calls these professional psychic hustlers "street-wise criminals". He emphasizes that they are not magicians but criminals who will resort to anything from tapping telephones to tampering with the mail to extort money from you. Perhaps this is why Houdini hired private detectives to deal with many of these villains.

Maskelyne went on to say that if experts in sense-deception, such as capable magicians, could not detect chicanery, then there would be a case for the supposed phenomenon; BUT he added that such negative evidence would not constitute absolute proof. Finally, he pointed out that where clear existence of fraud is found it "renders all non-expert opposition entirely ridiculous". Sadly, this too relates to Conan Doyle.

Should Maskelyne's attitude still apply today? The answer is yes. Richard Wiseman (Deception & Self-Deception, 1997) states that he would include in a report on research that had produced successful phenomena that he was impressed by the results, and has no conventional explanation. Richard would then note that further research is definitely warranted, but he would not issue a statement that he believes the claimant has 'psychic' ability. Perhaps Doyle should have taken a similar stance on Houdini's phenomena.

Finally, I will leave this subject with Verrall Wass' criticism of mediumship from his 1936 book (Astound Your Audience): "My criticism is on a higher plane. The triviality of such phenomena is what makes me hold aloof. Once dead, great poets no longer write great poems and great scientists produce no great scientific treatise; instead they occupy their time by throwing paper balls across rooms, returning to their schoolboy days, and when they speak it is to tell us nothing we could not have told them."

DOYLE

Okay, now you've absorbed all the above background, let's return to what this category is all about, and ask another 'why': "Why was Conan Doyle supporting Spiritualism?" Sir Arthur gave his answer in a London newspaper article (Daily Express, Sept. 17, 1925) describing his "Religious Evolution." Although born into a Roman Catholic family, he eventually lost his religion. After some years of agnosticism, he was drawn into psychic investigation, and in early 1916 was converted to Spiritualism. His wife shared his feelings, so together they determined to devote the rest of their lives to handing on the knowledge and comfort it brought to others. Kelvin Jones' book (Conan Doyle and the Spirits, 1989) confirms the 1916 date of Doyle's conversion when he says that Sir Arthur publicly declared his belief in spiritualism in an article in 'Light' magazine (Nov. 4, 1916).

MAGICIANS

'Why' were many magicians also drawn to Spiritualism? American writer and literary critic, Edmund Wilson, gave the possible reason in his book (The Shores of Light, 1952) when he wrote: "Doctors, psychologists and physicists are no better qualified to check up on spiritualistic phenomena than lawyers, preachers or poets....The problem is whether the 'medium' is a real medium or merely a conjuror, and this is something that only a conjuror is really equipped to find out." He then stated that Houdini had "collected a library of books on trickery, occultism and kindred subjects which is said to be the largest in the world....Where he once challenged the world to tie him up, he now challenges it to convince him of the supernatural."

As others have already stated above, Wilson was correct. Just because someone is an expert in one field does not mean that he knows any more about another area than anyone else does. Conan Doyle may have been an excellent Doctor, and a wonderful creator of detective stories, but he was most definitely not qualified to assess whether spiritualistic demonstrations were actually being done by means of conjuring. It takes a trained eye to spot trickery; BUT, there is no way any conjuror can categorically state that all the manifestations are due to trickery without thoroughly investigating each case. Just because Doyle was an honest man, did not qualify him to judge another's honesty. An expert con man can easily swindle an honest person by appealing to their emotions.

HOUDINI

So, was the above the reason 'why' escapologist Houdini was especially attracted to Spiritualism? There are two conflicting opinions as to why Harry became a psychic investigator.

Walter B. Gibson made the first suggestion in an article (The Sphinx, Mar. 1951) on "Good Box Office". Gibson, who Houdini had hired as a ghostwriter, said that Houdini's greatest "newspaper space getter" for his full evening show, was his campaign against fraudulent mediums. But Gibson doubted that Houdini would have gained so much publicity without Conan Doyle having first caused the tremendous stir with his lectures supporting Spiritualism. Gibson believed that Houdini was smart enough to jump in on the other side of a boiling controversy.

J. Malcolm Bird, in his 1925 book (Margery the Medium) wrote of Houdini's clash with the famous medium, Margery:

"Houdini is past fifty years old; and he faces the necessity for building up something new to keep him among the headliners of his profession when, as must inevitably happen, he no longer has the physical resources for his fatiguing escape tricks. In building up a new stage personality as exposer of mediums, he 'must' behave toward all mediums as he has toward Margery. He 'must' assume in advance that the phenomena are fraudulent, 'must' at all hazards make them so appear, 'must' in every way put the idea across that he is the author of mediumistic exposures, infallible 'bad medicine' for mediums."

Although a lot of what Bird says is probably true, you 'must' also remember he was not exactly a friend of Houdini's. Houdini biographer Kenneth Silverman (Houdini!!!, 1996) talks of Houdini's clashes with Bird, and how both Bird and Hereward Carrington were having an affair with Margery. [Yes, that's the very same Carrington who co-authored the book describing our slate trick!]

So, it would seem that Houdini was cashing in on the latest fad, or was he? Houdini's friend, John Mulholland (Quicker Than the Eye, 1932) declared it cruel that Houdini was usually thought to have campaigned against fraudulent mediums merely from a desire to see his name in print. John asserted that Houdini's crusade of enlightenment was to save people from their own ignorance, and the fraud of those who have no qualms about fleecing the bereaved. William L. Gresham (Monster Midway, 1954) seemed to agree with Mulholland when he said that although Houdini was a violent foe of fraudulent mediums, he was a sincere psychic researcher to the last.

Melville Cane, poet and Ernst's legal partner, knew Houdini for more than 15 years, and also formed an opinion. In his book (The First Firefly, 1974) he suggested that Houdini's investigation into the domain of the spirit, and communication with the dead, was an overpowering attachment to his dead mother. Harry's first impulse on returning from a tour was to visit her grave. Cane thinks that is why Houdini unselfishly "exposed the creatures who preyed and profited on the susceptibilities of the bereaved." Sid Radner's wonderful Houdini collection (described in The Linking Ring, Oct. 1947) had many letters from Harry to his brother Hardeen, which seem to confirm Cane's opinion. Houdini wrote repeatedly about the void left in his life because of the loss of his mother.

So, were the suggestions of the more cynical individuals that Houdini was moving into middle age and beginning to lose his drawing power correct? Well, Spiritualism was definitely the flavour of the moment, and Harry, like other magi before him, did jump onto the bandwagon and regain his celebrity status. The March 1924 issue of 'The Sphinx' reported Houdini drawing great crowds to his illustrated lectures on Spiritualistic Fakers and Miracle Mongers. He also wrote a book (A Magician Among the Spirits, 1924) giving his experiences with fraudulent mediums. My initial reaction was that it was probably a bit of both publicity seeking, and a bit of wanting to contact his mother. Then, I discovered yet another possible reason to add to that idea! It is something that is not often suggested.

Thanks to the Conjuring Arts Research Center's wonderful Ask Alexander Data Base, I was able to gain online access to Houdini's own personal scrapbooks. They contain many clippings of reviews of his early shows, especially during 1898 and 1899. They revealed: "The very unique entertainment Prof. and Mlle. Houdini gave" contained a "mixed bill of magic and spiritualism." As well as his "amusements" with "sleight of hand with cards", he was doing "slate writing and reading and answering unseen questions which had been written by the audience."

So, Houdini had definitely been involved with the occult very much earlier. I located supporting evidence in an article by Houdini's brother Hardeen (The Sphinx, Oct. 1940). It included a playbill for an early Professor Harry Houdini and Mlle. Beatrice Houdini performance of a "Startling Spiritualistic Séance". It was said to have been used shortly after their marriage. Another Houdini playbill from Jan. 1898, in Harold Kellock's Houdini biography (Houdini His Life Story, 1928), showed that "A Spiritual Séance" was being performed as part of their act. Within months of that date, Houdini was being billed as "The Famous Handcuff King". 'The Sphinx' for July 1904 points out that Houdini does not claim to use supernatural power; he simply tries to entertain and mystify. So, in the 1920s, was Houdini actually returning to his roots when he campaigned against fake mediums, and not just gaining publicity from the latest fashion trend, as so many authors have claimed?

Yes, it's quite possible that as Houdini approached middle age he had the urge to return to his roots [just like I did]. Even more fascinating was the other item he presented. He was freeing himself from audience supplied handcuffs like "alleged spiritual mediums do"! It would seem that Houdini's incredible escape act grew out of his imitating fake mediums. A clipping in his scrapbook quotes him as saying, "Mediums do the handcuff trick somewhat after the same manner that I do, but they are not quite so deft at it." Houdini seems to have found success by imitating the mediums and then dropped the spiritualistic side of the act completely to become the World's Greatest Escapologist. It would appear then that in exposing fake mediums during the 1920s, he was NOT just jumping on the latest bandwagon, as many of his detractors maintained; he was merely getting back on it after falling off some twenty years earlier! Was it a case of poacher turned gamekeeper?

Another important 'why' at this point is, "Why is Houdini usually said to be a doubter of spiritualistic phenomena?" A long Houdini scrapbook article, dated Sept. 24, 1920, entitled "Why I Am A Skeptic" might give the answer. Here is a very small extract to give you an idea of Harry's views:

"First let me say that I do not deny that there may be such a thing as spiritualistic manifestation, but I do say that my own careful research covering a period of over 30 years has brought to light nothing to convince me that inter-communication has been established between the spirits of the departed and those still in the flesh.... The vast majority of the mediums [employ] trickery....My friend, Sir Arthur Conan Doyle, tells me in all sincerity that the reason that I do not get convincing results is because of my skepticism, which fact closes all doors of enlightenment. I wish to put on record for all time that I am not a scoffer.....Doyle is an honest and sincere believer, and as honorable a man it has ever been my good luck to meet....

I do not care to discuss the religious side of spiritualism, as I fail to see that it has any relation to the manifestations of the

56

mediums.....It is the question of inter-communication that has claimed my attention, and....I attended over 100 séances with the best known mediums.....but the result has left me further than ever from a belief in the genuineness of the manifestations...."

Fulton Oursler's autobiography (Behold This Dreamer!, 1964) probably accurately summarized his friend Houdini's attitude when it asserted that Harry wanted to believe in the phenomena of spiritualism, but tragically his common sense would not let him. Houdini spent much time vigorously pursuing fake mediums because they would not give him what he wanted. Oursler claimed this was confirmed by the pacts Harry made with friends to try to contact each other if they died first. I tend to agree with Oursler, as this would seem to be Harry begging for proof. Why go to all the bother of making after death agreements if you didn't long for it to be possible to communicate with those left behind?

After spending much time looking into Houdini's character [see the 'WHO' section for details], I tend to agree that he was genuinely looking for a sign from his late, very much missed, mother. But unlike Conan Doyle who was content to accept any indication as comfort, Houdini's magical training led him to realize he was being conned. As his ego would not allow him to be duped, he became more, and more anti-mediumistic the more he saw of the sham, and determined to stamp it out. Of course, there was also definitely the element of publicity, with the resultant financial gain to be had, but in trying to maintain the self-esteem that came from being a pal of such a well known academic, he was being torn in two directions. Although Doyle was often painted as one, he was certainly no fool. He knew that if he could get Houdini on his side the resultant boost for the Spiritualist movement would be tremendous. The strain of trying to keep one foot in each camp must have been extremely hard on Houdini.

NON-DISCLOSURE

Another major 'why' before we move on has to be: "Why did Houdini refuse to tell his guests how he accomplished his mystery?" The intriguing thing here to me is that during his stage act he demonstrated how classic mediumistic phenomena were produced by giving the audience a pseudo-séance in full light. To simulate normal dark room conditions, a blindfolded spectator sat opposite Harry on an isolated platform, and held Harry's hands and restricted his feet. Even with that much control, Houdini was still able to use his head and mouth to carry out various tricks in full view of the rest of the audience. So, with all that exposure, 'why' not let Doyle in on the secret of this mystification as well?

After much thought I've decided the reason must have been one or more of the following:

A) Houdini was obsessed with secrecy. This isn't hard to understand when you realize that his escape act had been ripped off repeatedly by pirates and copyists. In his era, it was not in a magician's interest to make his greatest magic secrets common knowledge. He not only lost prestige, but his income as well. Houdini spent a great amount of time and money fighting those he considered to be plagiarists. It had become second nature for Houdini to protect his methods. Most magicians of his day had only a single, major, trusted assistant. The others were not allowed near the stage area until just before the time of their precise duties. That way they could not take the secrets of the other tricks with them when they defected to the magician's rivals. Anyone who worked for Houdini had to sign a secrecy agreement. Ernst, as Houdini's lawyer, was responsible for producing those contracts. It must have been quite a laugh for Houdini's assistants who were involved in the slate test to keep its secret from the very person in charge of them signing the non-disclosure document!

B) As Houdini explained, he had spent all winter working on the illusion. Having devoted a large amount of time, thought, and money, to its creation he was very loathe to give its secret away. He intended to use part of the method again, as a publicity stunt. [This he did, gaining headlines in many papers. More on that affair in the "HOW" section.]

C) Probably the main reason Houdini did not explain his 'trick' to Doyle was that he'd learned the hard way that it would spoil what he was trying to accomplish. As soon as Sir Arthur knew how the test was done it would be devalued as a possible deterrent to jumping to conclusions that other phenomena were not trickery. He would then only think of Houdini's test as a simple magician's trick and not a possible miracle. Magicians of his era often discovered that once they showed believers in Spiritualism how bogus mediums had faked their pseudo-séances, the believers would reply that it was not the way it had been done when they had seen the manifestations 'for real'.

BUT the problem non-disclosure caused here, as Ernst explained, was that Doyle then grouped Houdini's performance with other 'genuine' phenomena. By stressing it was just an unexplained trick, Houdini hoped to place doubt in Doyle's mind the next time he witnessed a medium. Not knowing how it was done would still keep it unexplained and a yard stick to compare other unexplained phenomena against. The best example of what I'm trying to get at is that you too wouldn't also be wondering now how he did it [and reading this book] if Houdini had explained his secret.

D) Another "why" for keeping the secret, was that Houdini wanted his best friend, and pupil, Ernst to know that his mentor was still well ahead of him. If he could fool Ernst, as well as Conan Doyle, the slate illusion would be audience proven for both magicians and laypeople. In magic there is a hobby within a hobby. Some magic enthusiasts only perform before other magic 'nuts', and never before non-magicians. Magic clubs and conventions are their usual venues. They often sell tricks and books to each other containing complex methods for doing tricks, when simple solutions would do for any performance before non-magi. Magicians frequently invent new solutions to standard tricks to fool their peers, while a layperson watching it would not see any difference at all.

Not revealing his method to Ernst must have been both partially frustrating for Houdini, and at the same time ego boosting. To pull off the stunt, and still be fooling today's magicians after all those years, Houdini would have had to go to a huge amount of effort. Unlike most other arts, the problem with magic is that you have to completely hide how skilful you are. It would have been very tempting to boast to another magus just how clever he'd been. BUT at the same time, it was great to know that his friend would continue to ceaselessly puzzle over how the trick was accomplished.

This falls into a class of magic known as "conjuring for conjurers", which is magic specifically designed to "fool another fooler". Most of the stunts used are not very magical to lay people, as they usually involve a different secret technique than is ordinarily employed, and doing it like that often downgrades the overall magical effect. But in this case, Houdini made it very difficult for himself – his 'slate test' not only had to fool a knowledgeable magus, but as well an ordinary person, and at the same time create maximum amazement.

As Houdini wrote in a magazine article (Popular Radio, Oct. 1922), "I love an honest-to-goodness trick that mystifies and entertains me. It is my business to know them all and try to perform them better than other magicians." In fact Houdini's pupil Ernst was so taken with the mystery that he included it in his book, thereby passing his mystification along to us. So, now just like Ernst had done, we can wonder, over and over, "How did Houdini do it?" Yes, the Master was still the Master.

E) Finally, we also can't discount the fact that Houdini got a 'buzz' or 'high' from knowing he had fooled the creator of the great detective Sherlock Holmes. Why should he put the man out of his misery? It must have been very satisfying to keep him guessing.

After thinking it over for a very long time, I've decided the reason 'why' Houdini was so secret about the method behind his slate test was probably a combination of several, if not all, of the above. I'll leave the last thought on the subject to Sam Sharpe, who wrote in his 1946 book (Neo-Magic) that Conan Doyle said: "A conjurer gets no credit once his trick is explained."

BACKFIRING

The last 'why', before we move on, is a combined one: "Why did Houdini's slate deception fail to convince Conan Doyle that all mediums could be potential fakes?", and "Why did Doyle think Houdini had truly accomplished his experiment by paranormal means and not trickery?" Ernst tells us that Houdini did not succeed in his aim, which was to convince Doyle to be more wary of accepting all mediums as genuine. Fulton Oursler, famous journalist and friend of both Houdini and Doyle [see 'WHO' section for Oursler's particulars] stated that Houdini's 'test' completely backfired. Fulton wrote (Behold This Dreamer!, 1964) that Doyle did not believe Houdini was a magician at all. Doyle declared that Houdini was a man who sold his soul to evil spirits! Yes, Oursler emphasized, "Doyle really believed that!" Houdini confirmed it when he wrote (A Magician Among the Spirits, 1924): "Sir Arthur thinks that I have great mediumistic powers and that some of my feats are done with the aid of spirits."

I won't go too deeply into trying to explain Doyle's attitude, as I'm far from qualified to do so, but it obviously has to do with the science of psychology, and the deep realms of the subconscious. It also includes Houdini's aggressive arrogance. Houdini was certain that he could easily persuade the great man that he was the victim of self-deception. To win the day all Harry had to do was present an unfathomable demonstration that created even greater results than the people Conan Doyle was championing.

What Houdini failed to realise was that he was dealing with Doyle's belief system as well as his model of the universe. Houdini didn't grasp what a complete upheaval it would have on Doyle's mind, and his outlook on life, to admit that he'd been wrong about something he felt so passionate about. The outcome would be shattering. The necessary 'proof' to bring about such a major change had to be extremely strong. Often it is better for the mental well-being of self-deluded people to ignore the proof, even if it is irrefutable, and for them to remain comfortable in the way they see the world, just carrying on as before.

Conan Doyle had such a trusting nature that he could not conceive of someone using religion to gain money and notoriety. His need to believe the cause he was championing somewhat clouded his rationality. Doyle's view of his life situation, and his wish fulfilment, made him accuse Houdini of being an unconscious medium. Although Harry stressed he was not attacking all mediums, only the unscrupulous ones, he was indirectly pointing out that Conan Doyle was mistaken in his beliefs and a bit gullible. Houdini was declaring that all mediums should be subjected to full rigorous and properly controlled tests by demonstrating what he could do under supposedly similar conditions.

Houdini's mistake was in assuming that he was merely attacking Conan Doyle's ideas, and would easily make him change his mind. Had Houdini been able to see himself, as others saw him, then he'd have realised that Conan Doyle would have reacted as Harry himself would have done in a similar situation. Houdini could not stand to be fooled. Sir Arthur, who was emotionally committed to his subject, took it that Houdini was attacking him and not his viewpoint.

David Marks and Richard Kammann (The Psychology of the Psychic, 1980) list three possible responses from someone who is confronted as Doyle was by Houdini's slate marvel. First, he could quote certain authorities he holds as infallible as evidence. [This, of course, was what Houdini was trying to stop Conan Doyle from becoming – a quotable authority.] Secondly, he could place non-believers into the category of bad people. [Conan Doyle was not one to think too badly of someone, so he put Houdini into the category of 'unconscious medium', i.e. if you can't beat him then make him join you!] Lastly, he might turn against you and accuse you of bad motives or stupidity. [This was partly what Conan Doyle did when he told Houdini to either explain his trick or admit to being an unconscious medium.]

It seems that once Houdini had apparently eliminated the possibility of digital skill, or cleverly faked apparatus, to Doyle that only left some inborn wondrous power, or the ability to organize unknown external forces to do his bidding. I believe Doyle was completely misinterpreting the facts. Why am I so sure Houdini did not possess mystical powers beyond our conception? Well, to start with, Harry wrote in a magazine article around the time of the experiment (Popular Radio, Oct. 1922): "I am simply a mysterious entertainer. Everything I do can be explained by natural means as illusions." In the years after the slate test, Houdini continued to emphatically deny having any supernatural or mediumistic powers. He was merely a conjuror [although he more than likely would tell you he was The World's Greatest Conjuror]. Even after his death, his wife continued to state that he was just a magician.

Today, we have even more proof of Houdini's non-occult status. Since Houdini's death many magicians have not only duplicated his tricks, that were supposedly supernatural, they have, in many cases, surpassed what Houdini did. Yes, I admit it; there is one exception to this – it's the slate trick Houdini did for Doyle. So, the onus is on me to prove that it too was an extremely well-constructed and performed illusion.

There's another way of looking at 'why' Doyle was so sure Houdini was an unconscious medium. Psychologists have recently investigated the tendency to jump to incorrect conclusions and classed it as "inattentional or unconscious blindness". They have defined it as a failure to see what is in plain sight, and they often group it with "confirmation bias". The latter is the inclination to interpret new information in a way that conforms to preconceptions, and to overlook anything that contradicts existing beliefs. These observers make fictional deductions and assumptions, which, of course, is just what a magician tries to make you do.

Again, Houdini's character would have made it easier for Doyle to ignore Harry's pronouncement of not possessing uncanny powers. Houdini's friend, magician Joseph Dunninger, referred to it (Inside The Medium's Cabinet, 1935) when he explained, "In speech, Houdini was direct, blunt, and unemotional when delivering an important statement." If someone is being almost rude in trying to force his or her point on you, what do you do? That's right, you turn off and stick to your side of the argument even more.

Sir Arthur was not the first one to come to supernatural conclusions about Houdini. Fulton Oursler pointed out that Houdini's mysteries were so baffling that people were ready to believe anything about him. Typically, Dr. Wilson, the editor of 'The Sphinx', wrote (Dec. 1911) that a Mr. W. H. Edwards of England had advanced a "nonsensical explanation" for Harry's escapes. In the December issue of 'The Occult Review' Mr. Edwards attributed Houdini's escape to the fact that he was a medium. It seems that "Houdini is first entranced by the spirit control and his body is then dematerialized, his soul having first been withdrawn."

Edwards said that after telling Houdini he had discovered he was a secret medium, Houdini did not reply. Editor Wilson called Edwards' conclusion "rot", and wrote, "Sure Houdini would neither deny nor affirm that he was or was not a medium: like all good showmen he leaves conclusions to his audience." Another Spiritualist, J. Hewart McKenzie, accused Houdini of being a medium (quoted in The Sphinx, Dec. 1925). McKenzie said Houdini did not dare admit it because he did not wish to upset Music Hall proprietors and managers. The short answer is that people often see what they expect to see. Yes, it is a form of subliminal blindness. Hopefully I will be able to avoid it here.

By refusing to explain his trick to Conan Doyle, Houdini was in fact reinforcing Doyle's expectations that only a medium could do what Houdini had done. Of course, the burden of proof is always on the person making the claim. If Conan Doyle was right about Houdini being an unconscious medium then it was up to him to prove it. As Doyle is no longer with us, and didn't satisfactorily prove his case while alive, I believe Houdini was using magician's tricks. Yes, having made that statement the onus is now on me to prove it. Others have tried and failed. Can I do it? Read on to find out.

Chapter 4: WHO?

I'm very proud of myself. I resisted the temptation to begin this "WHO" section with a joke about WHOdini. Hmm, maybe I just did..... Take that as a warning as to what too much concentrating on Houdini can do to you. - Now, where was I? Oh, yes....

If you're going to solve a mystery then you must examine 'who' was involved in it [the suspects] as well as their relationship with each other. Hopefully doing so will provide clues toward a solution. In our case, there were several unique social interactions between the characters 'who' were involved in Houdini's 'experiment'. Conan Doyle and Ernst were Houdini's guests. Houdini and Ernst were fellow magicians. Conan Doyle and Houdini were Ernst's clients. Conan Doyle and Houdini were both important celebrities. Conan Doyle and Houdini were fellow investigators of the paranormal, and each was trying to persuade the other that his point of view was the correct one.

THE TWO MAJOR CHARACTERS

I decided that in this 'Who' section I would concentrate on the characters, and idiosyncrasies, of those involved in the slate test. So, I began with our legendary magician, Houdini, then looked at his distinguished spectator, Conan Doyle, and finally gave the other bit players a quick once over. As I had found with the other sections of this book, everything I looked at was far more complex than I had first imagined.

Both Doyle and Houdini were major public figures, and arguably the two most well-known individuals of their era. Unlike so many modern so-called 'superstars', who soon go out of fashion, they remained at the top of their professions until their deaths. Both had the 'drawing power' needed to 'top the bill'. In addition to their public 'images', each was endowed with that intangible something known as 'presence'. Charisma is impossible to learn; you are born with it. Both stood out from the crowd. Their personal magnetism drew people to them. So, it was only natural that they would be drawn to each other.

I will only give an overview of Conan Doyle and Houdini's characters. It would take a whole book to do each of them justice. In fact, more than one book has been written on each. I'll just provide enough information here to let you know what you'd be up against if you decide to study them further. [If you do wish to investigate them in detail, then see my list of biographies at the end of the book.]

+ **HARRY HOUDINI** (1874 - 1926): Houdini is usually remembered today as the man they couldn't imprison – "The self-liberator!" He escaped from every conceivable type of restraint, including: handcuffs, chains, leg irons, death cells, and even a Siberian transport van. As well, he freed himself after being strapped into straitjackets, sealed into cans, nailed up inside boxes, and tossed manacled into rivers. In short, he released himself from every possible type of dangerous, 'foolproof' confinement. "To do a Houdini" still means to succeed against hopeless odds. If that was all he had done it would be quite something, but that's far from all.

What else did Houdini accomplish? Well, Magical Master of Ceremonies, Dorny (The Sphinx, Apr. 1945) quite succinctly summed Harry up by saying that as well as an escapologist he was a magician, illusionist, publicist, movie star and producer, and in addition, an author and humanitarian. To that list I'd add that he was also a magic shop owner, President of several magic clubs, a pioneer magic researcher, collector and historian, and furthermore a psychic investigator, an early aviator, an athlete, and finally, a great animal lover and trainer. I'm going to ignore the rest! Okay, okay, I'll mention one more - in their recent book William Kalush & Larry Sloman, (The Secret Life of Houdini, 2006) speculated that he was also an undercover intelligence-gatherer for the Secret Service and Scotland Yard!

To expand on each of those areas would take several books the size of this one. Fortunately those books have already been written. So, if you are interested in learning all about Houdini's remarkable career, then see my list of the major Houdini volumes under "Further Reading" at the back of this book. No, that's not a cop out! Although I'd love to tell you a great deal more about Houdini's many exciting exploits, space considerations [and the number of years I've left to live] restrict me. So, for now, I'll only briefly summarise his career as a self-liberator and psychic investigator.

Before going any further, from personal experience, I must advise you that Houdini can become completely addictive. He is a magical icon and a great hero for many young wannabe magicians. The danger is that you can definitely waste a large portion of your life attempting to confirm, or refute, events that have been attributed to him. So, if you wish to look into other areas of his life, please, please, do remember my warning - keep looking for signs of him beginning to take over.

An extremely concise description of Harry Houdini's life would say that he was born Erik Weisz ['Eric White' in English], in Hungary, in 1874, and taken to the U.S.A. at the age of four. Somewhere around the age of 9, the showbiz bug bit him, creating the deep-seated determination to perform in public, and bask in the buzz that comes from creating a captivating theatrical experience. For the first half of his life [26 years] he faced the gruelling challenge of struggling to succeed, enduring the daily grind that was the fate of entertainers in medicine shows, dime museums and circuses, adopting and adapting as he went. After experimenting with everything from Punch & Judy to acrobatic work, he at last found, in the early 1900s, his unique niche as "The Undisputed King of Handcuffs". As a magazine of that time (Black And White Budget, Jan. 5, 1901) put it: "He...can readily accomplish what would appear to be the impossible task of extricating himself from securely-locked manacles without the aid of a key or other implement."

The road to magical stardom is a tough one. You can usually count the number of successful publically well-known magicians on the fingers of one hand. Most magicians only dream of being a success, Houdini did something about it. He was a self-made man whose passion and determination to learn from failure, pushed his career from an unpromising start to fulfilment.

You can be the world's greatest magician, but if people don't know about you, you won't find work. Houdini was one of the first great self-publicists. He not only understood the business side of "show business", but also how to work it to achieve longevity of career. When it comes to maintaining your popularity, how many entertainers manage to remain at the top of the tree for over a quarter of a century, let alone novelty acts, which Houdini was? Harry provided theatre managers with full houses by combining his showmanship and publicity skills. He wasn't just a magician in the minds of the public and theatre owners – he was "Houdini!!!" With his Substitution Trunk, and challenge escapes, Houdini became an international celebrity, associated with presidents and kings, and broke box-office records in the top venues wherever he went.

As Dorny's above list pointed out, Houdini moved on to other areas of magic while managing to maintain his headlining star status during a time of great change in the entertainment industry. By 1908, he'd stopped escaping from shackles to concentrate on large, spectacular set pieces such as his Milk Can Escape, and Water Torture Cell. He employed many publicity stunts to keep his name on the front pages of the papers, such as jail breaking, escaping from packing boxes, and jumping from bridges or piers while heavily restrained. He even released himself from straitjackets while hanging by his feet from tall buildings. His exploits were watched by up to 50,000 amazed onlookers. Typical of his non-escape publicity exploits was being the first officially recognized man to fly a plane in Australia.

By 1918, he was performing such miraculous illusions as The Vanishing Elephant, and Walking Through a Brick Wall. Offstage Houdini was producing and starring in serial, cliff-hanging, motion pictures. During the period we are investigating here [the first half of the 1920s] he concentrated on attacking spiritual charlatans, and building a full evening show featuring escapes, illusions and fake psychic exposés.

That's the legend, but what about the man behind it? How do you separate the man from the myth? At first glance, it seemed fairly simple - Houdini is the most talked about magician of all time. The literature on him is constantly expanding. There are even published bibliographies to help navigate your way through the mass of Houdini material. All I had to do then was give that literature the once over. I rapidly discovered this approach only leads to total confusion. Why?

In reviewing yet another book on the master escapologist, Jamy Ian Swiss (Genii, Feb. 1995) said he already had more than a dozen Houdini-related volumes on his shelf, and most were flawed in some, if not many, ways. Was the book Swiss reviewed any different? No! He went on for several pages pointing out the errors.

Why are so many Houdini biographies unsound? Well, magic is the art of deception, which involves making normal things seem miraculous. This usually extends to the magician's life as well. In Houdini's era magicians were expected to be glamorous, and this usually involved creating a fictitious, fascinating background. Houdini was no exception. I'll give just two examples of how difficult it is to pin down anything about him. They concern both ends of his life. The first is about his birth. Apparently Houdini told Londoners he was born in New York, while he told New Yorkers he was born in Wisconsin. So, where was he actually born? His birthplace was Budapest! As for Houdini's death, the late, great collector/historian Bob Lund identified seven different 'true' versions of Houdini's death! Those variations were in how, when and where the great magus had escaped from life. [Yes, I admit to adding an eighth variation in a 'Magic Circular' article marking the eightieth anniversary of his death. No, I won't go down that road here as it's off topic - maybe someday I'll elaborate on it.]

So, if you can't trust the information at either end of Houdini's life, then what does that say about the stories in between? To get as near to the truth as possible, I'll only give an overview of his life and personality, while concentrating on the details that could affect our current quest. I'll start with the very few things that all the authors of Houdini biographies agree on. We can be sure he was born into a large, poor, immigrant family. With very little formal education, he set out at an early age to take care of his family. Surviving many hardships, he worked his way up through show business, and managed to achieve international fame due to his masterly skills of showmanship and generating publicity. The two outstanding character traits that all agree on are that he was exceedingly fond of his mother, and that he had an extremely large ego. His ego often led to him going to extremes to eliminate someone he saw as trying to steal his act, even if they were so 'small time' they could not possibly have harmed him.

As for Houdini's enduring fame, two years after Harry's death, A.M. Wilson, the editor of the leading magic magazine of its day (The Sphinx, March 1928), wrote that Houdini "will be forgotten within a generation or two". Nearly two decades after that, Dorny (The Sphinx, Apr. 1945) noted that Houdini's name was still "a household word all over the universe". Does that observation remain true today, more than half a century later? Well, just before the eightieth anniversary of Houdini's death, I gave a lecture on his exploits to several top Hollywood stars as part of the pre-production phase for a feature length, fictional movie including Houdini as a major character. Yes, the legend of Houdini is still alive, and his myth continues to build. As one magic magazine put it (The Bat, Nov. 1950) Harry "dominated the magical scene during his life [and] made such an impact, magic will never recover from his presence." The Oct. 1948 'Sphinx' noted that Houdini's name is now "used as a synonym for magic".

How did Houdini's legend grow, and how difficult is it to separate fact from fable? After Harry's death, his wife Bess commissioned a book on his life (Harold Kellock, Houdini: His Life Story, 1928). It tended to be the information source for many of those that followed. Sidney Radner (The Yankee Magic Collector #11, 2004) quoted Houdini's brother Hardeen as saying the book was "full of lies". Another major source of information for would-be Houdini biographers was the 1953 movie – "Houdini". George Johnstone declared, (The New Tops, Apr. 1969) that the only part of the film that rang true was its name. Bruce Cervon & Keith Burns, writing on another magic legend, Dai Vernon, wrote (Dai Vernon A Magical Life, Vol. 4, 1992) what tends to be the common assertion today concerning Houdini's lifestyle. They said that Houdini "never smoked or drank and led a very clean life without a word of scandal ever attached to it." Were they correct?

Well, George Boston, advisor to the 1953 Houdini movie, wrote in 1947 (George L. Boston & Robert Parrish, Inside Magic, 1947) that Houdini "smoked very little and drank no liquor." Yes, 'very little' would suggest that he must have smoked at least a bit. As for drink, Kreskin (Magicol, Feb. 1999) quotes Houdini's friend, Al Flosso, as saying that the last time he saw Houdini was just before his ill-fated final tour, and Houdini "was so drunk he had to be almost carried home." So, which do you believe?

As for scandal, Max Holden, who knew Houdini, and his wife Bess, quite well, wrote (The Linking Ring, Mar. 1943) that they "were a wonderful couple and always very devoted". I should just leave it at that, but I can't resist telling you that Kenneth Silverman's authoritative biography (Houdini!!!, 1996) strongly suggests a "love affair" between Houdini and the wife of Jack London the author, Charmian London. Other magical literature hints at a similar happening with the busty, "wildly sexy", "legendary beauty", magic shop demonstrator, Daisy White. Maurice Zolotow seems to have been convinced that Houdini had an affair with Daisy (quoted in William V. Rauscher, The Houdini Code Mystery, 2000).

Just when I was beginning to wonder if I was ever going to be able to distinguish the real man from the myth, I came across a statement by my friend, the distinguished Historian of the prestigious Magic Circle, Professor Edwin Dawes. Eddie wrote (Magigram, Oct. 1976) that the published assessments of Houdini's character traits were so diverse as to give psychologists nightmares. He explained that he'd asked the late John Mulholland, [the last editor of The Sphinx], who knew Houdini well, what he was really like. Mulholland replied that every story you'd heard about Harry was true. He could be mean, generous, harsh, gentle, hostile or friendly. Eddie concluded that Houdini's personality defied categorization.

That opinion was confirmed by Will Goldston, who also knew Houdini very well. Goldston acknowledged (Great Magicians' Tricks, 1931) that Houdini's "character was so complex...that it would not be possible to convey him with justice in a volume ten times the size of this present work". In addition, Kreskin (Magicol, Feb. 1999) quoted magical character, and Houdini colleague, Al Flosso, as saying that the fiction and myths surrounding Houdini were nowhere near what he was really like. Finally, Walter B. Gibson, Houdini friend and ghost writer, wrote (quoted in William V. Rauscher, The Houdini Code Mystery, 2000) that the only thing you can be sure of about Houdini is that you can't be sure about anything!

So, after reading all those words of warning, I decided not to attempt the impossible – trying to get into Houdini's head - I'd just gather statements from those who knew him and hopefully get an overall flavour of the man. I positively wouldn't try to psychoanalyse him, or make excuses for his conduct. Too many authors had gone wrong trying to do just that. So the following extracts, from my findings, are to allow you to draw your own conclusions on Handcuff Harry's eccentric character.

To make some sense of it all, I decided to separate the opinions of Houdini's magical contemporaries into two major categories.

Houdini seems to have had the knack of making people either love him or loathe him, with no middle ground. You can't become the number one in any enterprise without making some enemies along the way; so, before his many foes get their say, let's look at the more polite things people wrote about him.

Starting with where I began, magicians Ernst and Carrington's book, we find that Houdini was a strange mixture of vanity, generosity, arrogance and kindness. Ernst's legal partner, lawyer and poet, Melville Cane, described Houdini in his book (The First Firefly, 1974) as indeed a complex personality. He called him a consummate showman, and attributed the world-wide supremacy in his profession to years of self-discipline, self-denial, and study. Cane talked of Harry's "legitimate egotism and tenacity of the dedicated artist, an egotism which so often undermines acceptance and popularity." But in Houdini's case the egotism was "interwoven and spiced with a winning charm and a liberal supply of humour", and when off-stage, and out of the limelight "he was a genial, warm-hearted companion, essentially a serious person, [having an] affectionate nature."

American writer and literary critic, Edmund Wilson, tended to concur with the above in his book (The Shores of Light, 1952). He agreed that Houdini was a tremendous egoist, but was "remarkable among magicians in having so little of the smart-aleck about him." He also described Houdini as: "a short strong stocky man with small feet and a very large head. Seen from the stage, his figure, with its short legs and its pugilist's proportions, is less impressive than at close range, where the real dignity and force of the enormous head appear. Wide-browed and aquiline-nosed, with a cleanness and fitness almost military, he suggests one of those enlarged and idealized busts of Roman consuls or generals. So, it is rather the man himself than the stage personality who is interesting." Thomas J. Shimeld (Walter B. Gibson and The Shadow, 2003) quoted Houdini's friend Gibson as saying that in the Houdini film "Tony Curtis wasn't a very good Houdini…He made him suave. Houdini was rough and ready."

Another non-magician close to Houdini was his last Press Agent, George Atkinson. He is quoted (The Conjurors' Magazine, May 1948) as saying that initially he was completely won over by Houdini's good-natured sporting attitude. The author of the article, Bruce Reynolds, speculates, "Houdini, it would seem, as are many great geniuses – and he was truly a great genius – was a most inconsistent personality." Atkinson also gave his impression of Houdini as a person: "I thought he was a wonderful, a rare human being. He was natural, unaffected, democratic, and actually most generous....had the most eloquent hands I ever saw on a man; like chiselled marble. And he had a massive brow and a most poetic forehead."

Another Houdini Press Agent, Russell Holman, wrote (M-U-M, Aug. 1953) that Houdini had the brains of a super-press agent himself. Russell called Houdini privately an interesting but disturbing man. Holman said that, during the period we are looking at, Houdini appeared to be 10 years younger than he was, short but stocky, steel muscled and barrel-chested. He had a lithe carriage and movements of a trained young athlete. His coal black penetrating eyes burned straight through you when he talked. He was a man of supreme self-confidence.

Houdini's English magical chum Will Goldston (Great Magicians' Tricks, 1931 & The Magazine of Magic, May 1921) tells us that Houdini was a strong, determined man of iron, possessing "to an extraordinary degree the will to win". Milbourne Christopher (The Yankee Magic Collector #11, 2004) talks of his drive and determination. Houdini biographer Kenneth Silverman (Genii, Sept. 2003) describes how hard Houdini laboured, while Harry's great friend John Mulholland (Quicker Than the Eye, 1932) stresses that Houdini would work eighteen hours a day.

Bill Kalush (Magic Magazine, Nov. 2006) says Houdini slept only 4 hours a night and did not waste any of the 20 he was awake. William Lindsay Gresham (Monster Midway, 1954) speculates that during his days of hardship, Houdini must have constantly hammered at himself with a barrage of autosuggestion that he would one day be great. So, one of the main reasons for Houdini making it to the big time had to be his strong willpower and work ethic.

Stanley Collins (The Linking Ring, May 1945) remarking on Houdini as a magic historian, says that in collecting and co-ordinating his data there had never been a more painstaking researcher. Houdini went to great lengths to pay homage to past magical 'Greats'. John Mulholland (Quicker Than the Eye, 1932) remarks on Houdini's veneration for magicians of other days. Houdini was also a keen book collector and author, amassing a large collection of magic and theatrical works, which he willed to the public. Milbourne Christopher (The Yankee Magic Collector #11, 2004) agrees that Houdini had a love of old books.

Dorny (The Sphinx, Apr. 1945) called Houdini a humanitarian, while Will Goldston (Great Magicians' Tricks, 1931 & Sensational Tales of Mystery Men, 1929) said he was kindly, warm-hearted, gentle and loving, and mentioned his maudlin sentimentalism for animals and children. Stanley Collins (quoted in Edwin A. Dawes, Stanley Collins, 2002) agrees with the 'sentimental' assertion. Houdini is often said to have been a wonderful family man. Augustus Rapp, who claimed to have known Houdini from childhood, emphasized (The Life and Times of Augustus Rapp, 1959) that Harry was strictly a mother's boy. Edwin Dawes (The Magic Circular, June 1994) wrote that it is interesting to note how Houdini's devotion to his own mother extended also to concern and respect for the mothers of his friends. Syd Bergson puts it slightly differently when he says (The Linking Ring, Oct. 1975) that one can't help concluding that the immortal escape artist couldn't escape from his mother's apron strings. All I can say is that it's a shame more people aren't that way today. The world might be a better place for it.

Milbourne Christopher (The Yankee Magic Collector #11, 2004) refers to Harry's generous contributions, and how he was a soft touch for anyone needing cash. Goldston (Sensational Tales of Mystery Men, 1929) agrees with the generosity, and says he was always willing to help a brother or sister in distress. John Mulholland reveals (Quicker Than the Eye, 1932) that no one knew until after Houdini's death of the many aged magicians he was supporting. Christopher also writes of Houdini being at the same time a penny-pincher and a big spender. Although he spent practically nothing on his own clothing and abode, he would spend lavishly on his wife and family's clothing and residence, as well as other projects, to the point of near bankruptcy. Typically, he spent 25,000 dollars on a house, and moved in his mother, sister and brother, and as well, paid out 20,000 dollars on an exedra dedicated to his parents in Machpelah Cemetery. Sidney Radner (The Yankee Magic Collector #9, 2000) quotes Houdini's brother Hardeen as saying that Harry spent more than 50,000 dollars over the years in perfecting his Chinese Water Torture Cell trick. All this was at a time when the average weekly wage was approximately 15 dollars.

Houdini also visited hospitals, asylums, and prisons performing his magic without pay to bring cheer to the less fortunate. He spent his last Christmas Eve performing magic [and escapes!] for the 1,200 prisoners of Sing Sing Prison. [Yes, well before Johnny Cash thought of doing it!] Houdini's childhood friend, Joseph Rinn (Searchlight On Psychical Research, 1954) says that Houdini helped nearly every reporter whenever he found him broke. Of course, this generosity made all reporters his friends, and they'd go to any lengths to help him. This, added to the fact that he was constantly on the lookout for any opportunity to gain publicity, helped greatly to keep him at the top of his profession until his untimely death. T. Nelson Downs, the great coin manipulator and Houdini pal, called Harry (The Sphinx, Nov. 1930): "the world's greatest press agent for himself". To this tribute Gresham (Monster Midway, 1954) adds the word "mythmaker".

While writing about Houdini's death (quoted in Magicol, Nov. 2003), the great humourist Will Rogers described a showman as a man who can sell himself to the public in the very best way possible, and called Houdini the greatest showman of his time by far. Will Goldston (Great Magicians' Tricks, 1931) agreed that

Houdini was certainly the greatest showman of his time, and elsewhere (Secrets of Famous Illusionists, 1933) talks of Houdini's "amazing genius for showmanship". Charles B. Cochran (The Secrets of a Showman, 1925) called Houdini: "one of the most remarkable showmen I have ever known....[his] sense of showmanship was almost uncanny." John Mulholland explained (The Sphinx, Oct. 1948) that Houdini's presentation created a thrilling spectacle due to his masterful showmanship and striking personality. Sam Sharpe said (The Magic Play, 1976, & Magigram, Aug. 1982), "I was not only completely baffled, but felt that Houdini was one of the very few magicians whom I had seen who came up to expectations."

Sharpe not only mentioned Houdini's charisma, and his ability to handle an audience, but also made an interesting point. He added that Houdini was also a master of stagecraft, and the handling of atmosphere, which is not quite the same as showmanship. Sharpe says Houdini did not do tricks – he made magic. Being a master at anticipating spectator expectations, Houdini was able to time his triumphant reappearance to coincide with audience suspense reaching a peak. He had the ability to make people want him to break free. They would go wild when he succeeded. So, one thing we can be sure of is that his many years performing in sideshows and dime museums, taught him to be the very best when it came to 'working' a crowd.

Those above comments are just a very few from the many writers who called Houdini the greatest showman, in fact, almost all of the people who criticised him as a person seem to have acknowledged his incredible showmanship, and ability to dramatize conditions with his immense stage personality. A typical person who admitted to writing "uncomplimentary" things about Houdini, was magical elder statesman Dai Vernon, but at the same time Vernon referred to Houdini's "remarkable showmanship" and said (Genii, Apr. 1979) "People witnessing his performances were sure his life was in danger." Houdini was a genius at creating audience suspense. Bill Kalush (Magic Magazine, Nov. 2006) called Houdini the most exciting man alive during his lifetime.

Several authors have written that Houdini had no sense of humour. That is wrong. Although he wasn't a funny man in the way that a comic would be, he did possess an excellent sense of situational humour. This is confirmed in the annotated bibliography of William Lindsay Gresham's book (Houdini: The Man Who Walked Through Walls, 1959), where he writes of Houdini's lively sense of humour. George Shultz gives a typical instance of Houdini humour when writing on the subject of "Saying The Right Thing At The Right Time" (The Sphinx, Dec. 1913). Schultz explains that one of the best moments of Houdini's recent performance occurred when a committee was strapping him into a straitjacket. As Houdini was being pulled and tugged about the stage, he stopped, looked at the audience for a moment and remarked, "This is one way to make an easy living." And then began to struggle to free himself.

Although Houdini's quick mind and marvellous powers of observation enabled him to sensationalize any feat he performed, to carry out his escapes required a powerful, outstanding physique, coupled with the pliability of a contortionist, and the agility and delicate touch needed to pick locks. Houdini had the instincts of a true daredevil, as Gresham (Monster Midway, 1954) points out. Although, as some authors have suggested, he might have made sure his escapes where foolproof before doing them, you only have to look at his pioneering flying in dangerous kit-like planes that were more apt to kill you than fly.

Gresham (Monster Midway, 1954) reveals that Houdini was always on the lookout for skills that he could adapt to his escapes. When he found them he mastered them. As John Mulholland explained (Quicker Than the Eye, 1932), Houdini took advantage of everything nature endowed him with. As an example of using everything at his command, Mulholland explains that Houdini told him to find a way to use his most generously proportioned ears to serve him in his magic. John at first thought he was being teased but found out that Houdini was very serious. Does using your ears sound farfetched? Well, if you think so then refer to the June 1898 issue of 'Mahatma' magazine. There you'll find an article by Houdini that describes ways to secretly signal to a partner. What does he tell us? He says, "I have even trained my right ear to move up and down and thus give my assistant the tip." Yes, Houdini used every part of his body to its utmost capability!

As well as being ambidextrous and agile, with unusual endurance, Houdini also needed an exceptional knowledge of locks, and above all courage and a brazen confidence. So - his magnetic stage personality aside - what was his physical appearance like? David Bamberg (Illusion Show, 1991) talks of seeing Houdini stripped to the waist and says he (Bamberg) "was awestruck by his marvellous physique". Did this make Houdini an imposing figure? Although you would think so, the answer is "No!" In reality he was short and stocky, and quite unlike the tall Hollywood heroes who have played him – but he would have loved them for it. Nevertheless he had a unique captivating appeal that still exists today.

I can't leave the subject of Houdini's physique without giving you my favourite quote. One of Edwin Dawes' excellent columns, in the journal of The Magic Circle (The Magic Circular, Sept. 2001), featured an advertising promotion book of magic tricks. In it was a description of Houdini: "A short, vain man with hypnotic eyes and Brillo pad hair, who had a genius for scaring the wits out of people." When I repeated that quote to a well-known Hollywood leading lady, she turned to her famous heart-throb co-star, who was about to play Houdini, and took great delight in pointing out the "Brillo pad hair" to him.

Okay, now we've covered the praiseworthy side of Houdini what did his detractors write about him? [Why is it that the weaknesses and failings of super stars always seem more interesting than their respectable sides?] What you'll now discover is that it was possible for Houdini to have all the above commendable attributes, BUT at the same time behave in completely the opposite way, for example he could be both charitable and vindictive.

Who better to start us off on the darker side of Harry's character than a person we quoted above when looking at his commendable attributes - Will Goldston? He knew Houdini as well as anyone, and refers to him (Great Magicians' Tricks, 1931; Secrets of Famous Illusionists, 1933; & Sensational Tales of Mystery Men, 1929) as an enigma with an incongruous mixture of human virtues and failings. Some of those failings, Will says, were being utterly childish, boastful, ungracious, aggressively brutal, and having the vanities of a woman, along with a quick temper that bordered on insanity, as well as often being unscrupulous and dishonest. Stanley Collins (quoted in Edwin A. Dawes, Stanley Collins, 2002) called Houdini 'hard', while Martin Sunshine refers (The Linking Ring, Mar. 1998) to him as "a tough little guy". William Lindsay Gresham (Monster Midway, 1954) explains that having come up the hard way, via dime museums, circuses, and carnivals, Houdini acquired the toughness of an old-time "carny", which never left him.

'The Bat' magic magazine (Nov. 1950) talks of his many bitter enemies, and refers to Harry's egotism, his unscrupulousness, and his use of devious means to attain his ends. David Bamberg (Illusion Show, 1988) confirms the enemies when he says, "Houdini was disliked by most of his fellow magicians; it might have been envy, I don't know. To me he was a kind man." But Bamberg elsewhere gives us a clue to what may have caused the 'dislike'. He says, "Houdini had a dominating character and it was part of his personality and drive to always try to be greater and bigger than anyone else." Milbourne Christopher (The Yankee Magic Collector #11, 2004) confirms this when he refers to Houdini's ceaseless effort to become the best known magician of his time, and talks not only of Houdini's ruthless battles with spirit mediums, but as well his viscous attacks on rival escapologists. William Rauscher mentions (The Great Raymond, 1996) Houdini's relentless efforts to literally control the magic world. Gresham (Monster Midway, 1954) asserts that it was the heart breaking number of years to reach the top that made him defend his position so forcefully.

Just three of the major magi of Harry's era, who were strongly anti-Houdini, were Blackstone, Raymond and Dante. George Johnstone, who worked for Blackstone, asserted (in The Yankee Magic Collector #8, 1998) that Blackstone and Houdini despised each other. While Thomas Ewing said (in the same magazine) Houdini recognised no other escape artists, and wound up in a fist fight with Raymond during a magicians' banquet. Raymond accused Houdini of having his accomplices gimmick a pair of handcuffs that Raymond was attempting to escape from so that the cuffs had to be sawn off. William Rauscher (The Houdini Code Mystery, 2000) stated that Dante's feelings for Houdini could be called vitriolic, and a bitter hatred. As Daniel Waldron (Blackstone: A Magician's Life, 1999) pointed out, Houdini's attacks on competitors were not just limited to the big boys; he also harassed the small man.

Houdini had many bitter feuds. A typical one was with Dr. Wilson, the editor of 'The Sphinx'. Although they eventually settled their dispute, during their "acrimonious disagreement" Wilson wrote (The Sphinx, May 1908): "....self conceit has caused him to idolize himself. I am sorry for him for he has not yet learned the lesson that others have the right to live (if they are in the same line of business as himself) but must pervert his manhood by trying to abuse and crush them." Walter Gibson added (quoted in William V. Rauscher, The Houdini Code Mystery, 2000) that Harry had a genius for finding out someone's weakness and using it on them. It would seem that although Houdini's will power, showmanship genius, and magnetic performance, coupled with his self-publicity talent, got him to the top, a bit of underhanded dirty dealing helped to keep him there, and crush his opponents.

As for Houdini's ungovernable, quick temper, Walter B. Gibson described (The Sphinx, Mar. 1951) an incident where Houdini mistakenly raged at a poor messenger. Houdini's brother Hardeen told Walter not to bother trying to stop him because it was impossible. Gibson says it was Houdini's technique, he just hammered away at people, sometimes getting results, and sometimes not. John Mulholland (Quicker Than the Eye, 1932) confirms the extremely quick temper, but adds that his anger could cool off just as quickly as it flared up. After talking to many old stagehands of Houdini's era, George Johnstone concluded (The New Tops, Apr. 1969) that Houdini was not really the nicest of fellows.

According to Daniel Waldron (Blackstone: A Magician's Life, 1999), Houdini's utter seriousness attracted magical pranksters. He did not take kindly to being the butt of their jokes. As Dai Vernon put it (Genii, Apr. 1979) being an extreme egotist Houdini could not bear to have anyone fool him. Vernon then tells how Bess Houdini, the Godmother of Vernon's older boy, wrote him a letter describing how Houdini had sat up nearly all night trying to solve the card trick Vernon had fooled him with. This hatred of being fooled also extended to fraudulent mediums. Dick Cavett recalls (Magic, June 2013) how he and Johnny Carson "laughed heartily at Vernon's tales of what a shit Houdini was."

Houdini lost many friends in magic by publishing a book spitefully attacking his former hero J. E. Robert-Houdin (Harry Houdini, The Unmasking of Robert-Houdin, 1908). Harry had got his stage name by adding a letter "i" to Houdin's name. It seems that when members of the late magician's family refused to meet the brash young American, Harry turned against the great magician. It's sad because if Houdini had not made that attack, and just published his work as a conjuring history tome, he'd have received the congratulations of the magic world. So, it seems Houdini also had failings like his former hero, but was unable to see them.

There are so many references in magical literature to Houdini being arrogant and egotistical that I won't attempt to argue the point. My favourite 'big-head' quote is by P. T. Selbit who asked (The Wizard, Nov. 1906): "Does Houdini fully comprehend the meaning of egotism?" John Mulholland, who Harry hired to teach him to be a little more cultured in his lecture presentation, wrote (quoted in William V. Rauscher, The Houdini Code Mystery, 2000) that Houdini could be both charming and insulting, and that he never apologized. But although many hated Houdini,

Mulholland said he still liked him. Elsewhere (Quicker Than the Eye, 1932) Mulholland says that Houdini did use his capabilities to their utmost, which could possibly justify his self-conceit, but [something most of the others don't mention] he also was well aware of his limitations. If he didn't know something he would seek out an expert and learn from him. This included everything from knotting ropes with your feet [acquired from an armless sideshow freak] to gathering information from authorities on theatrical history. Gresham suggests (Monster Midway, 1954) that for someone as egocentric as Houdini to flatter the press in each country he visited must have been hard to learn, but learn it he did in a very big way.

Many writers have said that Houdini was a poor magician. Perhaps top illusionist David Bamberg put it best when he wrote this about Houdini: "Alongside his sensational escapes, his tricks and illusions were flat. The background of suspense and danger were lacking....However, Houdini's lectures on anti-spiritualism were sensational." It would appear that his critics did not include escapes and anti-spiritualism under the category of 'magic'. All I'll say on the subject is that the next time someone tells you Houdini was a poor magician, just mention the unique performance piece he did for Conan Doyle and Ernst. That artistic presentation caused the creator of Sherlock Holmes to believe the illusion was real, while the man who succeeded Houdini as the President of America's premiere magic organisation, was still puzzling over how it was done when he died. Oh yes, and so have subsequent generations of magicians.

On a lesser note, for someone who was constantly in the public eye, Houdini was not exactly a fashion icon. Bamberg (Illusion Show, 1991) described Houdini as "wearing an old sloppy pair of pants...". Augustus Rapp (The Life and Times of Augustus Rapp, 1959) calls Harry a notoriously bad dresser, and says he nearly mistook the star of the show for a janitor. Yes, as I've said already, although he was very generous with his wife and family's clothing, he was a penny-pincher when it came to his own attire.

Walter Gibson states (quoted in William V. Rauscher, The Houdini Code Mystery, 2000) that Houdini was not one of the suave, elegant magicians that many of his competitors were. He lacked class and even rudimentary refinement. He always remained what he started out in life as, a carny man. It has been suggested that he was too illiterate to write anything. The truth seems to be that his lack of formal education was covered up by secretaries, and ghost writers, but in the main he dictated the material, as no one else would dare to be as insensitive as his writings often are. When it came to truthfulness, what was true was what would boost Houdini. Like most magical performers, he was adept at exaggeration, and this extended offstage as well. Of course, Houdini is certainly not the first or last entertainer who made the big time and then re-invented himself. Most tell the press what they think they want to hear.

Finally, although I wrote that Houdini was an expert at the business side of show business, I must clarify that statement. I was referring to the generating of income. As David Hibberd reported (Chronicle of Magic 1900 - 1999, 2003), Houdini is said to have earned a salary of 750 pounds per week for a two week engagement at the London Palladium. This was when the average weekly wage was well below 5 pounds. But, like many other magicians, Harry had great difficulty in keeping his money. Typically, he wasted a great amount on his film ventures. Sadly he also lost the money of some of his friends who'd invested in the movies as well, turning them into non-friends. Although he was one of the highest paid entertainers of his era, he spent money faster than it came in. As Bob Lund revealed (Magicol, Aug. 1992), Houdini died broke. His estate was insolvent.

So, to sum up those derogatory remarks, Houdini had, as George Johnstone wrote (The New Tops, Apr. 1969), like all of us, many faults and foibles. As several brave people have suggested in magical literature [and usually ignored by the vast majority, who actually fit it] most would-be young magicians use magic as a crutch, or a mask to hide behind. Many are 'geeks', who use the power of their special secret knowledge to overcome a lack of social confidence. The self-image of being someone who possesses supernatural abilities is a tremendous ego booster. [Yes, sadly, I'm talking from personal experience!]

If you ask any magician's wife about magicians you'll nearly always get the same reply - magicians are just big kids who never grew up. They are all little boys at heart, still playing with their 'toys'. Many wives say the average mental age of their magic nut husbands is thirteen. [After reading this paragraph, my wife said it was not thirteen, it's more like eleven! Another magician's wife told me that was entirely wrong....it was five!] The classic magic anecdote is about the young lad who tells his parents he wants to be a magician when he grows up, but is told that he can't do both. Hence Will Goldston's assertion that Houdini was utterly childish is probably quite right.

My gut feeling is that Houdini used magic to overcome his height disadvantage, i.e. little guys get beaten up in the school yard unless they have an 'equalizer' like magic. Yes, I think Houdini was one of the typical, height challenged, socially inadequate fellows using magic as a prop to raise themselves to an equal level with the bigger boys. It is interesting to note that Houdini's major magic rival, Howard Thurston, was also short. At least Houdini didn't resort to lifts in his shoes and plastic surgery as Thurston did. Often the insecurity remains hidden just below the surface image of the mystery man. I'll leave the psychologists to argue the point with regard to whether Houdini 'needed' magic as opposed to 'wanted' to be a magician. But it could help explain why he didn't reveal the secret of the slate test to fellow magician Ernst. Was it low self-esteem coupled with a huge ego?

I won't try to justify any of Houdini's above actions, but, to help you understand them a little better, I'll attempt to put them into a more modern context. Today, nearly a century later, you can find a similar attitude that Houdini had toward his competitors by perusing your daily newspaper for stories about the nefarious goings on of some big businesses. Another parallel is the conduct of many current superstars. During a recent interview, on a U.K. TV chat show, a top movie actress and entertainer [who will remain nameless] admitted that off-camera she was spoilt and petulant. Her behaviour was of a dramatic nature. She had "the most spectacular tantrums". Hmm, somehow that sounds familiar. Is that conduct a requirement to making it big in the entertainment world?

Okay, there you have it. Houdini was unquestionably a paradox. As stated above, his personality defies categorization! Rauscher talks of the extraordinary views held about him; but, as John Mulholland wrote, a decade after Houdini's death (The Sphinx, Oct. 1936): "Houdini was so great that even those few, who were his enemies, had to admit that he was great." The last words on the subject have to be Syd Bergson's who declared (The Linking Ring, Feb. 1980): "Long after the current crop of detractors and defamers of Houdini are gone and forgotten, he will be remembered by the public."

Right, now it's time to move on to Conan Doyle, but before doing so there is something connected with Sir Arthur that really belongs here. What is it? Well, you've just read many different opinions of Houdini's character from many people, but not from the most important person. We need Conan Doyle's assessment of Houdini to help in evaluating his reaction to the slate trick.

My first thought regarding quoting Doyle was to question the judgment of someone who believed Houdini might be escaping from restraints by dematerialising himself. Fortunately Milton Bridges cleared that difficulty up. In reviewing Conan Doyle's 1930 book, Bridges said (The Sphinx, Dec. 1930) that the question of Houdini's supernatural powers aside, Doyle's characterisation of Houdini is the most exact that had been presented in writing to the public. Bridges added that Doyle "not only was totally familiar with his subject but his ability of description was in no sense diminished in his declining years."

Instead of repeating that specific chapter from Sir Arthur's 1930 book (The Edge of the Unknown, 1930), I'll include extracts from an even earlier 1927 Conan Doyle magazine article (The Strand, Aug/Sept. 1927) on which the book's chapter was based. The article is better for our purposes as it was written closer to the time we are investigating. It just might help shed some light on why Doyle thought Houdini could have been, in addition to "the greatest medium baiter of modern times", also "the greatest physical medium". The article was spread over 16 pages in two issues of the magazine. For your ease of reading, I have ignored the claim that Harry was a medium, extracted the major bits on Houdini's character, and then extensively edited it down to only a few paragraphs. [Yes, I realize I should have done that in many other places as well!] Doyle had this to say:

"I knew Houdini well. I will give some of my personal impressions of him. Houdini is far and away the most curious and intriguing character whom I have ever encountered. I have never met a man who had such strange contrasts in his nature, and whose actions and motives it was more difficult to foresee or to reconcile. First, the great good which lay in his nature. He had courage to a supreme degree allowing him to undertake reckless feats of daring. He was in constant training. Nothing in this world or the next could permanently abash him. He was a very astute man, and what he did he would do thoroughly. He had a poker face and gave nothing away as a rule.

He was remarkable for his cheery urbanity in everyday life. One could not wish a better companion so long as one was with him, though he might do and say the most unexpected things when one was absent. He was estimable in his family relationships. His love for his dead mother seemed to be the ruling passion of his life. He was devoted also to his wife. Another favourable side of his character was his charity. He was the last refuge for the down-and-outer. On one side of his character he was a fine fellow.

So much for his virtues – and most of us would be very glad to have as goodly a list. But all he did was extreme, and there was something to be placed in the other scale. A prevailing feature of his character was a vanity which was so obvious and childish that it became more amusing than offensive. This enormous vanity was combined with a passion for publicity which knew no bounds, and which must at all costs be gratified. He had a desire to play a constant public part. He loved to be important. Where there was an advertisement to be gained Houdini was a dangerous man. Houdini's attitude in private was quite different to what it was in public. He always published my letters, even the most private of them. His curious mentality caused him to ignore absolutely the experiences of anyone else, but he seemed to be enormously impressed if anything from an outside source came in his own direction."

Sir Arthur finished his article by saying, "He was a great personality, with many outstanding qualities, and the world is the poorer for his loss. I shall always retain an affection for him...."

That article was written after Houdini's death. Fortunately I located evidence of Doyle's opinion of Houdini, written three years earlier, while Houdini was still alive, and even closer to the time we are looking at. Harry Price, the great Ghost Hunter, whose library was of enormous help in this quest, included an extract from a 1924 Conan Doyle letter in one of his books (Leaves From a Psychist's Case-book, 1933). Often someone will write something in a private letter that they would not include in an article for publication. This seems to have been the case here. Doyle wrote a single sentence that is quite revealing He declared that Houdini was "a very conceited, self-opinionated man".

Okay, that's Houdini out of the way. All right, I admit it. My look at him probably caused more confusion than provided answers. But it shows you what I was up against in trying to solve the master magician's slate mystery. After finishing the above I turned to Sir Arthur's personality. I hoped to find that he was much less complex – but wasn't too sure I would!

+ SIR ARTHUR CONAN DOYLE (1859 - 1930): After learning how complicated Houdini was, I suspected his illustrious spectator Sir Arthur would prove to be just as difficult to pin down. Unfortunately I was right!

The average person is a mixture of good and bad traits [yes, that includes both you and me]. Since Houdini and Conan Doyle were well above average, I opted to begin my examination of Doyle by looking for similarities between the two. My assumption was that those likenesses had probably attracted them to each other. As any good con man will tell you, how much a person will trust another is usually dependent on how much they resemble each other.

To begin with, as I did with Houdini, here is a very brief history of Sir Arthur Conan Doyle's life. He was born in Edinburgh, Scotland, in 1859 and died four years after Houdini, in 1930. Like Houdini, Sir Arthur came from a poor background. His upbringing was blighted by the alcoholism of his father. Unlike Harry's limited schooling, Doyle managed to study medicine at Edinburgh University. [The self-educated Houdini graduated with distinction from 'the school of hard knocks'.] Qualifying as a Doctor, Conan Doyle practiced from 1882 to 1890.

Facing poverty practicing medicine, he turned to writing, and achieved literary immortality by creating the super-detective Sherlock Holmes and his good-natured friend, and chronicler, Dr. Watson. Just as there are many magic clubs named after Houdini, there are at least 400 Holmes appreciation societies worldwide. My wife and I had the great pleasure of being present on a special Holmes night at the famous old time music hall, The Players Theatre, in London. We went there every week, but hadn't realized that it was fully booked that evening by members of Holmes' societies from around the globe. The doorman, who was the brother of a good friend, managed to sneak us in to sit in a corner of the balcony. Those Holmes aficionados had come to London, from as far away as Japan, to attend the Baker Street unveiling of Sherlock Holmes' statue. Many were in costume. We saw several judges and villains, as well as Sherlocks. It opened my eyes to the fact that magic nuts weren't the only strange people in the world.

Of course, Doyle's detective novels weren't his only writings. He penned many historical romances and adventure stories. He even launched a whole genre of pre-historic animal, scientific adventure type films when he created 'The Lost World', in 1912.

Turning to our Scottish doctor's nature, I decided to commence slowly by looking at his physical prowess. Houdini had been extremely athletic. Was Conan Doyle also, or was he more a desk bound novelist? While leafing through the sports section of my daily paper one day, I discovered the answer. Sir Arthur had not only been a founder member of the Portsmouth Football Club, in 1884, he was also the team's first goalkeeper. This alone would have been quite something, but it wasn't his only sports claim to fame. He was a member of the MCC, and once bowled out W. G. Grace in a cricket match at Lord's. [Note for American readers: For 'football' think 'major league soccer', and for cricket performance imagine him striking out Babe Ruth in Yankee Stadium.] Doyle was also an amateur pugilist, and wrote the boxing story, 'Rodney Stone', in 1896. In addition, he was instrumental in making skiing a fashionable new hobby. So, our two leading characters were very similar in the sphere of sports.

Okay, so both of them were sporty, but what about Doyle's physical appearance? Well, it seems that he and Houdini were opposites in the height department. Where Houdini was very short and stocky, Doyle was well over 6 feet, and burly. An incident during Conan Doyle's visit to America, will illustrate the point nicely. Sir Arthur attended the Society of American Magicians banquet [June 22, 1922] as the principal guest of honour. There Houdini did a trick using Doyle's jacket. Harry's hands were securely tied and he stepped into his cabinet carrying the jacket. Almost immediately he reappeared wearing the coat. 'The Sphinx' (June 1922) described Houdini as: "wearing the rather gigantic coat belonging to Sir Arthur Conan Doyle." Sir Arthur has also been described as jovial, with heavy eyelids and a drooping moustache that seemed to make him look like a genial walrus. Milbourne Christopher (Seers, Psychics and ESP, 1970) called Sir Arthur a tall, moustached British writer who had a serenity rare among men. Doyle was convinced that there was an afterlife.

The next Conan Doyle attribute I considered was his sense of adventure. Houdini had been game for almost anything, such as risking his life on the other side of the world to become the seventh man ever to fly a plane. Was Doyle equally courageous, or was he just an armchair adventurer? Well, his first job after graduation was as a ship's surgeon on a whaler. For 11 months he sailed from the west coast of Africa to the Arctic. At the age of 40, when most men would be settling down, he volunteered to serve as an army surgeon in the Boer War, working in dreadful conditions. This action, and his written history of the conflict (The Great Boer War, 1900), earned him a knighthood in 1902. No, it was not, as you might imagine, for his Sherlock Holmes stories (The Adventures of Sherlock Holmes, The Strand Magazine, 1891-3).

Perhaps Conan Doyle's most appealing characteristic was being a champion of underdogs. In several celebrated cases he fought to redress miscarriages of justice. Typically Sir Arthur's personal investigation secured the freedom of George Edlaji, who had been falsely imprisoned for animal mutilation. Doyle's hard work also secured the release of supposed murderer Oscar Slater. Like Houdini, Conan Doyle was a public campaigner, giving himself heart and soul to his undertakings. In Carl Murchison's book (The Case For and Against Psychical Belief, 1927), Sir Arthur wrote that he had given a lecture on spiritualism in 1916, and found that it gave so much comfort to others that he determined to devote all his time to the subject. He then travelled the world for ten years as spiritualism's ambassador giving over 500 lectures on the subject.

I revealed above that Houdini died broke. So, was Sir Arthur equally careless with his cash? Did he leave anything behind? On his death, Conan Doyle's estate amounted to 63,491 pounds. That would be worth about 3 million pounds today! Yes, I think we can safely say they were dissimilar in that department.

Now, as I did with Houdini, I have to look at Conan Doyle's not so favourable points. He upset many people, just as Houdini did when he attacked his former hero J. E. Robert-Houdin (Harry Houdini, The Unmasking of Robert-Houdin, 1908). Sir Arthur caused a worldwide outcry when he killed off Sherlock Holmes, in a struggle with his arch-nemesis, Professor Moriarity, after a mere 2 years of publishing his stories.

Like Houdini, Doyle was more likely to distort or ignore something that did not agree with a cherished belief than to discard that belief. Harry Price, who could also be said to be on the opposite side of the occult fence to Conan Doyle, confirmed Sir Arthur's short temper and often unreasonable attitude. Price wrote (Leaves From a Psychist's Case-Book, 1933) that he would brook no correction, and in many respects was like a child, but a child with a heart of gold. That is very close to what has been written about Houdini. Doyle wrote that Houdini attacked him behind his back, so it's interesting to note that Price accused Sir Arthur of denouncing him [Price] during a lecture, while he was not there to answer those accusations.

Price had this to say about Sir Arthur: "A born fighter, sometimes intolerant, and often open to criticism, there was hardly a journal in the country to which he did not contribute....dynamic personality, driving force, dogged grit, tenacity of purpose, fighting qualities, large-heartedness, and word-wide prestige." That certainly could apply to Houdini.

Houdini's boyhood friend and sometime undercover assistant, Joseph F. Rinn, mentioned Sir Arthur several times in his book (Sixty Years of Psychical Research, 1950). Magician and psychic investigator Rinn said: "Doyle was a nice, kind, cultured old gentleman....but gullible....an easy mark for tricksters....a sincere but deluded person. The trouble is that Sir Arthur does not understand how tricks are performed and therefore does not know how to protect himself from frauds."

Editor of 'The Sphinx', John Mulholland, told how (in the Jan. 1931 issue) when riding in a train with Sir Arthur's fellow English writer G. K. Chesterton, he asked his opinion of Sir Arthur. Gilbert Chesterton, the author of the Father Brown detective books said, "Doyle had the mentality of Dr. Watson much more than that of Holmes." Mulholland added, "It is true the agile, quick deductive mind of detective Holmes does not represent Doyle as much as the believing and rather ponderous mind of Watson." Magician, best selling author, and prominent magazine editor, Fulton Oursler, wrote that when it came to mediums: "Sir Arthur Conan Doyle is the most deceived man in the world." Why was that? Well, Harry Price, who described his relations with Sir Arthur as often being "strained", gave a view that is probably very near the truth. I've condensed Price's several pages of comments (in the above book) into one paragraph - he wrote:

"Sir Arthur, who was High Priest of spiritualism in the eyes of the public, was content to forgo any real control of a medium, and accept spiritualism as a religion, which appealed to the emotions. His great big heart ran away with him and he was no match for the charlatans, who, like parasites, battened on his good nature. Doyle simply could not bring himself to believe that any medium was vile enough to trade on the most sacred feelings of the bereaved, and it was on this magnificent trait in his character that dishonest mediums traded. Too honest himself, he could not imagine his too sympathetic credulity being imposed upon by unscrupulous rogues. He was a great and wonderful man with the heart of a child."

Harry Price had many debates with Sir Arthur. He said his own relations with Doyle varied from month to month. When Price was not exposing Doyle's mediums, his letters to Price were full of praise for his efforts in interesting scientific orthodoxy in psychical research. It sounds as though Doyle had a similar relationship with both of the Harrys.

Earle J. Coleman (Magic: A Reference Guide, 1987) says: "The more knowing a reader is in the wiles of the magician... the more gullible Doyle appears and the more jolting is the realization that his fictional character, Sherlock Holmes, the very personification of rational thinking, is still cited in logic textbooks." Sherlock Holmes' method of detection was in two parts. The first was scientific investigation, which included great attention to detail, such as cataloguing cigarette ends. Secondly it included insight into criminal psychology. Magician John Booth's book (Psychic Paradoxes, 1984) states: "Sir Arthur Conan Doyle, the creator of Sherlock Holmes, although shrewd at perceiving how fictional persons might carry out deception, was often gullible in assessing the true character of real life individuals. A generous and honest man himself, he projected his own qualities into others."

I can't resist inserting a quote from 'The Sphinx' (Aug. 1922) here to give you the attitude of most magicians toward him: "At a Toledo séance Sir Arthur Conan Doyle had his arm stroked by a spirit. It must have been an agreeable change from having his leg pulled." H. L. Mencken, in a review of Ernst and Carrinton's book (American Mercury, June 1932), said that although Doyle was treated very politely "the fact that he was an almost fabulous ass cannot be concealed."

It would be easy to class Doyle as a fool; BUT, in his crusades against blatant miscarriages of justice, he certainly used all the Sherlock Holmes' techniques. At Edinburgh University, Dr. Joseph Bell had taught Sir Arthur the use of minute observation and diagnostic deduction. Where Doyle failed to employ those Holmesian deductions was when faced with anything to do with the occult or supernatural. He was even hoaxed by two little girls who supposedly took photographs of real live fairies. This incident was made into a 1998 film, Fairy Tale. It would seem that Doyle's complex mind could create the world's most logical detective, while at the same time fully believing in fairies.

I referred to Houdini's possibly complicated love life, so to be impartial, I'll just mention in passing that Sir Arthur fell in love with his second wife before his first had died of consumption. And finally, Kalush & Sloman (The Secret Life of Houdini, 2006) suggested another aspect of Conan Doyle. They described him as a man who clearly wanted to hijack Houdini's legacy. If Houdini was using Conan Doyle during his lifetime to gain publicity, as many have stated, then Doyle seems to have been doing the same with Houdini once Harry left the scene.

I won't play the amateur psychologist here, as I've already done that in the 'WHY' section! I'll just sum up my feelings on him from the very little I've read on the subject of human reactions. I think Doyle was so into Spiritualism that when Houdini pandered to it during his experiment, Doyle's brain set itself to expect a paranormal occurrence, and the 'feedback' triggered the 'intuitive' appropriate response.

I finished looking at Houdini by giving Doyle's opinion of him, so it's only fair to give Houdini's opinion of Conan Doyle here. The May 1922 issue of 'The Sphinx' reviewed a Houdini performance at a private club, and gave his response to a question about Sir Arthur and others as follows: "Houdini replied that he is convinced that they were absolutely sincere in their spiritualistic beliefs, and stated that in his opinion, these gentlemen are mistaken in what they have seen and, what is worse, that in their eagerness to believe they are imposed upon by unscrupulous tricksters. Houdini has attended several thousand séances and has investigated practically every well-known medium in the world, and doesn't hesitate to say they all practice frauds and that only the most childlike can accept their revelations seriously. And Houdini should know, for he is today undoubtedly the best posted man in this particular field."

So, there you have it. Houdini thought Conan Doyle was absolutely sincere, but mistaken, and due to being childlike, easily deceived.

Now, before finishing my assessments of both Houdini and Conan Doyle I'm going to give you a little test to see if you've been paying attention. Eric J. Dingwall's book (How to go to a Medium, 1927) refers to someone's character and has this to say about it:

"....highly complex emotional and mental, extremely suggestible and touchy, whilst at the same time capable of warm friendships and equally strong dislikes. Often of a childlike nature, easily forgives and forgets, although at the same time a strong sense of justice is found. Quick temper and waywardness are other characteristics,....more apparently self-centred than normal people."

So, having read my comments on both Houdini and Conan Doyle, who does the above paragraph apply to? Well, although it sounds very much like both of them, bizarrely Dingwall was giving the traits of an average medium. Could this also be partly what attracted them both to spiritualism, and also why Doyle thought Houdini was an unconscious medium?

THE TWO AUTHORS

To properly evaluate the description of Houdini's slate 'test', in Ernst and Carrington's book, I decided it was also necessary to look at the authors themselves, and their relationships with Houdini. Did their connection with him colour their reporting of the slate experiment? Harry had a strange effect on people. Those who knew him either admired him or were hostile. Which camp did each of our two authors fall into when Houdini was alive? Were they pro-Houdini or anti-Houdini? I found the answer to be intriguing.

+ **BERNARD M. L. ERNST** (1879 - 1938): Bernard Morris Lee Ernst - Bernie to a small group of friends - was Houdini's great friend and lawyer. A partner in the law firm Ernst, Cane and Berner, he specialised in copyright and theatrical matters. As well as advising Houdini, Ernst was also the lawyer of Conan Doyle.

Noted American poet, and fellow legal counsel, Melville Henry Cane, was Ernst's partner. So, who better to begin with when looking at Ernst? In his book (The First Firefly, 1974), Cane states that Bernard must have been born with the love of magic in his blood, because it was his favourite boyhood hobby. He delighted in entertaining his friends with parlour tricks. Ernst eventually qualified as a member of the Society of American Magicians where he met Houdini, and they took to each other forming a life-long friendship. When Houdini died Ernst succeeded him as President of the Society.

Ernst's obituary, in 'The Sphinx' (Dec. 1938) referred to his great generosity, not only in time, but also with help and money, and pointed out his many kind acts for the needy. It went on to say that all who knew him thought of him first not as a scholar, lawyer, or magician, but as a friend. The Sphinx's editor, John Mulholland, wrote that Ernst was a most wonderful friend and his idea of a gentleman. This would seem to answer why Houdini chose Ernst to act as an independent, trustworthy witness for both himself and Conan Doyle during the performance. Ernst was not only the lawyer of both men, but also a friend.

Apart from mentioning that Ernst was Houdini's lawyer, there is very little written on him in magic historical records. Two years after Houdini's death, Bess Houdini asked Harold Kellock to write a book about her late husband (Houdini: His Life Story, 1928). It was the first of a long line of biographical works on the self-liberator. The book's dedication read: "To Bernard M. L. Ernst, Houdini's dearest friend and adviser." The next mention of Ernst in a book, that I came across, was in David Bamberg's Illusion Show (1988). Although the manuscript had been written in 1965, it was not published until some years after Bamberg's death. In writing about a magic shop Bamberg said: "...satisfied customers were Harry Kellar, Frederick Eugene Powell, Bernard M. L. Ernst, Samuel Leo Horowitz and many other leading magicians of the U.S.A." This was quite a distinguished magical group for Ernst to be included in, and written by a man who would definitely recognise fellow "greats."

In the November 1985 issue of 'The Yankee Magic Collector', Henry Hay (Barrows Mussey) listed the men he met and used as role models. The roster could be said to be a who's who of magic's greatest magicians. There are 26 people listed including T. Nelson Downs, Houdini, Thurston, Blackstone, Annemann and Cardini. The list ended with "....and B. M. L. Ernst, Houdini's attorney and long president of the Society of American Magicians." The others only needed their names, but by 1985 Ernst had slipped down the list and now needed justification for being there. In 1996 Kenneth Silverman published his definitive biography on Houdini, aptly entitled 'Houdini!!!'. In the book I could find no mention of Bernie Ernst! How soon we are forgotten?

Ernst had a long association with The Society of American Magicians. He was a Delegate to the National Council, Vice-President, President, Honorary Life President, and Life Member of the Executive Committee of the Parent Assembly. He was also an Honorary President of The Board of Directors of The Sphinx Publishing Corporation. According to John Mulholland, Ernst was instrumental in The Sphinx continuing its publication when its editor, Dr. Wilson, died. For many years, Ernst also wrote a page on the 'doings' of magicians for what was the leading magic magazine for nearly half a century.

Although his peers held Ernst in great affection, it was necessary to determine the extent of Ernst's knowledge of the actual performance of magic. Was the description of Houdini's trick written by a very experienced magician, or just someone who was interested in magic? Often the officers and committees of magic clubs are dedicated amateurs, who are not performers but love magic. Professionals are frequently too busy working to have the time to run magic organisations. Was Ernst actually an expert performer? Will Goldston's Who's Who In Magic (1934) listed Ernst in his amateur section noting that Ernst was a close friend of Houdini's. Ernst was said to present a very polished act in all-round magic, frequently appearing at educational and charitable institutions, schools and colleges.

While investigating Ernst's magical abilities, I came across the following report in the 'M-U-M' (Magic Unity Might) - The

Society of American Magicians' (SAM) bulletin, which cast a very interesting light on Bernie's character:

"After the regular business of the meeting of April 2, 1921, the hour from 11 to 12 o'clock was given to recreation.

Illustrious B.M.L. Ernst started things with his magical lily cups. Several dozen cups were arranged in rows upon the table and from a glass cylinder was poured a fluid, which had been carefully protected from light by wrappings of paper.

After the contents of the jar or cylinder had been transferred to the cups, the performer called attention to the magical changes - or, as he announced - each cup, upon examination would be found to contain a different colored fluid.

A close and intimate examination of the contents of the cups convinced the examiners (comprising all present) that the color suited all tastes - and in a very short interval of time the cups were found to be empty - whether by the continued magic of the professor - or through unanimous co-operation of volunteer assistance - was not clearly proven."

My first thought was that this must be a version of Karl Germain's Water Jars Trick. I recalled that lily cups were paper cups, and found that Germain had invented his trick around 1908. To check out my supposition that it was, in fact, a Paper Cup Water Jars Trick, I started to reread the above description. I got no further than the first line when I realized what had actually taken place. Are you ahead of me? Well, just in case you aren't, the date was April 1921. Prohibition started in 1920, and the lack of alcohol was beginning to bite. 'The long dry spell' would go on until 1933. If you reread the above description with this in mind, it takes on a whole new meaning. Most interesting of all is the fact that there was unanimous co-operation in vanishing the interesting liquid. President Houdini, who was supposedly a complete teetotaller, according to magical history, was present! I was beginning to like Mr. Ernst.

Two months later, at the Annual Banquet of The Society of American Magicians (SAM), Ernst was at it again. The official report said:

"....Illustrious B.M.L. Ernst was called upon to do a trick and asked for a committee to help him along. He selected our worthy President Houdini and said he was going to do a production act. In the midst it turned out to be a loving cup for our worthy president and a magnificent cluster of flowers for a little lady, magnificently gowned, (hear, hear) Mrs. Beatrice Houdini. It was a great surprise to them both and they are truly grateful for the remembrance..." The report also said, "Mrs. B.M.L. Ernst presided at a table and she was some hostess..."

Reading between the lines again, it would appear that Bernie delighted just as much in fooling Houdini, as Houdini did in fooling him. Hence my conclusion that there was a second agenda to Houdini's performance for Conan Doyle and Ernst. Houdini was not only fooling a layperson who had no magical knowledge, he was also showing his fellow magician that he still had quite a bit to learn.

As for Ernst's magical competence, John Mulholland explained (The Sphinx, Dec. 1938) that Ernst received lessons in magic from him for several years. After each lesson they would talk about magic and magicians. It would be quite natural to assume that Houdini's appearing message performance would also have been thoroughly dissected and no answer found. Ernst had gone to Mulholland on the suggestion of Houdini. Will Goldston explained that Mulholland occupied a unique place in magic. He had performed in most countries of the world and had been hailed as the leading magical authority of his day.

So, can I say that Houdini also fooled the leading magical authority of his day? As for Mulholland's coaching abilities, he had been a teacher in a boys' school for several years, which would make him well qualified to tutor Ernst. His pupil would also seem to be well qualified to write up Houdini's enigma. With a mentor like

Houdini, and a tutor like Mulholland, I don't think we can question Ernst's magic abilities, even if he couldn't unravel what he had seen.

In examining 'WHO' might have been involved in the test, it's quite possible that Houdini had "hidden assistants", who were unknown to both Ernst and Conan Doyle. In a moment I'll suggest who some of them could have been; BUT, I am forced to ask first if Ernst himself was a "secret assistant". Crooked mediums often had a confederate, or stooge, acting as part of the audience. It would not be the first time Houdini had used such a subterfuge. Several books have suggested this might be the case. A typical one is Patrick Culliton's 2010 book Houdini: The Key.

After much consideration I decided that Ernst was not covertly helping Houdini. The urge for Houdini to fool his fellow magician, as well as the great fictional detective's creator, would have been too great. As Ernst wrote, Houdini was always fooling him, and refusing to explain how he did it. As well as Houdini, Doyle was also a client of Ernst's. If Houdini had afterward explained that Ernst had helped to fool Doyle, what would that have done to Ernst's reputation as a lawyer? I tend to agree with the Grand Old Man of Magic, Dai Vernon, who knew both Houdini and Ernst intimately. Vernon wrote (Genii, Apr. 1979), "Bernard Ernst was a true gentleman beloved by all." I couldn't see someone like that being a willing 'stooge' in this case.

+ **HEREWARD CARRINGTON** (1880 - 1958): Carrington's real name was Hubert Lavington. He was born in the Channel Islands and moved to the United States in 1899. As well as a prolific writer on the subject of psychical research, he was also a clever public speaker and lecturer. For someone who wrote over 100 books, there is surprisingly little written on him.

I spent quite a bit of time investigating Hereward because he could have had a major impact on my success. I believe that although Ernst supplied the information for the book, Carrington wrote it up. I came to that conclusion because Ernst, who inherited

Houdini's private notebooks, as well as much of his correspondence, had supplied data from the notebooks to another author [Walter B. Gibson] who produced two books based on them. Ernst only wrote the prefaces to both those books (Houdini's Escapes, 1930, and Houdini's Magic, 1932). In the 'Houdini and Conan Doyle' book, Ernst is credited as co-author, but when describing Houdini's slate 'test' the text refers to Ernst as "Mr. Ernst". So, it would appear that Carrington did the writing, and was somewhat distancing himself from the description of the event – possibly because he could not work out how Houdini had accomplished it, and thought Ernst might not have remembered the events quite correctly. The intriguing thing to me is why Houdini's friend Ernst chose Carrington to work with him on the book.

Joseph Rinn's autobiography (Searchlight On Psychical Research, 1954) mentions Carrington. It states that Carrington's attitude, from his earliest days, was that while there was a large percentage of fraud in psychic phenomena or Spiritualism, there was still some genuine phenomena. Rinn described how Carrington promoted, managed, and both acted as a master of ceremonies and translator for the famous Italian medium, Eusapia Palladino, on her 1903 American tour. Carrington had stated that he was bringing her to the United States so scientists could study her case. Somehow he forgot to submit her for examination until after many séances had been held and entrance fees collected. She was subsequently unmasked as a faker employing simple trickery. One of the exposers of Palladino, W. S. Davis, said, "After my investigation of Spiritualism for over twenty years, my conclusion is that Spiritualism is a gigantic delusion and that Mr. Carrington is a very good talker." The New York Times of May 14, 1910 wrote that Mr. Carrington assumed too much when he assumed that no deception existed when he could see none.

'Magic Magazine' (Sept. 1998) explained that magician, author, and psychic researcher Hereward Carrington appeared on the "You Asked For It" television show, in the 1950s. There he exposed tricks employed by "spook crooks" and phoney mediums. In his 1989 book (The Experience Of Magic), Eugene Burger, the award

103

winning magical lecturer, listed magical presentations that had a profound emotional impact on him. One of those presentations was the You Asked For It show on which Herewood (sic) Carrington talked about and demonstrated the tricks of spirit mediums.

Perhaps the best way to describe Carrington, for our purposes, is to read what the editor of the Society of American Magicians' magazine, M-U-M, wrote in the April 1921 issue. By the way, the editor was a fellow called Houdini! :

"We are pleased to inform our readers that after the regular meeting, May seventh, Professor Heward (sic) Carrington has kindly offered to give a lecture on Spiritualism. Professor Carrington is quite as well known as a lecturer on matters Spiritualistic as he is as a Spiritualistic investigator and writer."

The review of that lecture was published in the May 1921 issue:

"Mr. Hereward Carrington, of the Society of Psychical Research, having accepted an invitation to give a talk on the subject so familiar to him through long investigation, was received with prolonged applause, and for half an hour the members were treated to the narration of incidents in the experience of one who has, with but few exceptions, failed to unearth anything supernatural or contrary to known laws in presentations of Phenomena in any form. At the close the speaker was given a rising vote of thanks.
        The subject was then open for general discussion taken part by.....Illustrious Ernst....."

So, Ernst had met Carrington as early as 1921. From this report it would seem that Carrington would be eminently suitable to assist Ernst in recording the matters that transpired at Houdini's performance. At least that is what you would think until you read what editor Houdini had to say four years later in the February 1925 issue of the M-U-M:

"....Hereward Carrington, who for many years has endeavoured to serve two masters, posing as an honest investigator, exposing fraud, denouncing practitioners of occultism in one breath and in the next advocating the cause, endorsing its devotees, and exhaustive scientific (?) research endeavouring to prove its genuiness and sacredness...."

Rather scathing! Something had happened in the intervening years. Milbourne Christopher (Houdini: The Untold Story, 1969) wrote that Houdini had scorn for Carrington and thought he was an opportunist who professed to believe in spiritualism because the "pro" books he wrote sold more copies than "anti" volumes. Bart Whaley (Who's Who In Magic, 1990, 1991) said that Carrington was a famous although self-servingly credulous investigator of psychic phenomena.

Houdini had at least two major confrontations with Carrington over fake psychics Hereward was promoting. They became enemies over Margery [Mrs. Crandon] the medium. While Carrington claimed the Boston medium had produced genuine phenomena, Houdini branded her a fraud. Houdini also charged Carrington with being her confederate. Kenneth Silverman (Houdini!!!, 1996) explained that Houdini believed Carrington had helped Margery fake her manifestations and feared being found out. Houdini had told the press that Carrington was not qualified to sit or pass judgement on any spiritualistic investigation and had purchased a phoney Ph.D. degree for 75 dollars in Oskaloosa. Carrington denounced Houdini calling him a pure publicist and said that he had no standing as a Psychist. Houdini countered by saying that Carrington's actions in the Margery incident should be investigated.

Who was right? Possibly Ruth Brandon (The Life And Many Deaths Of Harry Houdini, 1993) has the answer. Looking at the situation from a woman's point of view, she declared that Mediums had rarely hesitated to use their sexual charms whenever this seemed appropriate. Margery was a very beautiful and very

105

sexy lady who had no compunction about displaying her highly desirable body. Brandon says that Carrington was undoubtedly in love with her. I leave the rest to your imagination.

One other major clash between Houdini and Carrington was over an "Egyptian Miracle Man" named Rahman Bey, who Carrington was also promoting. Carrington publicly challenged Houdini to duplicate Bey's underwater endurance feat - if he could. Houdini rose to the challenge and triumphed over Bey and Carrington, gaining maximum publicity along the way.

Up until his death, Houdini continued to have Carrington investigated. In a February 2, 1925 letter to fellow psychic investigator, book collector and magic nut, Harry Price (from the files of the Harry Price Library, at the University of London), Houdini wrote, "...I am very suspicious [of] Carrington..." In August of that year he remarked, "...I know that Carrington is going to open up a sort of exhibition at a hotel here, charging fifty cents admission. Will keep you informed...."

Houdini's 1924 book (A Magician Among the Spirits) explains that magic dealer Francis J. Martinka supplied apparatus to many magicians and "indirectly to well-known mediums." Houdini gives a Martinka example as "selling luminous paint to Hereward Carrington at the exact time he was the manager of the celebrated medium, E. Palladino." Houdini's "undercover man" Bob Gysel [see below] wrote in his letters (from David E. Price's collection): "H. Carrington is not an honest investigator....I would not buy a book that Carrington wrote on any subject...."

Milbourne Christopher (Seers, Psychics and ESP, 1970) stated that Carrington was a prolific writer on occult subjects and a psychical researcher who was always willing to sponsor a mystic whose name was in the news. It was his ambition to head a well-endowed laboratory for occult investigation, but the widely circulated exposure of Palladino shattered his hopes. Just to show you the other side of that situation, Sir Arthur Conan Doyle (Our Second American Adventure, 1923) asserted: "Dr. Carrington though he

106

acted well in the matter of Eusapia (Palladino), is not popular with Spiritualists." So, it seems that both pro and anti Spiritualistic camps were very wary of Carrington. By the way, Carrington's use of the title "Dr." is mentioned in a Gysel letter where he talks about Carrington's degree and says, "I know where he bought it for 75 dollars, I have asked him several times to stop using it." So, that's where Houdini got the information mentioned above.

Loren Pankratz sums up Carrington (The Linking Ring, Dec. 1989) by saying that it is easy to conclude that Hereward's loyalties changed from exposing the tricks of mediums because more money was available from endorsing the occult than writing about fraud. Finally, Patrick Lindley (Magicol, Aug. 1987) points out that Ernst and Carrington's book, on Houdini and Doyle, is sub-titled "The Story of a Strange Friendship". Patrick says that with Ernst a loyal Houdini supporter and Carrington having every reason not to be, "their collaboration is the story of a strange partnership!" I think he's right. Perhaps M. L. Mencken's review of their book (American Mercury, June 1932) had the answer when he said that presumably Mr. Ernst represented Houdini in the reported combat, while Mr. Carrington was in Doyle's corner.

Silverman (Houdini!!!, 1996) called Carrington a well-versed amateur magician. But Paul Tabori (Pioneers Of The Unseen, 1972) gives us a glimpse of a different Hereward. Tabori interviewed Henry Gilroy, who knew Carrington well during the last 20 years of his life. Gilroy talked of how Carrington was a great psychical researcher. He then went on to say that Carrington was a persistent, but awful, amateur magician fumbling almost every trick he tried. Most interesting of all was the comment that Carrington often talked of his "friendship" with Houdini and how he had visited him in his home!

It would seem that by the time Carrington and Ernst wrote their book, Carrington had forgotten his battles with Houdini and was willing to bask in the glory of being the co-author of a book about the two well-known legends of magic and writing. The monetary side of him probably took over. As I've already pointed out, when you read the description of Houdini's experiment you will notice that Carrington seems to have distanced himself from Ernst's description of the event by the use of the curious device "Mr. Ernst". The important point here is that it seems Ernst's exact description was used, and Carrington only tidied up the grammatical presentation. So, hopefully correctly, I decided to ignore my initial suspicion that Carrington might have altered Ernst's description in an attempt to get belated revenge on the man who had humiliated him.

HOUSEHOLD STAFF

In the description we have of Houdini's slate mystery the only people mentioned are Houdini, Ernst and Conan Doyle. It would be easy to assume that the house was otherwise empty; BUT, having watched too many detective stories on television, I wondered if there were other undisclosed suspects that could be lurking about. For example, there was no reference to household staff. They would normally have been 'invisible', but could very well have been a secret part of the plot. [Yes, I've seen too many second rate detective films in which the butler did it!] So, did Houdini's house have a hired workforce, or at least people employed for the day to make a good impression because a celebrity was visiting?

In Silverman's Houdini biography is a mention of a German servant, Anna Aulbach, looking after Houdini's mother, sister and brother, when they resided in Houdini's house on West 113th Street, in 1908. Did that still apply to the time period we are looking at here? I uncovered an item suggesting there were definitely still servants in the house a decade later than the above. It was from the November 1918 issue of 'The Sphinx', and is interesting for several reasons. Houdini had obviously sent it out as a press release:

HOUDINI OUTRANKED BY MAID IN ESCAPE ACT

Harry Houdini may be among the greatest little escapers in the world, but Bethel May Dove, 21, pretty and weighing about 135, according to the description Houdini gave the police yesterday, did an escape act in the handcuff king's house at 278 West 113th Street, Thursday night that he admits out-ranks any of his achievements.

Six years ago, Mrs. Houdini engaged Bethel as a maid, when the Houdini's were touring Scotland. They brought her to America and she has been with them ever since. At 9:40 p.m. Thursday, Mrs. Houdini went to the girl's room and left some minor instructions for the morrow. She remembers distinctly that the maid's wardrobe trunk and other habiliments were in their normal places.

Ten minutes later, Mrs. Houdini had occasion to pass the room again. The door was open and the room was seen to be empty of all of Bethel's belongings. Bethel herself had likewise vanished.

Houdini told the police that he believed the girl had run away to marry a young soldier who had been paying her much attention of late, though he hasn't figured out how she managed to get trunks, bags and everything else out in such record time.

To me that story established three things:

A) Household staff were employed to manage the large residence. So, there would definitely be others in the building at the time of the performance as well as the ones mentioned in the book.

B) Houdini could turn any negative happening into a publicity piece. If that situation had happened to me, I would have just mumbled something slightly impolite, and set about seeking someone to replace the runaway maid.

C) Most important, there were surreptitious ways in and out of the house, which must be kept in mind when we get around to looking at "HOW". Photos of the family, taken at the front door of the house, show them on a set of steps that led up from street level. There was a separate basement entrance, which Houdini often used to sneak his many purchases of magic memorabilia into the house so that Bess didn't know about them. She, along with many other magic spouses, had obviously complained about his over-spending on what was clearly junk!

TEAM HOUDINI

George Boston wrote (Inside Magic, 1947), "Houdini's success depended just as much upon his assistants as does that of all other illusionists". Although Houdini was generally what we'd call today a control freak, the biggest secret of his success was accepting that he could not do everything himself. Unfortunately, many would-be magi lack that awareness. They attempt to be one-man bands, and often fail. Collaboration was the answer to Houdini lightening the load so he could devote himself completely to the performance of magic. He also had the good sense to choose co-workers that were unlike him. [If you are going to spend your money on assistants, then to be successful you must hire those whose skills compliment yours, i.e. avoid 'yes men'.] Houdini not only surrounded himself with the most talented people available, he also chose those who completely believed in him, and understood that their own success depended on his success. His other strong point was being able to completely trust them to work unsupervised, in harmony, toward a common objective.

Houdini's 'control freak' mind-set was especially evident in his employing several levels of 'associates', who were usually unaware of the existence of each other. Sid Radner's wonderful collection of Houdini material (described in The Linking Ring, Oct. 1947) had an item that confirmed Houdini's pursuit of confidentiality. It is the oath of secrecy that his assistant James

Collins signed in Manchester, England, in Dec. 1910. In it, Collins agreed to never under any circumstances reveal a Houdini secret to anyone. As, around the time Houdini's slate test took place, Ernst would have administered this oath. It must have been particularly galling to not be able to ask Harry's assistants how he did the slate trick. If he had questioned them, they, of course, would have either thought he was testing them and refused to explain, or, more than likely, taken great pleasure in reminding him of their oath and adding to his embarrassment at not being able to figure out the method.

I discovered that Ernst had omitted his business partner Crane when describing a Houdini incident in which Cane definitely participated [as explained in the 'WHAT' section]. So, I believe others besides the household staff were in the house at the time of the experiment. Typically, Ernst made no mention of Lady Conan Doyle or Bess Houdini. Both most likely would have been present.

As Houdini relied heavily on his team, quite probably some [if not all] of them were secretly operating in the background. So, the question was, "who could these hidden operatives be?" Just some of the possibilities were:

HOUDINI'S STAGE ASSISTANTS

These were his high profile aides who were seen onstage as an integral part of his act. Their duty was to visibly help Houdini, but not draw undue attention to themselves. They were usually multi-skilled, 'jacks of all trades'. Having people to bounce ideas off is always important, but proper feedback is even more vital. Having 'yes men' who merely boost your ego is no help at all. Houdini's assistants knew their jobs depended on him being the best he could be, so they lived with his inflated ego. It takes a special relationship to invent magic. Over the years working with him, they had developed an understanding of what would 'fly' theatrically. They were not afraid to tell him what ideas would 'work' and which wouldn't. Yes, he often fired them, but they had quickly learned to re-appear the next day and act as if nothing had happened.

His main assistants at the time of our slate experiment were the two English Jims, Collins and Vickery. Patrick Culliton, in Walter B. Gibson's book (The Original Houdini Scrapbook, 1977), said they must take a major part of the credit for turning a mortal man into a legend. He added that in his opinion they were the finest magician's assistants that ever lived. So, it was inconceivable that they did not have some major input to the slate experiment. So, here is a quick look at them [plus one more!]:

+ **JAMES COLLINS** (early 1860s - 1942): A typical member of this group, Collins wrote (The Sphinx, Oct. 1936) that he was with Houdini for twenty years. He had joined Houdini in England, around 1908, as a carpenter/metal worker. Although initially hired as a technician, for the last eleven years of Houdini's life, Collins was Harry's Chief Assistant. James called his boss a fair, generous and great man. After Houdini's death he went on to assist Houdini's brother Hardeen.

William L. Gresham (Monster Midway, 1954) described Jim Collins as a tall, sandy-haired Englishman, an obscure figure, a shadowlike companion, and Houdini's chief assistant for nearly 20 years. Collins was an absolutely reliable, faithful assistant. Gresham says that Jim was so nondescript people hardly noticed him, which is the perfect appearance for a magician's assistant/back room boy. He could easily pass for a member of a committee [on hand to make sure no trickery was being done, and then do the necessary unsuspected "gaffing"]. Collins was Houdini's right hand man and, as a master mechanic, the real brains behind many of the "Boss's" escapes. He built many of the gimmicks that Houdini did not trust to outside mechanics.

As an onstage assistant, Collins was able to handle and direct know-it-all, awkward committeemen. If necessary, he could stall for time until he received the secret signal from Houdini that all was ready. James constantly monitored events on the lookout for anything going wrong, and anticipated Houdini's needs before he knew them himself.

+ **JAMES VICKERY**: He was Houdini's number 2 assistant, from about 1908, and also performed the same role in Hardeen's act. He has been credited as a co-inventor of Houdini's Milk Can Escape. To show how close James was to his employers, Vickery was a pallbearer for both brothers. An extremely intriguing statement, in Culliton's above article, was that Vickery often appeared as a police detective, an insane asylum attendant, or whatever official-looking character was needed. [Keep this in mind when we get around to looking at the outside part of the experiment.]

+ **FRANZ KUKOL**: I had originally excluded Austrian army officer Franz [Houdini's chief assistant pre-War] from being involved, because Houdini had reported that he had been re-called to duty in Germany in 1914. I had seen reports that he had probably died in the war, but had also noticed that Houdini had left Kukol money in his will. His demise was worth checking out, but as seemed to have no direct bearing on the subject in hand, I shelved it until later. In the meantime Patrick Culliton did a fantastic detective job that put Kukol right back in the picture. Patrick (Houdini – The Key, 2010) discovered that Kukol had not returned to Germany, but stayed in America in the new identity of Frank Williamson. Kukol was definitely [secretly] working for Houdini during the period under investigation as he was in Houdini's 1922 film, Haldane of the Secret Service. [Yes, a very apt title for him.]

FAMILY MEMBERS

We can't just look at Houdini's hired assistants without also considering the many members of his family who also worked directly with him:

113

+ **BESS HOUDINI** (1876 - 1943): Melville Cane, Ernst's legal partner, who knew Houdini for at least fifteen years, wrote in his book (The First Firefly, 1974) that Houdini's early marriage to Beatrice Rahner [1894] prospered devotedly. Cane confirmed, "Bess served him as helpful assistant, supplying the accessories for his performances and working at times as a confederate in his mystifications."

Lewis Goldstein is quoted (in Patrick Culliton's Houdini – The Key, 2010) as saying that when he was an assistant to Houdini, it was Bess who kept the crew together and kept us all working smoothly. He added that Houdini was a poor payer but Bess would supplement the salaries by playing cards with the crew and intentionally losing.

Houdini's last Press Agent, George Atkinson is quoted (The Conjurors' Magazine, May 1948), as saying: "Mrs. Houdini....a trim, tiny little person...I was impressed with the exotic atmosphere about her. A pretty little woman, too, and completely charming....she was not only wife, stage assistant and business right arm, but a mother to her husband as well. John Booth wrote (The Linking Ring, Nov. 1941) of meeting Bess a decade and a half after Houdini's death, and how she was extremely gracious, completely unassuming and delightfully cordial.

Typical of the many other similar comments is that of Houdini's friend Walter Gibson. He liked Bess and found her very sweet. Sid Fleischman recalled (Magic Magazine, May 2003) meeting Bess Houdini, after Houdini's death, when he (Sid) was young. He described her as being tiny on very high heels, and said she was warm and generous. Milbourne Christopher (The Yankee Magic Collector #11, 2004) called Bess calm and complacent so that she complemented Houdini's volatile character, comforting him in times of stress and turmoil. She was always in the background, acting the gracious hostess to his friends. The hostess remark is confirmed in a description (The Sphinx, Aug. 1924) of an "informal reception" at Houdini's residence, where Mrs. Houdini acted as the hostess for the event. Finally, 'The Sphinx' (Mar.

1924) states: "Houdini has one trait that is greatly admired and that is he always gives Mrs. Houdini credit for her help in helping him make the grade."

In line with the modern tendency to portray people in a 'warts and all' manner, as I did for Houdini and Doyle, I feel I must balance the above with a quote from an Eric Mead review (Genii, April 2007) of William Kalush and Larry Sloman's 2006 book (The Secret Life of Houdini): "Kalush and Sloman bring Bess out of Houdini's shadow to reveal a complex woman of fragile health who was often jealous, liked to drink whiskey and smoke marijuana, and who lived in her husband's shadow largely because he wouldn't have it any other way." That assessment of Bess may be true, but I'd sooner think of her in terms of the previous paragraphs. So, was "confederate" and "stage assistant" Bess involved in the experiment? At the very least she must have been the hostess for the distinguished guests, and involved in keeping Lady Doyle out of the way while Houdini performed his slate illusion.

+ **THEODORE HARDEEN** (1876 - 1945): Houdini's brother, Hardeen, explained (The Sphinx, Oct. 1936) how he had originally been a partner with Harry in the 'Brothers Houdini' act. When Bess arrived he left the act. Hardeen mentioned Harry's resourcefulness in picking him to be Harry's leading rival once he made the big time. This eliminated other imitators, and kept the rich pickings in the family. Hardeen also revealed that Houdini had chosen Theordore's stage name, and that they both eventually made those stage names the legal ones.

Hardeen said that when he retired as Houdini's rival, he devoted himself to Harry's motion picture interests. Then after Houdini's death Hardeen toured with the "Houdini Show" featuring many of the tricks his brother had made famous. Hardeen wrote: "My brother and I were always close and always friendly. He did a great deal for me and I was at times able to do things for him." Was our slate illusion performance one of those times Hardeen helped his brother?

+ **NIECES AND NEPHEWS**: William Kalush & Larry Sloman's book (The Secret Life of Houdini, 2006) shows a picture of Houdini's niece, Julia Sawyer, and states that she infiltrated séances for him. So, Houdini's nieces and nephews were quite used to undertaking covert actions for Uncle Harry. Did any of them help here?

+ **INLAWS**: Houdini's niece, Marie Hinson Blood, reveals (in Kenneth Silverman's Houdini!!!, 1996) that her father John built tricks for Houdini. John was the husband of Bess Houdini's younger sister. Did he contribute to the slate test?

HIGH PROFILE ASSOCIATES

+ **JOSEPH F. RINN** (1868 – 1952): Rinn, a successful New York businessman, and Houdini childhood friend, became very wealthy from his fruit brokerage business at an early age, and was able to devote much time to his hobby of investigating and harassing deceivers. Houdini gave him the title of "The Ghost Breaker". Tough, street-wise and not easily intimidated, Rinn offered enormous sums of money in challenging anyone to demonstrate a psychic event that he could not duplicate. He attended hundreds of séances, and was involved in exposing many of the great mediums of his era. George LaFollette (The Linking Ring, Jan. 1956) listed 16 of them.

A Vice-President of the Society of American Magicians, as well as a psychic investigator, Rinn wrote (Sixty Years of Psychical Research, 1950) that he assisted Houdini "in his feats whenever he required help of someone he could trust." So, did Rinn assist Houdini during our slate feat?

+ **CHARLES FULTON OURSLER** (1893 – 1952): Fulton Oursler, a prominent member of the Society of American Magicians, was the famous American journalist, and writer, who edited both 'Liberty' magazine and 'The Readers Digest'. He wrote the world-wide best seller, 'The Greatest Story Ever Told' (1949), as well as the book that was made into the movie 'Boys Town' starring Spencer Tracy. In his autobiography (Behold This Dreamer!, 1964) Fulton talked of his "friendship with Sir Arthur Conan Doyle which lasted until he died." He also said that he and Houdini worked together on many exposures of fake mediums for "more than twenty-five years." As someone who knew all three participants of the experiment, Houdini, Ernst and Doyle, he would have been an excellent person to undertake any undercover work involved.

APPARATUS DESIGNERS & BUILDERS

Behind all great illusionists are those craftsmen, who can take a magical vision, and construct a piece of equipment to accomplish what the entertainer originally imagined. Usually those 'backroom boys' are unknown to the public. Often their existence is also kept secret within the magic world as well. Barbi Walker & Robert Seaver (The P & L Book, 1992) explained that Houdini never revealed how much research and experimentation he commissioned others to do, in working out ways to duplicate a supposedly genuine medium's act – or queer it.

Although Houdini's assistant, Jim Collins, constructed many gimmicks for Houdini, I suspected the one required here was far too complex to complete in-house. Why? Well, as no one has discovered what it was so far, I suspect it was very intricate. The risk of going outside the 'company' to manufacture apparatus was that the secret could leak out. It was not unknown for an outside producer to make a duplicate piece of apparatus, which would then be sold to a competitor to obtain a bit more profit from the deal. One way to stop this was to keep it in the family. In Silverman's 1996 biography of Houdini, Houdini's niece, Marie H. Blood, reveals that her father was a cabinet maker, who would often meet with Houdini and Jim Collins to discuss tricks they wanted him to build.

Craftsmen Houdini definitely used were:

+ **RUDOLPH S. SCHLOSSER**: An eccentric German master magical mechanic, Schlosser lived in New York. The gifted magic builder made quite a few pieces of apparatus for Houdini. Tad Ware (Magicol, Feb. 1995) calls Rudy "one of Houdini's favourite builders." It seems that Schlosser's mental stability was always a little unstable, and Rudy was eventually committed to a mental institution where he died. [No, I won't comment on the mental stability of anyone who is into magic, but Houdini did secretly employ several magic eccentrics. A typical one is Bob Gysel (see below).]

+ **JOHN A. HINSON**: As mentioned above, John was the husband of Bess's sister, Mae. He was a cabinet maker who often carried out any carpentry work on new tricks that Houdini and Jim Collins wanted done (see also 'Inlaws' above).

THE INVISIBLE MEN & WOMEN

Houdini's friend, Joseph Dunninger, wrote (Magic and Mystery, 1967) that Houdini had an army of private operators who secretly worked for him. Uriah Fuller's book (Confessions of a Psychic, 1975) included tips on the use of confederates [or secret accomplices], which I believe Houdini must have used. The first was to make sure they were old trusted friends. This Houdini did. The other I strongly suspect was that he asked them to never get photographed, as they were more useful when nobody knew who they were. Houdini had many people in many countries carrying out investigations for him. A typical one was magician Alex De Vega, the First President of the Scottish Conjurers' Association in Scotland. But I'll only mention the ones in America here, as that's where our slate test took place.

This group included unseen assistants like Vacca and Gysel. The public were unaware of them, but they often took an unknown part in Houdini's act, or did covert preparatory work. They would usually not even be aware of other similarly employed individuals. For example Vacca mentioned that he was pledged to the strictest secrecy, and not even Hardeen or Bess really knew what he did for Houdini.

+ **AMEDEO VACCA** (1890 - 1974): Top of the bill, professional magician Vacca was born in Italy, and moved to America at the age of 14. Only Vacca's wife, and a few very close friends, were aware that he was a part of Houdini's unseen team. He worked for Houdini for at least the last three years of Harry's life, but that fact did not become generally known in the magic world until nearly 50 years after Harry's demise, and just before Amedeo's. An article by Bruce Reynolds (The Linking Ring, Dec. 1947) gave an excellent example of the enormous extent Houdini went to in hiding his relationship with his undercover people. To be unobserved in his discussions with Vacca, Houdini purchased a Barber Shop a few blocks from his home, and installed Amedeo as the Boss Barber. It necessitated Vacca going to Night School to learn the barber trade! Frank Garcia & George Schindler's book on Vacca (Amedeo's Continental Magic, 1974) reveals that each morning Houdini would go to the Barber Shop for a shave - and a secret planning session.

Vacca's many duties for Houdini not only included him being an ideas man, creating new and mysterious stunts, but also being a "front" or "advance" man. When Houdini was "on the road" Amedeo would travel ahead of him, and carry out secret necessary alterations, adjustments and installations to theatres Harry was about to play. Richard J. Weibel quoted a letter (M-U-M, July 1982), from the President of one of the vaudeville chains, introducing Vacca to the various theatre managers. It stated that he was connected with Mr. Harry Houdini's act, and would carry out "experiments" in the theatre. They were to be "conducted in absolute secrecy", and at night when no one was around. I was very fortunate to uncover certain other covert actions of Vacca's that had a direct bearing on the secret of Houdini's slate mystery. All will be revealed in the "HOW" section.

+ **ROBERT HENRY GYSEL** (1880 – 1938): I had some difficulty in deciding how to describe magician Bob Gysel's connection to Houdini. 'The Linking Ring' (Oct. 1952) said he was someone "who acted at one time as undercover man for Houdini." Kenneth Silverman (Houdini!!!, 1996) called Gysel the 'brassiest and most knowing of Houdini's undercover agents'. But, Kalush and Sloman (The Secret Life of Houdini, 2006) declared that Gysel was NOT a formal member of Houdini's investigation team, although he provided valuable inside information. David E. Price, in a lecture on Gysel, suggested that today we'd say Gysel worked in Houdini's "dirty tricks" department. [David very kindly gave me a copy of his lecture. It was based on the vast number of letters in David's collection that Gysel had sent to English journalist and magician, Henry Sara – a fellow eccentric.]

Oswald Rae (The Demon Telegraph, Oct. 1947) described Bob as "certainly somewhat eccentric...[but] darned interesting," and "full of magical ideas, some extremely clever, and some shall we say debatable." Wayne Wissner points out (in Houdini & Gysel, 2013) that Gysel exposed crooked mediums well before Houdini did. Leslie Guest (M-U-M, Mar. 1971) called Gysel a "Peculiar Genius of Magic." Will Goldston (Great Magicians' Tricks, 1931), said Gysel "is a much misunderstood man." But my favourite description of him is by Silverman, who revealed that Houdini considered his "one-of-a kind friend" to be "dangerous – crazy- in fact."

I also discovered there was some discrepancy as to how long Gysel worked for Houdini. In a Jan. 16, 1928 letter to Harry Price (in the Harry Price Collection at the University of London), Gysel wrote, "I have known Houdini for over 35 years....I taught him many of the stunts he used to do." Kalush and Sloman say Gysel became a friend of Houdini's in 1907, when Harry found that they shared many interests. This would be nearly 20 years. The Jan. 1917 issue of 'M-U-M' lists Robert Henry Gysel among those applying for membership in The Society of American Magicians, with Harry Houdini recommending him for membership. This was 9 years before Harry's death. An article in 'The Buffalo Times' (dated June 10, 1936, and reprinted in 'The Jinx', July 1936) says Gysel "was right-hand man to Harry Houdini for five years." Bob's April 12, 1929 letter to Sara asserts that he "travelled weeks ahead of him to get the dope on mediums so when Houdini got into town, he was ready for the exposure." In the end I concluded that Bob Gysel worked off and on for Houdini for a long period of time, and the clues I unearthed showed he was quite likely involved in the slate test Houdini did for Conan Doyle. [I'll reveal those clues in the "HOW" section.]

PRIVATE DETECTIVES

Ernst and Carrington tell us that Houdini employed a regular network of spies to conduct his investigations. Martin Sunshine (The Linking Ring, Mar. 1998) describes arriving at Houdini's hotel room, and discovering Harry talking on the phone to one of his detectives, who was investigating spiritualists. Fulton Oursler confirms this (Behold This Dreamer!, 1964) when he describes a telephone conversation with Houdini, in which the escapologist declared he had detectives investigating fake mediums, and paid them thousands of dollars for their services. Samri Frikell [an Oursler pseudonym] (Spirit Mediums Exposed, 1930) further explained Houdini's "detective system": "Houdini employed a most comprehensive system covering the entire United States. Some of those detectives were members of spiritualistic churches and of 'circles'."

One of Harry's leading undercover special investigators was Miss Rose Mackenberg, who exposed many important mediums of her day. Julien Proskauer (The Dead Do Not Talk, 1946) called Miss Rose Mackenberg, Houdini's chief confidential investigator of psychic frauds. George LaFollette declared (The Linking Ring,

Jan. 1956) that Houdini's special investigator, Rose Mackenberg, exposed many leading mediums, including Rev. Renner of Cleveland, and Peirri Keeler of Washington.

Loren Pankratz says (Skeptical Inquirer, July/Aug. 1995) Rose Mackenberg was so dedicated that after Houdini's death she continued to pursue fraudulent mediums for more than 20 years. During investigations for Harry, Rose often paired up with Houdini's niece and secretary Julia Sawyer [see Nieces and Nephews above]. Houdini's staff nicknamed Rose "The Rev." because she had been ordained a medium by so many spiritualist churches. A master of disguises, she declared that marriages were made in heaven, because, although unmarried, Rose had received messages from 1,500 departed 'husbands'! Apparently not one spirit ever told a medium who Rose actually was.

I've included Rose here as typical of the many Private Detectives Houdini employed, BUT, she was probably not involved in the slate test, because Pankratz says she did not start working for Houdini until 1925. To give you an idea of how many detectives Houdini had working for him, Patrick Culliton (Houdini – The Key, 2010) quotes a Rose Mackenberg article. In it she says, "Houdini's personal staff of investigators numbered 20 men and women – mostly girls like myself." So, how many other covert operatives did Houdini have?

OTHERS

I went on to discover several other people 'who' probably had a hand in Houdini's slate test; but I will not cover them here. To give you something to look forward to, I will discuss them in the 'HOW' section, and explain how I managed to find them.

Chapter 5: WHEN?

Although this might not seem like a major category, it was important to discover 'WHEN' the performance took place, to establish the magic techniques available to Houdini at the time. Magicians love to use the latest gimmicks to fool each other. Houdini was no exception.

Although 'When' is not the first of Kipling's categories in this book, I actually chose it first to look at in depth. I selected 'when' because I thought it would be an easy area. That way, after completing it, I would feel more confident in attacking other more challenging sections. In fact, to make the task even easier, I decided to begin with something 'easy' within this 'easy' field. I began by looking to see 'when' Houdini and Conan Doyle had struck up what Ernst called their "strange" friendship; BUT, I soon discovered conflicting information. [I would eventually learn that nothing to do with this project was going to be 'easy'.]

Ernst and Carrington's book was based on the letters between Houdini and Conan Doyle that Ernst had inherited from Houdini. So I looked to see what the authors said was the date of the first communication between the two famous personages. The book stated: "Owing to the fact that some of the earlier letters do not seem to have been preserved, the correspondence begins somewhat abruptly." The first letter quoted was dated March 15, 1920. So, I looked for information on the first meeting of Harry and Sir Arthur before that date.

As part of the ongoing search for Houdini/Doyle data, I came across a clue in Kelvin Jones' book (Conan Doyle and the Spirits, 1989). He explained that while Harry was touring Britain in 1920, Doyle learned he was performing at Portsmouth. Sir Arthur apparently took his family to see Houdini's show, and a firm friendship was cemented between the two men. That sounded like the answer until I read Houdini's 1924 book (A Magician Among the Spirits).

Harry wrote, "The friendship of Sir Arthur and myself dates back to the time when I was playing the Brighton Hippodrome, Brighton, England. We had been corresponding and had discussed through the medium of the mail, questions regarding Spiritualism. He invited Mrs. Houdini and myself to the Doyle home in Crowborough, England, and in that way an acquaintanceship was begun which has continued ever since." So, as I repeatedly discovered, you often have to make an educated guess as to which expert to believe. Was it Portsmouth or Brighton? As it does not have a direct bearing on the outcome of the investigation, I'll leave you to find out who was right. Yes, that's a challenge! [So, why not believe Harry because he was there? Surely he would know? Well, unfortunately he often 'embellished' his memories of events to make a better story.]

Now, on to the more important 'WHEN' – when did our performance actually take place? If we assume it was a magic trick - 'when' trying to discover a magic secret, it is helpful to know the exact date the particular piece of legerdemain was first performed. The state of current magical invention and knowledge can then be applied to resolving the problem. Ernst's report stated: "One of the most striking cases of this character was a 'test' which Houdini gave to Sir Arthur and Mr. Ernst - for the former's especial benefit - in his own home, some years before his death." He also wrote: "All this happened years ago. . . and the mystery of that slate-test remains as great a mystery as ever!" Yes, not very exact. The only solid clue was that it was some years before Houdini's death in 1926.

So, with just "some years before his [Houdini's] death" and "years ago" to work with, it was going to be difficult to put an exact date on the performance, but a look in the "WHERE?" category helped. [Yes, I know I said I started with this one, but I soon decided that running them in parallel would be more useful.] Ernst had written: "...in his [Houdini's] own home..." So, with the performance happening in Houdini's New York home, it was possible to narrow the period down. It had to be during one of Doyle's American tours. After becoming friends with Houdini in 1920 [according to Kelvin Jones' above book], Doyle journeyed to the U.S., to promote Spiritualism, in 1922 and 1923. On both of these visits he met with Houdini. So, which was it - 1922 or 1923? [And before you ask, no, 'which' is not one of the categories!]

I began to think that a year either way wouldn't have a major influence on how Houdini had done his test, when I was suddenly hit by a shattering concept - the bottom line for "When?" was, "Did it actually happen?" i.e. When? - Possibly never! Yes, I had to question the validity of the occurrence. Was it merely a device to sell a book? After considerable thought, I could not see what Ernst and Carrington would have gained by fabricating the performance. It was only a few pages of their book. In fact, after reading it, I got the impression that the description was so detailed that Ernst must have gone over it in his head nearly every day, trying to find a solution. After all, when Houdini died, Ernst replaced him as the President of The Parent Assembly of the Society of American Magicians. A man fit for that elevated position must have thought that he should have been able to work out how Houdini had pulled it off. Carrington had craftily distanced himself from the description, by using the literary device "Mr. Ernst..." when describing the event.

So, I accepted that the performance really did take place, but doing so brought me back to the original question - When? I decided the best place to establish the dates of Conan Doyle's tours was from the writings of the man himself. Doyle wrote two books covering his lecture tours of America, 'Our American Adventure' and 'Our Second American Adventure'. The dates he mentioned in the first book are:

April 9, 1922 - arrive in NEW YORK;
April 24, 1922 - on to Boston;
April 27, 1922 - travel to Washington, Philadelphia, then back to NEW YORK, then on to Buffalo; ['The Sphinx' (May 1922)

reports that Sir Arthur Conan Doyle was lecturing at Carnegie Hall, NEW YORK, on May 4, 1922.];

May 14, 1922 - in Toronto, then on to Detroit, Toledo, and Chicago, before returning to NEW YORK;

June 2, 1922 - attend Society of American Magicians' banquet in NEW YORK, then rested in Atlantic City, before spending last days in NEW YORK;

June 24, 1922 - leave America for England.

I established that Houdini was in New York during all of the above Doyle visits, so any of the periods in New York could have been the date of the performance.

With regard to the second tour, Pulitzer Prize winner Kenneth Silverman's book, (Houdini!!!, 1996) says that even before the second visit, in April 1923, Doyle and Houdini's friendship had soured. A month before they had a sharp exchange of letters on spiritualism in the 'New York Times'. So, I thought, it would be easy to eliminate a New York meeting during the second visit. It seemed that Houdini and Doyle never met in New York during 1923, only in Denver. At least I assumed this from reading Silverman, then I made the mistake of following the golden rule of "investigating everything". Doyle wrote in his second book that he landed in New York on April 3, 1923. He left there April 15th on his western American tour. He says he did not return to New York until a week before boarding the Adriatic, on August 4, 1923 to return to Europe.

Houdini was absent from New York when Doyle arrived. Ernst and Carrington's book says: "And so Conan Doyle set sail, and soon began the second tour of the states, lecturing from coast to coast on Spiritualism. Houdini meanwhile was also on tour, and the two men met in several cities - Denver and elsewhere..." Did the elsewhere include New York? Although the first period in New York can be eliminated, can the second one be as well? Ernst quotes from a Houdini letter to Doyle written on May 28th, 1923, saying that Houdini was now back in New York, "...It is too long to write about it, but will tell you in person when you arrive..." So, it would appear that there was a definite plan to meet in New York, but did that meeting take place?

In The Harry Price Library, at the University of London, I obtained confirmation that Houdini was definitely in New York when Doyle returned at the end of the 1923 tour. Harry Price and Houdini often corresponded on their two favourite subjects - psychical research and magic book collecting. On May 10, 1923 Houdini wrote to Price from Denver, saying that he had just had a long chat with Sir Arthur Conan Doyle, and that Doyle had left for Salt Lake City that morning. Houdini added that he would be back in New York in two week's time. Further letters were sent to Price from New York dated June 6, 9, 16, 18, and most important of all, August 2, 1923. At the end of this last letter, which was dated during Doyle's period in New York, was a hand written note saying that Houdini was busy on his books. A letter sent from Sioux City, Iowa dated August 30, 1923 stated that he was on the road once again.

So what conclusion can be drawn from the above? Well, there was an opportunity for them to meet in New York at the beginning of August 1923, with the performance possibly taking place then. Houdini mentions a potential meeting. Factors against that meeting being the performance are:

a) The discordant state of their friendship by that time.

b) Neither of them appear to have mentioned a New York meeting in writing. Houdini tells Price he is working on his books and does not mention meeting Doyle. Only the Denver meeting appears in Doyle's book.

c) In Ernst's description, Houdini stated that he had been working on the slate illusion on and off, all winter, while the possible 1923 meeting was in August.

This last item seems to point toward a 1922 performance. Knowing how eager most magicians are to show off a new trick, I estimate the performance date of Houdini's 'test' for Doyle was somewhere between the April 9, 1922 arrival, and the Society of American Magicians' banquet on June 2, 1922. Their friendship at that time was still on a firm foundation. We will probably never be able to tell the exact date for certain, but if any of you dedicated Houdini nuts out there want to try, good luck. Yes that's a challenge. [Strong Hint: Kenneth Silverman (Houdini!!!, 1996) says that Sir Arthur came to 278 for lunch on May 19, 1922, and the guestbook from Houdini's home has recently surfaced!]

Chapter 6: WHERE?

The more I investigated Houdini's "experiment" in detail, the more problems I seemed to encounter. So, when I first approached the "WHERE" category, I decided to start very gently by considering the psychological 'where' as opposed to the physical 'where'. Yes, I know, that sounds like the confusing "jargon" magicians often use to baffle you with, but it isn't. So, if it isn't then what am I on about?

Well, I mean that Houdini was creating a 'major' piece of magic outside his normal 'comfort zone'. I specifically wrote "major" because the whole experiment had to work or it would be a disaster. If Houdini didn't completely mystify Doyle using trickery, as he claimed others had been doing, his whole premise would be negated. I also used the words "comfort zone" because Houdini's expertise, built up over many years, was performing in front of many hundreds of people, who were on the other side of the footlights, i.e. he was normally onstage with the spectators at the theatrical arm's length.

During his career, Houdini had achieved the considerable confidence needed to be a superstar by analysing what worked for him and what didn't. Through trial and error, he'd discovered how to maximize publicity by 'working the media', to boost the paying customer's expectations and ensure box office success. He had learned how to expertly use a theatrical setting, and especially how to get the best out of the people working there, i.e. the backstage technical crews, who can make or break your act. He became skilled in the use of lighting and music to set the scene as he wanted it. He mastered the technique of showing himself to the best advantage; for example, not looking awkward while getting into or out of boxes and large restraints. He became aware of how to gauge precisely the correct timing, to wring the last bit of emotional conflict out of seemingly impossible predicaments challengers put him into, before emerging triumphant.

In addition, he learned how to solve the many problems that arose every time he moved to a new town. Typical ones were: a) efficiently 'loading-in', and then 'striking' and repacking his equipment, b) checking for damage, and repairing his illusions, and c) ensuring that technical rehearsals went well. As well as the general preparations for his show, he had to consider how to constantly keep his show up to date and ahead of his competitors. In other words, he had to meet all conceivable challenges in putting together a top class magic spectacle.

His experience gained over many years of facing those challenges allowed him to relax onstage. Instead of worrying about his show, he was able to devote himself completely to using his personality, and his natural showmanship ability, to artistically connect with his audience. The rapport he created heightened the entertainment, BUT in the situation we are looking at here, entertainment was not the prime target. Houdini was in a completely different venue. His "where" in this case was a one off, non-paying performance, in an intimate setting, producing a supposed miracle 'close-up', for an audience of just two. On top of that, to prove his point it had to work perfectly the first time. There would be no learning by trial and error here.

Today many magi make a good living performing magic "close-up". They work in intimate settings such as restaurants, and "walk-around" corporate promotions. In Houdini's day, magic at close quarters was usually only performed 'supposedly impromptu' for non-magician friends, fellow magi, or potential bookers. [Note that I wrote "supposedly impromptu".] The nearest paid magic venue to "close-up" at that time was referred to as "parlour" magic; but, even there magicians were still at arm's length. They were standing at one end of a room performing for seated spectators. So, to leave the psychological "where", and move on to the physical, "where" exactly was the uncommon, intimate setting of Houdini's experiment?

Well, to add just one more exceptional restriction, it was in full daylight. As a member of The Magic Circle's Occult Committee pointed out (The Magic Circular, June 1932), "in order to make a spiritualistic séance a success the most important factor was 'atmosphere.' In a semi or completely darkened room with everyone present believing they were going to peep beyond the veil, manifestations of a wonderful nature would almost certainly result." Houdini had no such factor working in his favour; in fact, he chose to do exactly the opposite to a normal séance by working in completely lit conditions.

Okay, it was finally time to locate the setting for Houdini's experiment. Where precisely did he perform it? I mentioned 'close-up' magic above, so I decided to start close up, and work my way outwards. Ernst and Carrington wrote: "....Sir Arthur was asked to fasten the hooks over anything in the room which would hold them. He hooked one over the edge of a picture-frame, and the other on a large book, on a shelf in Houdini's library. The slate thus swung free in space, in the centre of the room ..." The answer to "where" appeared to be extremely simple. The setting was a room - Houdini's library - BUT, like nearly everything else I looked at on this quest, there was a problem!

I discovered two completely contrasting photographs, both supposedly showing Houdini in his library. The first one, in Ruth Brandon's book (The Life and Many Deaths of Houdini, 1993), was labelled "Houdini in his library". Houdini could be seen in shirt sleeves sitting at a desk surrounded by tall piles of papers and books, that appeared to be on the verge of toppling over. Nearby were shelves overflowing with books and other items. That room looked far too cramped to be a place where you'd entertain a distinguished visitor. The other completely different photo appeared in several other books. It showed a more spacious room. A well-dressed Houdini was leaning against a long, low row of cupboards with solid doors. Above the cupboards were glass-enclosed shelves full of books. Both the cupboards and the shelves above them ran the length of the room. In the near corner of the picture was a comfortable looking armchair. This picture was of an expensive looking room where a world famous magician could definitely entertain guests he was trying to impress.

So, I had two totally different settings, each claiming to be Houdini's library. It was important to discover in which of those rooms our 'experiment' took place, as it might give a clue to how the 'test' was carried out. [And it eventually did!] After an extended search, I managed to solve the problem, BUT that answer, like so many other times during this quest, raised yet another question! In talking of Harry's 'experiment' for Doyle in his library, William Kalush and Larry Sloman (The Secret Life of Houdini, 2006) said the term "library" was a misnomer because Houdini's entire house was filled with books and memorabilia. So, both rooms could have been considered a "library". I decided that one of those areas must have been a working library, while the other was a reference library, much like The Magic Circle Library is today, with its lending books separated from its reference works. To confirm that theory, I attempted to trace Brandon's picture back to its source.

I found the Brandon photo initially in Walter B. Gibson's earlier book (The Original Houdini Scrapbook, 1977). As it was mainly a compilation of earlier information, I continued looking. Eventually I located the Brandon picture in the first authorised biography of Houdini written by Harold Kellock (Houdini His Life Story, 1928). The photograph was labelled: "In his library, 1924. The picture shows the characteristic condition of Houdini's desk." It explained that there wasn't a spare inch that was not piled high with books and paper. Somehow it reminded me of my own desk. So, this would appear to have been Houdini's working library. Further research produced an interesting picture that confirmed my speculation.

William Lindsay Gresham's book (Houdini: The Man Who Walked Through Walls, 1959) included a photo of the same room shown in the Brandon/Gibson/Kellock "library" picture, but taken from a different angle. Gresham called it Houdini's "crowded study". Kenneth Silverman (Houdini!!!, 1996) also had the identical picture to Brandon/Gibson/Kellock, but called it "his office". So, it seemed that the congested room containing the desk crammed full of books, diaries, scrapbooks, etc., was the study/office, which was located upstairs, while our experiment took place in the downstairs library. The final proof for me was that there was no way the 'test' could have been carried out in a room that you had to "enter sideways" to avoid knocking over a maze of books and papers.

As usually happened on this quest, after I decided which one was the correct "library" picture for Houdini's experiment, [the less crowded one] I came across it in several more books and magazines. Frustratingly, once you finally discover an answer to a vexing question, you often find it, over and over again! A typical place to see that library photograph is in Silverman's book. The amazing thing about the picture is that not one of the authors who reproduced it seemed to have noticed the photo was a COMPLETE DECEPTION!!! Yes, like most things in magic, it contained trickery. How? Well, in the upper left hand corner of all the library pictures I located was the writing: "To my friend Al Snyder". Below that was Houdini's signature and the date. At first glance it appeared to be perfectly normal, as Houdini signed many pictures for many friends, BUT when The Executive Librarian of The Magic Circle, Peter Lane, looked at it he noticed something odd. Peter pointed out to me that it was dated 1927. Yes, a year after Houdini's death!

After Peter mentioned the date discrepancy, I looked very carefully at the signature, and realized it was definitely not Houdini's! The way the letter "H" had been written was certainly not the way Houdini wrote it. To be absolutely sure, I examined as many Houdini signatures as I could locate. I even found an article by Stuart Lutz (Autograph Collector, Feb. 1999) that examined Houdini's signature in great detail. Not one of the many examples Lutz gave matched the signature on the photo. Lutz warned that there were forgeries of Houdini's signature about. The photo definitely appeared to contain one of them. So, I was back to where

I'd begun! Now I had to determine whether the picture itself was genuine, or as bogus as the writing on it?

I had to begin somewhere, so my first approach was to assume the picture was authentic, because it had a genuine look and feel about it. But that then raised the question of why, if it was legitimate, would someone forge the message? So, I investigated Al Snyder. - Alvin L. "Al" Snyder (1902 - 1970) had been a magician since 1919, and a full-time professional in his early years. He was said to have been "a personal friend" of many of the top magi of his day, including Houdini. If that was so, then why wasn't the inscription genuine? Well, after much contemplation, I suspect the reason was because of the magic magazine Al had edited (The Osarian Magazine). In it Al been rather unkind about a series of articles Houdini wrote in the 1920s. So, Houdini would most likely have put Al on his 'troublesome people' list.

Peter Lane suggested several solutions as to why the spurious signature and message had been added to the photo, which, like me, he felt was genuine. One was that Bess could have signed the picture after Houdini's demise. Peter also thought it might have been an "inside joke". It seems that the "Society of American Magicians Dean of Magicians" Jay Marshall had once produced an obviously fake Houdini souvenir. Jay had manufactured and distributed a Houdini advertising ballpoint pen. [Yes, Houdini had died many years before that type of pen was invented.] So, Jay was a possible candidate for the perpetrator. As well as Bess and Jay, I began to think that the hoaxer might even have been Al Snyder himself poking fun at the Society of American Magicians (SAM). This was because Houdini's tombstone had been engraved with the fact that Harry was the SAM President from 1917 until 1927! It wasn't until 1964 [nearly 40 years later] that the SAM discovered their error, and had to rectify it by changing the 1927 to 1926. So, was Al mocking them?

After many frustrating hours of searching, and with a little help from both the wonderful Magic Circle Library, and the magnificent Conjuring Arts Research Center's Ask Alexander database, I eventually discovered who had first unearthed the photo. Frances Marshall wrote (Abracadabra, Apr. 29, 1972) how over 75 people had attended the Magic Collectors' Weekend, held then [1972] in Chicago. She explained that a "souvenir of the weekend" was "a hitherto unknown photograph of Houdini in his personal magic library." Apparently: "This Jay Marshall property caused much comment."

Yes, Frances's husband Jay was the same person who had produced the Houdini hoax ballpoint pen. A Magic Inc. advertisement in 'The New Tops' a month later (May, 1972) confirmed what Frances had written. [Magic Inc. was the Chicago magic retailer, and publisher, co-owned by Jay and Frances Marshall.] The ad read: "Also introduced at the Collector's Weekend - Houdini Photo: A never-before seen 8 x 10 photograph of Houdini in his magic library, autographed in his own hand." So, I suggest someone else had given "his own hand" a little help. This appearance of the photo was two years after Al Snyder's death, so it was just possible the picture, and signature, originally came from Al's estate. As it was not going to affect the outcome of the present quest, I decided to leave it to you to discover the truth of that conjecture.

My priority then became to establish whether the picture itself was genuine, or as fake as its dedication, because it could influence the outcome of the present pursuit. It seemed that the first time the picture appeared in print, after its initial Magic Collectors' Weekend outing, was in the Nov. 1973 issue of M-U-M. The caption said it appeared through the courtesy of Magic Inc., who were selling glossy copies of it. It seems the photo was then reproduced from time to time over the years, with no one noticing the date discrepancy [or, at least, pointing it out]. Fortunately, I eventually confirmed the picture was genuine from an impeccable source - Houdini's niece.

In a long, detailed article on Houdini (The New Tops, Sept. 1985), Robert Olson described his meeting with the renowned escape artist's niece, Marie Hinson Blood. Marie said that as a child, "she used to spend weeks at a time at the Houdini residence on West 113th Street." That statement made her the ideal person to confirm whether the picture, with its counterfeit inscription, was in fact "Uncle Harry's" library. You can imagine my joy when, in the middle of the article, I spied a copy of the infamous picture, complete with the bogus dedication in the corner. Accompanying it was the caption: "This is the library where Houdini spent much of his time off the road. Marie knew it well, even remembering the picture of Philippe and the bust of Kellar on top of the bookshelves." Apparently Olson showed the picture of the library to Houdini's niece, and she confirmed its authenticity. [Yes, they both appear to have missed the spurious date on it!]

Before I travel outward from that room to give you the bigger picture of "where" Houdini's library was located, there is one additional, small puzzle about the library that cropped up during my research. After I thought I'd satisfactorily determined which room was the library, and which the study/office, I made the mistake of looking in Walter B. Gibson's book (The Original Houdini Scrapbook, 1977). Gibson talked about a visit to Houdini's house and how the library, on the first floor next to the reception room, was filled with stacks of books standing waist high on the floor, while the upstairs study was less cluttered! That gave the impression that everything I have just said above was wrong! But, after I solved the date of Gibson's visit, it all became clear. Although Walter did not give an exact date, he said Houdini "was then in his mid-forties." So, the date would be around 1920, which was a few years prior to our experiment. Gibson also gave a clue as to why the library and study were different to the situation I described above.

He said a professional librarian and two assistants were reorganizing Houdini's library. It included "cross-indexing all the tricks found in standard works on magic." This allowed me to get a picture of the background to the room in which the experiment took place. A news item (The Magic Key, Mar. 1918) said: "The New York papers made considerable comment on the 'moving day' of Harry Houdini. It required four large vans to move his library." My supposition is that he had all his collection relocated to his home, from storage, in 1918, and then set about organizing it. Once he had the library arranged to his satisfaction, everything else, including his personal files, was shifted up into his study/office, which then became the cluttered room shown in the pictures mentioned above.

By mid-1921 the downstairs library was in a suitable condition to entertain guests in style. Again, how do I know? Well, the Sept. 10, 1921 issue of 'The Billboard' reveals: "Surrounded with magical literature of all ages and with the world's famous magicians looking down upon them from their portraits on the walls, the council of the Society of American Magicians held its meeting in the library of President Houdini's home."

I was halfway there. I had found the picture of one side of Houdini's library, but what was on the other side? Did it contain bookcases and cupboards as well? I looked at what Ernst and Carrington told us. They said Doyle had chosen to position the slate in the middle of the room by hooking one supporting wire "over the edge of a picture-frame, and the other on a large book, on a shelf in Houdini's library." Based on that, coupled with the above paragraph mentioning "surrounded with magical literature of all ages and with the world's famous magicians looking down upon them from their portraits on the walls", I surmised that the one side, shown in the photograph, contained the cupboard/bookshelves while the other was a wall full of portraits of magicians. Was there any way I could actually confirm that after all these years? Amazingly there was!

Before Houdini died he vowed to contact his wife with a coded message through a spirit medium if it was at all possible. After he passed away, Bess held séances attempting to contact Houdini on the anniversary of his death - Halloween. After nothing was received from Harry for ten years she gave up. But Houdini's brother Hardeen carried on. Then Sid Radner continued the séances. Two of them are important to us.

In 1960, Radner held The Official Houdini Séance in Houdini's library. Nearly 40 years later, in 1999, he staged it in the headquarters of The Magic Circle here in London. I was able to talk to Sid then, and asked him about Houdini's library. Without me prompting, he said that it had a bookcase on one side but the other wall was plain. As this was a few years before the building was made into apartments [see below], I didn't think anyone would go to the trouble of just removing the bookcases from one side of the room. They looked too substantial to be easily removed. So, there you have it - books on one side, and pictures on the other, with the slate swinging between them.

Now, looking at the bigger picture, 'where' exactly was this wonderful library located? It's important to know because part of the action took place on the street outside. William Lindsay Gresham (Houdini: The Man Who Walked Through Walls, 1959) explained that Houdini purchased a four-story house with twenty-six rooms at 278 West 113th Street, Manhattan, to store his mountain of magical memorabilia. Gresham said: "Into it he moved his collection of magic books, playbills, old programs, letters, manuscripts, and odd pieces of magical apparatus acquired here and there on his travels....the house had plenty of space in the upstairs rooms and a capacious cellar."

To give you a flavour of the character of Houdini's house around the time of our experiment, I can do no better than quote Samri Frikell's colourful description of it (Spirit Mediums Exposed, 1930). Frikell was a pseudonym of the famous American writer, and Houdini friend, Fulton Oursler (see the WHO section for his details). Frikell talks of being summoned to Houdini's house and writes about the master magician's residence:

"Houdini lived on West One Hundred and Thirteenth Street, New York City, in a dignified old stone-front mansion that gave no hint of the weird wonders practiced, or the extraordinary relics collected within its walls. This was not my first visit to the abode of the mystifier; yet the house always exerted a new spell with each visit. Verily, the ghosts of old conjurers and old magicians seemed to glide up and down its corridors and stairs, with feet that made no sound upon the floor. For Houdini was a collector – he had letters and the wands and apparatus of sorcerers and sleight of hand men of many times and climes. As I trudged up the stairs – he was waiting for me in a room just under the roof – I fancied that behind me crept the stout spirit of Cagliostro; and out of the dark shadows of landing and balustrade peered the phantom faces of Herrmann the Great, of bald-headed Kellar who is no more, of my own ancestors, Wilbalja Frikell and Samri S. Baldwin...." [Oursler's reference to his "own ancestors" was acknowledging that he'd used part of those two magicians' names to make up his pen name.]

Frikell then went on to mention the "queer room" [which I believe to be Gresham's study/Silverman's office] that he entered:

"Amid cabinets and filing cases of historical, magical and spiritualistic data, trunks, bookcases, models of new illusions, a tangle and a jungle and a confusion of relics and documents, were Houdini and his guests....."

Frikell tells us that Houdini suggested they go downstairs, and says:

"I wish there were space to describe the front room of the lower floor of Houdini's house – an odd mixture of precious pictures, rare fine old furniture, magical curios, and a bronze bust of himself which now reposes above his grave. Also there were original letters of Cagliostro there, written from his prison. But that is another story...."

What a shame he didn't give us that other story.

Okay, now for a less colourful description, by a lawyer instead of a writer, which just might provide a clue toward solving our mystery. Melville Cane, Ernst's legal partner, in his book (The First Firefly, 1974) talks of a visit to Houdini's home "on West 113th Street near Columbia University," and "the atmosphere of the room lined with its book-filled shelves." Cane also tells us that "when Harry and Bess decided in their middle years to buy the house on 113th Street, a main consideration was to provide a permanent residence for his aging mother and her other children." Kenneth Silverman's Houdini biography also says that at the time his mother, sister and brother Bill moved in, a German servant looked after them. So, [as I pointed out in the "WHO" section] although Ernst and Carrington neglected to tell us, there definitely would have been others in the house at the time of the experiment.

More accurate physical details of Houdini's residence are given by magic collector Morris N. Young and architect Geoffrey Fulton (Linking Ring, Dec. 1979). In their excellent article, they thoroughly describe Houdini's New York house located 125 feet east of Eight Avenue at 278 West 113th Street. Construction of the twenty-six room building was completed in 1896, and the Weiss-Houdini family moved into it in 1904. The brownstone building consisted of a cellar, basement, and three floors. A key date is 1965, because that is when apartments were created on the first and second floor. So, it now no longer looks internally as it did in Houdini's day, or when Sid Radner held his Houdini Séance there, but the outside is still very much the same as it was when Houdini moved in.

I located a few other comments to help round out the picture of the building. 'The Sphinx' (Aug. 1924) described an informal reception at Houdini's New York City "palatial residence". Kenneth Silverman (Houdini!!!, 1996) talked of Houdini spending twenty-five thousand dollars for an elegant brownstone, in Manhattan, across Morningside Park from Columbia University. It had "a dozen rooms on three floors" [as opposed to the twenty-six above], with several fireplaces, baths, and kitchens, plus a cellar and basement.

Okay, so far I've described the performance area as being indoors, but that wasn't the full story? If you recall, Ernst and Carrington tell us that Houdini said: "...go out of the house, walk anywhere you like, as far as you like in any direction..." At this point, I was beginning to think I would have to fly from London to New York to look over the terrain, and then it happened! The 'Google' web site began visually mapping all the major roads of the world by sending trucks along them to take pictures. Of course, like everyone else, I had to see if they had included my house. After discovering they had come down my road in England as far as our house, a thought struck me - I could virtually walk down Houdini's street on my computer.

I was overjoyed when, through my computer's screen, I was able to stand in the middle of the block, in front of 278 West 113th Street, New York, and see the view that Doyle had seen as he reached the bottom of the steps [allowing for some rebuilding in the period in-between]. No, it wasn't just the huge saving on the cost of going there that was exciting. [Okay, just a bit.] The old saying is that Houdini nuts should get out more often. Yes, they can now go out without going out! I checked that I had the right house from pictures in several Houdini biographies, as well as from a web site that displayed a recent photograph. I was surprised to see how little the outside of the house, a few blocks north of Central Park, had changed.

I was able to exactly visually trace Conan Doyle's route - BUT how did I work out which way he went? Ernst and Carrington wrote: "Sir Arthur walked three blocks and turned a corner....and returned to Houdini's home." As the house was in the middle of the block, Doyle only had the option of going left or right. So, I opted initially for the left, setting off virtually to walk the three blocks, and around a corner. After crossing 8th Avenue I came to Manhattan Avenue, BUT could go no further! Ahead of me lay Morningside Park. So, Doyle could not have gone that way. He definitely went to the right, along West 113th Street, crossing both 7th Avenue and St. Nicholas Avenue. Then, when he reached Lenox, he went around the corner to write his message. He most likely turned the corner on the side that he was already walking on, which was probably the side that Houdini's house was on, but just to be sure I went the other way as well.

If you want to physically duplicate Doyle's walk today, my stroll above is as far as you can go because the road ends at Lenox. There is now a large housing development in the way, but in Houdini's day the road actually did carry on. I discovered that detail from a 1920s map of New York City and, to be completely authentic, used the street names of that era in my description above.

[VERY IMPORTANT NOTE: Please, please, please, do not knock on the door of Houdini's house. Over the years, I have seen many references to the owners being repeatedly annoyed by Houdini nuts wanting to look over the house. How would you like it if every week someone wanted to come into your house and search it in detail? Houdini is long gone, and the inside of the house has completely changed! You can now use the internet to examine the outside. You can even see a satellite view of the building, and virtually walk down his street. So, please, please, do not upset the people living there.]

After completing this 'WHERE' category, I had two thoughts that might have a bearing on the outcome. First, although I said Houdini was not in his normal comfort zone, i.e. onstage, he was actually on a stage of his own making. Theatre managers are not always happy with you messing about with their stage. Here he was in his own library where he could do any 'special' work he wanted. So, there was a definite advantage to the location. Secondly, could it have been that Houdini was actually performing the trick in a place that contained the secret of how he was doing it? Could the answer have been in one of his many books, and perhaps in the very book Doyle hung the slate from? All will be revealed in the "HOW" section.

Chapter 7: HOW?

PART 1 - THE EFFECT

Magicians make a sharp distinction between what they call the "effect" and the "method". The "effect" is what the spectators are supposed to perceive as happening.
- Bart Whaley (The Encyclopedic Dictionary of Magic, 2000)

"It is not really difficult to construct a series of inferences, each dependent upon its predecessor and each simple in itself. If, after doing so, one simply knocks out all the central inferences and presents one's audience with the starting-point and the conclusion, one may produce a startling, though perhaps a meretricious, effect."
- Sherlock Holmes (The Dancing Men)

Now you've explored all the other categories, it's time to reveal 'HOW' Houdini accomplished his impossible mystery. If you were tempted to skip all the other sections and begin here, then I suggest you go back and read them, because what follows is based on them, and could be confusing without having perused the preliminary chapters.

While searching for a solution to the problem, over the years I employed many different approaches. No single technique was completely successful, BUT each provided a clue toward the ultimate answer. Sometimes I put the problem away for months at a time. That way when I returned to it I was looking at it with a fresh mind and not seeking proof to support a theory. The following is a compilation of my findings at each stage of the investigation. See if you can guess my answer before I reveal it.

Supernatural vs. Trickery

In the beginning I decided I had to keep one essential thing in mind. Many past researchers came unstuck attempting to verify already held hypothesises. I needed to approach the problem from an un-biased viewpoint, and as well remember there were two opposing opinions:

A) Ernst stated: "Sir Arthur came to the conclusion that Houdini really accomplished the feat by psychic aid, and could not be persuaded otherwise."

B) Houdini declared: "This is as marvellous a demonstration as you have ever witnessed, given you under test conditions, and I can assure you that it was accomplished by trickery and by nothing else."

After much deliberation, I decided my initial task was to decide which of those two opposing assertions was most likely correct. That way I could investigate it, and then return to the other if I got nowhere. So, was Houdini really an unconscious medium producing the spirit writing by supernatural means, or had he employed magician's tricks to simulate the paranormal?

Dismissing Doyle's theory without proper research would be falling into the trap of preconceived investigation. At the same time, proving that Houdini had employed super-natural powers would be almost impossible. To me the most interesting aspect of the problem was that no person on either side of the question - neither the spiritualists nor the sceptical magicians - had managed to duplicate Houdini's 'psychic' performance exactly as Ernst had described it. After much thought, I decided I would never be able to achieve irrefutable evidence either way, BUT if I proved it could definitely be done by trickery, then I would have a strong case against Houdini being paranormal. That line of attack was strengthened by a paragraph in Dingwall's 1927 book (How to go to a Medium). He declared:

"There is no good scientific evidence that any slate writing has ever been genuine, and although tricks used by mediums have been repeatedly exposed there are still simple people who believe in the genuineness of the phenomena. A thorough training in the principles of deception is necessary before the average person can expect to understand how these very clever effects are produced. Many of the results obtained by skilful mediums appear almost miraculous, yet very often the more marvellous the effect, the simpler the trick. You must remember that the medium has been producing these tricks for a great number of years, and his trade has led him to exploit just those very weaknesses in human observation which are most difficult to avoid."

Further on Dingwall warned: "Because you cannot understand how a medium has obtained certain information, do not rashly conclude that spirits are responsible." It appears that Conan Doyle did this, as he does not seem to have supplied proof of his conjecture, other than to state that all skeptics would say it was merely a magic trick. Dingwall also warned that you should "remember the study of these subjects is apt to become so fascinating to some people, that their minds become enthralled and they become credulous without realising it."

So, to get started on my research, it came down to where best to concentrate my efforts. Should I investigate the possibility of it being an unnatural manifestation, or should I go for the natural, but hidden, magician's approach. Conan Doyle did not seem to give any evidence to back up his assertion. What about the other point of view?

NEVIL MASKELYNE, magician and magic theorist, said (Our Magic, 1911) that a magician's general purpose was to simulate supernatural effects. He also mentioned that in real life every effect is produced by some appropriate and sufficient cause.

ARTHUR BUCKLEY, magician and dabbler in fake mediumship wrote: "...it is well to reason that all things are explainable by natural laws, though the explanation may not always be within the limited comprehension or immediate understanding... When something is performed that cannot be immediately explained, it is no criterion for supposing it to be contrary to natural laws."

ARTHUR PRINCE, amateur magician and famed ventriloquist, declared (Magazine of Magic, March 1920): "I am getting rather tired of being confronted with Sir Oliver Lodge and Sir Arthur Conan Doyle. I acknowledge them to be great men in their respective spheres. But I do not acknowledge the right of the Editor, or of anybody else, to thrust them upon me as men of superior knowledge of affairs spiritual. They both suffered a sad bereavement during the Great War. That together with their wonderful imagination self-hypnotised them into the belief of spirit manifestations."

BESS HOUDINI wrote to Conan Doyle, after Houdini's death, saying: "If, as you believe, he had psychic power, I give you my word he never knew it... He buried no secrets. Every conjurer knows how his tricks were done - with the exception of just where or how the various traps or mechanisms were hidden..."

Those statements seemed to suggest that my prudent choice would be to investigate magicians' deceptive techniques. I decided, though, to keep my options open and to return to the supernatural if I could not explain the uncanny performance by means of natural mechanisms or sleights.

Houdini's Apparatus

"Discovery consists of seeing what everybody has seen
and thinking what nobody has thought."
-Albert von Szent-Gyorgyi

After coming across the above quotation, I thought I'd see if I could spot something others had overlooked. As often happens, the obvious seemed to have been missed by other investigators. What do I mean by the obvious? Well, no one appears to have asked whether Houdini's slate still existed. What was the first thing Sherlock Holmes would have done? He would have looked for clues, and then gone over them with his magnifying glass. Everyone appeared to have assumed that, after nearly a century had passed, none of Houdini's apparatus would still exist. I decided to see if it did. In other words, why spend a lot of time theorizing, as others had done, when one good look might solve the whole problem?

So, what happened to Houdini's magic equipment? Well, to begin with, Houdini was a collector, i.e. a hoarder who never threw anything away. One of the symptoms of being bitten by the magic bug is that the victims often save everything just in case they might need it. Houdini's house was crammed full of magic related items. He was one of the first great magic collectors. In fact, his slate test for Conan Doyle took place in the midst of his collection of books and paintings of past magi. So, I decided it was very unlikely that Houdini would have disposed of the slate himself; BUT, what happened after his death?

Houdini's brother, and fellow magician, Hardeen, inherited Harry's "secrets". After his brother's death, Hardeen even proclaimed it on a poster when he presented his "Houdini's Master Mysteries". The poster quoted Houdini's will, saying that Houdini bequeathed Hardeen "all my theatrical effects, new mysteries and illusions and accompanying paraphernalia, to be burnt and destroyed upon his death." So, did it all get destroyed when Hardeen went to join Houdini in the hereafter? No, Hardeen sold most of it before he died!

A large portion of Houdini's magic items, that Hardeen sold, were purchased by magician/escapologist/collector Sidney Radner. Sid was said at that time to have the world's biggest Houdini collection. I was able to have a quick chat with Sid in 1999, at The Magic Circle, in London, and asked him about Houdini's slate. Unfortunately, he said he had no idea what had become of it. So, I was about to give up on the idea of ever finding the slate, when I was able to have one more attempt at discovering it.

While looking through my "Appearing Messages" file, I noticed that many years ago I had collected a copy of page 56 of the October 1954 issue of 'Genii, The Conjuror's Magazine'. Started in California, in 1936, by William Larsen Sr., 'Genii' has gone on to become the world's oldest independent magic magazine still in continuous publication. When I subscribed to 'Genii', as a young lad, my favourite feature was the "Double Daring" column. It ran from 1947 to 1961 and was written by two extremely clever magicians, Frederick Michael Shields and Bascom Jones Jr. The page I had collected was one of their columns containing a letter from Shields to Jones, which included the following:

"....We used to talk about Houdini and Conan Doyle, and you were always intrigued with the story of the giant slate that Houdini hung in the middle of a home library, and then caused a name to appear upon, a phrase that Doyle had selected and written down while by himself, outside the house. Remember?

We were interested in it, because the big slate was in the Larsen studio for years. Or at least Bill told us it was the same slate. And how he liked to weave stories around the apparatus that was always about.

Maybe it wasn't the same slate, but we liked the idea, and you were always trying to figure how Houdini did the effect. Finally you decided that Bessie, who was very conspicuous by her absence on that particular day, must have had something to do with it.

Which gets me to the point of the letter.

No, I don't know how it was done, either. Relax....."

Was it possible that it was the very slate Houdini had used? On the plus side were several facts. First Bill Larsen was definitely a friend of Bess Houdini. She and her manager/companion, Dr. Edward Saint, had settled in California in the summer of 1934. Saint had written a column, "Thru The Monocle," in 'Genii'. Bill Larsen had been a guest at Bess's "Final Houdini Séance" on Saturday, October 31, 1936. And finally, Bess had donated Houdini memorabilia, including handcuffs, to magic clubs to be used as "Houdini Awards" in the late 1930s.

On the minus side was the fact that, according to 'Magic' magazine (Oct. 1995), some 300 Houdini props, not claimed by Houdini's brother Hardeen, were sold to Joseph Dunninger. Also Larsen was a well-known story teller and hoaxer. An example of that was Bob Weill's story (Genii, Nov. 1992) about "Horse Thief Larsen." He described how Bill Larsen Sr. had created a hoax controversy in the 1930's magic press that culminated in a fake punch-up at a major magic convention. Finally, the "Double Daring" column mentioned a giant slate. That seemed to be too big. [In the end I decided it just might have been Berol's slate, which I will get to shortly!]

I decided to see if Larsen's slate still existed. I took a chance and sent an e-mail to Max Maven. Max, at that time, was the official "consigliere" [advisor] to 'Genii'. Max is a top-flight mentalist, magic consultant, prolific author, trick inventor, and one of the most knowledgeable people in magic. In my e-mail I mentioned my quest, and asked if he was aware of what became of the slate that had been in Bill Larsen's studio. Max very kindly answered my request saying that according to Erika Larsen none of Bill Larsen Sr.'s props had been left behind. He went on to say that one must assume, that when Larsen died, his props were distributed to friends, but Max unfortunately was not aware of any record of that.

I did ask several Californian magic collectors if they knew what happened to the Larsen slate, but drew a blank. I also wrote to Bill Sr.'s son Milton to see if he would know, but got no reply. If he did get my query he probably wrote me off as another Houdini nut [and was probably correct!]. So, I assumed that the supposed Larsen/Houdini slate had gone the way of many famous pieces of magic equipment and memorabilia. Relatives faced with a huge pile of magic "junk" sadly destroy them. If you are a magic nut who owns an item of historical value, please, please, ensure its future is adequately provided for, before something unexpected happens to you. I decided to leave the quest for Larsen's slate to any interested reader. If you find it, please let me know. Okay, so I had to try to discover Houdini's secret the hard way.

Trick Selection

The first thing is to get your idea.
Having got that key idea one's next task is
to conceal it and lay emphasis upon everything
which can make for a different explanation.
- Sir Arthur Conan Doyle.

The above quotation amazed me when I came across it in a magic magazine (Genii, July 2006) because it was Doyle's explanation of how he plotted his Sherlock Holmes stories. The startling thing about it was that I think it was exactly how Houdini devised his slate 'experiment'. Perhaps Doyle should have paid more attention to what he had written instead of to his emotions. So, could I discover how Houdini not only 'concealed' his idea, but how he got that 'idea' in the first place?

At the beginning of this quest, I decided to totally ignore any ideas that had been published on how Houdini had supposedly accomplished his slate mystery. Hopefully doing so would prevent me going down too many wrong paths wasting time attempting to prove, or disprove, existing theories. I would wait until I had completely formulated my own hypothesis, and only then compare it against the ideas of others. So, anything I came across claiming to be the correct answer, I put in a folder marked "Do not look at until you think you have the answer!"

So, what was I up against in trying to determine how Houdini had accomplished his sensational sorcery? Many people think magic is only about doing 'tricks' with not much thinking involved. For a unique piece of powerful, theatrical art like Houdini's 'experiment' nothing could be further from the truth. Usually, the more a magician's illusion appears to involve no effort, the more both physical and mental labour has been expended on it. To create Houdini's slate illusion would have required an extremely, detailed amount of specialist technical engineering, coupled with major artistic input. In other words, it encompassed everything from invention to choreography.

Why would Houdini go to all that trouble for a single performance? I think it was his love of a challenge. He had perfected his professional act to the point where it was no longer mentally demanding, only physically, so he would probably have welcomed anything new in which he could fully immerse himself. Harry's young assistant Lewis Goldstein is quoted (in Patrick Culliton's Houdini – The Key, 2010) as saying that Houdini was so devoted to magic that he rarely thought of anything else. He lived for his magic. Harry would often wake up his assistants in the middle of the night to work on an idea he had just thought of.

There was only one way that Houdini could have eliminated the tremendous effort required to achieve the slate 'test' exactly as Ernst described it. What was it? It was to just use actual supernatural power, exactly as Doyle concluded. But, as Houdini repeatedly pointed out, he was not able to do that. So my quest was to find out what lengths Harry had gone to to accomplish his 'miracle'.

During the slate performance Harry's life was not being threatened. Unlike his dangerous escapes, there would be no physical mishap if it went wrong, BUT a blunder would damage something more precious to him – his huge ego. Most of those who knew him intimately said he was a supreme egotist, which, of course, you have to be to survive at the very top your profession for a quarter of a century. To avoid the wounding embarrassment of humiliating failure, Houdini would have gone to great lengths to produce his experiment, doing anything that was needed to completely fool his two important observers. [We are talking here about someone who hired private detectives to not only thoroughly investigate his foes, but his friends as well, and also employed "dirty tricks" to put his competitors out of business.] How do I know about his dedication? Well, Houdini's friend Walter B. Gibson said in his 1977 book (The Original Houdini Scrapbook) that Houdini's "inquiring mind was never satisfied until he got to what he regarded as the bottom fact of a question."

Over the years magical investigators had not adequately solved Houdini's slate performance. I believe they failed because they assumed he would not go to the great lengths he did, AND as no magic 'pirates' have stolen the 'effect' it must have been extremely complex to carry out, i.e. 'a great pain-in-the-backside to do'. Sadly piracy is rife in magic, BUT if an act takes a lot of trouble to set up and perform, no one will steal it. Pirates aside, part of the magic disease seems to involve spending vast amounts of time, and often money, to achieve something that is over in a few moments. [Yes, magic junkies get high on the adrenaline rush of presenting a perfect performance.]

Therefore, I decided to not discount any possible solution; no matter how great an effort would have been needed to accomplish it, or how farfetched it initially seemed! Of course, this would mean that I too would need to go to great lengths to uncover the truth. So, to get into the correct frame of mind, I speculated on how Houdini would have approached his initial trick selection. Could I recreate his thought processes?

It must have begun with Houdini realizing that it was futile to warn Conan Doyle about being careful about what he accepted as reality. Harry then must have decided to produce an example of extraordinary pseudo-phenomena that would hopefully shake Doyle into not accepting everything he saw as the truth. Yes the old adage, 'one good look is worth a thousand words'. The first question then was why did Houdini choose a slate trick for this crucial demonstration?

There are two contrasting sets of advice that are usually given to magicians on selecting the 'effects' [tricks] they perform. The first recommendation is audience driven. It suggests choosing items that will entertain your spectators - entertainment is considered more important than mystery. This theory stresses that people pay to see you, so they should derive maximum pleasure. The contrasting proposition is to choose tricks you like so you'll be more relaxed and able to 'sell' them well. The danger with this latter counselling is that magical 'dabblers' often tend to select items that fooled them, or looked great when executed by another magician or magic dealer. Trick selection because of novelty of method, or a new twist, is usually commercially unsuccessful. Many laypeople say that magicians all do the same thing. Sadly, that is often correct. Too many magi opt for tricks that are easy to do, and require little in the way of preparation. It takes courage to perform unique, original material like Houdini's 'test'.

It was certainly not going to be easy for Houdini. The experiment he chose contained many constraints to the creative process. A great amount of prior thought was needed, as it had to achieve maximum impact on two different types of spectators, a non-magician and a knowledgeable fellow 'magus'. Each was processing what he observed from a different viewpoint. Houdini could have easily pulled the wool over Conan Doyle's eyes. As Richard Wiseman's book (Deception and Self-Deception, 1997) says some of the easiest individuals to fool are those who are very confident of their ability to detect deception. Samri Frikell's book (Spirit Mediums Exposed, 1930) quotes from a Doyle letter that says: "I'm sure no medium has ever deceived me." Houdini would already have established that Sir Arthur had no idea of magicians' methods, when Doyle typically thought Houdini's good friends, and fellow magicians, The Zancigs, were genuine mind readers. They actually were using a very elaborate coding system.

BUT Houdini was also performing his slate mystery for someone who did possess a very good knowledge of magic principles. Houdini would have looked on it as a challenge, pulling out all the stops to fool Ernst. This would have involved leading him up the garden path toward a possible solution, and then proving that it was impossible to do it that way. At that point it would be too late to backtrack and pick up the threads again. That is why not only Conan Doyle was amazed, but, also generations of magicians who read Ernst's report of the mystery.

Devising a 'trick' to amaze two very intelligent spectators, from two completely dissimilar backgrounds, is very 'tricky' [sorry, I couldn't resist it]. Yes, Houdini and his 'backroom boys' were searching for the 'perfect' trick. [As I discussed in the WHO section, although magic is usually thought of as a solo occupation, Houdini shrewdly employed a small team of specialists with skills that complimented his.] To accomplish Houdini's 'sensation' would have required a large amount of 'brainstorming', by a knowledgeable 'brains trust', to establish the initial suggestions for an 'effect' that would create a common "Wow!" factor of amazement. After generating a suitable list of possible effects, the next stage was to reject unsuitable ones, and then finally choose a concept to be thoroughly developed. The chosen trick had to not only fit Houdini's audience, but also the limits and possibilities of the performance location [the physical structure]. It would take an extremely knowledgeable, and patient team to bounce ideas off each other, eliminate half-baked ones and then expand on suitable ones.

I believe Harry's team started by envisioning the 'effect' [what the spectator sees – the dramatic plot] rather than seeking a way to employ a secret method. Early on they must have recognized that if the magic were to be accomplished with everyday, readily available, common items, then it would greatly strengthen the performance. Tricky looking props do not create a strong magical experience. During the era we are looking at, small slates were everyday items used by students in schools. When I went to school we called the board the teacher wrote on a blackboard, but I'm reliably told that it is now called a chalkboard. In Houdini's day it was far cheaper to have pupils wipe chalk off small boards then to keep buying paper and pencils.

My feeling is that Houdini employed both of the above trick selection measures to create a 'test' that both he, and his guests, would be equally familiar with. Ernst and Carrington declared that Houdini was into slate tricks. He devoted two chapters of the book he was working on at the time (A Magician Among the Spirits, 1924) to slate tricks. I found that he had also written about slate tests in his magic magazine (The Conjurers' Monthly Magazine) as early as October 1907. He had even performed an appearing message slate trick for a past U.S. President.

From Doyle's point of view, spirit mediums had been using slates to receive spirit messages since the mid-1800s. Doyle had even described one of his characters writing on a slate in a Sherlock Holmes story (The Greek Interpreter). So, a slate would not be just a piece of magician's paraphernalia; it would evoke feelings for both of them. Ernst and Carrington also say that Houdini and Doyle had clashed over the famous "slate-writing" medium Slade. So, to Doyle, a slate would be a simple, guileless appearing prop.

The decisive factor in creating Houdini's experiment was that it had to be totally deceptive. There could be no question in his spectator's mind that Houdini was using a tricky device. It had to be as near as possible to what Doyle considered "real" when viewing other pseudo-mediums. Only by having Sir Arthur witness the impossible could Houdini prove to him that he should not accept everything at face value. In fact, the best target to aim at was to make it more "real" than any pseudo-medium could produce, which, as Ernst tells us, Houdini managed to do.

As I pointed out in the "WHERE" section, the most difficult part of the test was that Houdini was doing his demonstration in broad daylight. Pseudo-mediums have the advantage of doing their tricks in the dark. [Apparently the spirits prefer to work with the lights out.] I believe that Team Houdini invested hundreds of hours in

155

strategically planning, dramatizing, and perfecting the structure of this one trick, for an exclusive performance that was devastatingly emotional. They managed to devise an 'effect' that achieved the difficult double; it was not only intimate and meaningful, but also highly visual. [An interesting aside is that they also achieved the modern 'Holy Grail' of magic – packs small, plays big. But I don't for a minute think his 'effect' was portable. It must have certainly been venue-specific; or by now, others would have successfully duplicated it.] I decided to look at how magicians created their magic tricks to see if I could gain an insight into to how Houdini had specifically produced his 'test'?

Magic Creativity

"A magic performance consists of a collection of tiny lies, in words, and deeds, that are stacked and arranged ingeniously to form the battlement for an illusion."
- Jim Steinmeyer

"Magic is the only Art I can think of where lying is not only approved but is actually considered a requirement."
- Michael Ammar.

"Why do complicated sleights when you can just lie?"
- The late, Great, Ali Bongo.

From the above quotes, it would appear that the bigger the liar the better the magician. So, how does this big liar create his big lie, i.e. an astounding piece of magic that will not only apparently completely contradict natural laws, but also seem to have no possible explanation? Unfortunately the answer is that there is no ideal system or theory for inventing new tricks. Every trick is different, and each has to be individually logistically worked out. Magical 'effect' creators use various approaches. There is no right or wrong way. Some originators seem to find trick invention easy, while others have to work intensely at it.

Are there any helpful techniques? Well, sometimes a secret method is visualized first and then an analytical search undertaken for the best way to exploit it. The problem then becomes how to hide the method so well that it doesn't appear to exist. At other times the opposite occurs. A way of using an object in an effect [a plot] is envisaged, and then a hunt made for the best method to accomplish it. The ability to visualise the effect in the imagination is essential, as well as being able to exaggerate and not feel foolish while doing so. The 'effect' is what the spectators think they witness, so it is usually considered to be far more important than the 'method'; BUT, if the method is not completely hidden, the effect will not be achieved. The simplest 'method' is always the best, BUT 'simplest' does not necessarily mean the 'easiest'.

The most productive trick creation approach is often to not rush the process, but to mull over it. While sleeping on the problem, wonderful ideas often suddenly, mysteriously, appear from somewhere deep in the sub-conscious. The secret is to maintain the positive attitude that you will definitely solve the problem. If you do, then eventually the mind will find a solution. Unfortunately, it seldom produces a brand new, revolutionary, ingenious method. Most tricks evolve from existing ones. They are usually changes or adaptations of known principles. So, the would-be inventor must learn as much as he can about the history of secret sleights and special apparatus, along with the misdirection required to cover them. Then he must question why certain things are done as they are. In other words, he must eliminate critical thought, and let his mind freewheel in playful adventure. It is his education and training that will stop him from trying out new approaches. The rule is to be child-like but not childish.

For the reasons I've already mentioned, I think Houdini started with his desired category of effect - a slate trick - and was then determined to create a presentation that would far outdo anything pseudo-spiritual mediums had accomplished. The messages on slates that mediums produced tended to be created in secret, i.e. the slate surface was hidden, either in the dark, under a table, or by another slate. From the results Houdini achieved, I believe he wanted his slate trick to do several things: a) create a large impact in a small-scale location, b) work in an informal setting with maximum spectator involvement and minimum magician input, and c) be direct and uncluttered while producing a startling visual climax. Because Houdini's available time for creating the experiment was restricted to the fixed date of Doyle's visit, he did not have the luxury of waiting for inspiration to strike, i.e. having a "eureka" moment. There could be no short cut; he had to carry out a comprehensive, detailed design process of several stages, with each phase requiring different skills.

The first stage of that process, was visualizing, which involved Houdini mulling over the problem of what constituted an ideal slate effect. Any ideas that came to mind would be written down without worrying about how to accomplish them. Most books on creativity say that recording ideas is the best system. The mind is liberated to think of new ideas, instead of trying to memorize everything daydreamed. I'm absolutely certain Houdini wrote down those ideas. Why? Because Ernst inherited many of Harry's notebooks, containing trick ideas he had scribbled down as they came to him. Frustratingly, when he'd completed the work on a new trick, he usually destroyed all the paperwork involved with it. So the possibility of finding early design data for our trick in a magic collectors' hoard is extremely unlikely.

Once Houdini had gathered enough ideas from his daydreaming phase, he had to narrow down his imaginings. Each vision of the perfect presentation would be checked to see if it fitted the basic criteria he was aiming at. Was it a step further than anyone else had gone with slate magic? Would it attract, and hold, the attention of his two spectators from very different backgrounds? Would it draw them into his world? Would it maintain their interest throughout? Was there an emotional hook? Was it suitable for the restricted location? Was there a visually strong impact? Would the final climax completely astonish his viewers? Yes, quite a difficult goal to achieve. It would require compromise and a trade off between objectives.

When he had finally found the slate 'effect' most closely fitting those conditions, he would progress to the next step. At the same time he would not yet totally eliminate the other ideas he'd listed. If an overly complex method to accomplish the chosen effect was required it could send him back to the beginning to start over again.

At this point in considering Houdini's search for an ideal effect I wondered if the answer to why other magi had not been able to explain Houdini's performance was, in fact, because he had invented a unique magical method. Then, because of his obsession with secrecy, had it become lost to the following generations of magicians? If so, how could I possibly re-discover it? I concluded that the only answer was to thoroughly analyse in detail how magicians invented magic illusions. Here I was in luck. This area of magic had always intrigued me. During my many decades of magical secret searching, I had collected everything I came across on magical invention. I turned to my 'Invention' file.

The first item I noticed was a statement by prolific inventor, Peter Warlock, in a 1981 'Magic Circular'. Peter stated that there had been very little written on this important subject. [Was that why so many magicians' acts sadly looked the same?] The fact there was only a small amount available on invention in magical literature was both good news and bad news. The good news was that I could quickly cover the subject. The bad news was that I probably wouldn't find much. Here is a very short summary of what people had written:

PAVEL (The Magic of Pavel, 1981): "Theoretically, truly original tricks are, in the main, achieved in two ways:- (1) By a process of evolution. (2) By chance."

HENNING NELMS (Magic and Showmanship, 1969): "Complete originality is rare...."

159

STEVE LETT (Lett's Make Original Magic, 1989): "Research is the absolute keystone upon which originality in presentation or invention are based....creativity defined as the rearrangement of past experiences into new combinations of magical ideas, as nothing in magic can be completely original"

PETER WILKER (The Creation of Magic, 1991): "....the starting point of creation: ...effects one would like to alter and improve upon...the number of tricks invented from scratch is extremely small."

ERIC C. LEWIS (Magical Mentality, 1934): "...a new idea is generally only the joining together of old ideas....reassembling."

MICKY HADES (The Make-Up of Magic, 1962): "It is rare indeed when an entirely new principle or an original plot makes an appearance. Almost every 'invention' is a variation of an established effect, with some modification in the mechanism, design or presentation."

BILL SEVERN (Bill Severn's Guide to Magic as a Hobby, 1979): "Magical invention is no different from other kinds of invention in that it starts with what is known and develops the new out of the old.... But the creation of a totally new effect or discovery of an entirely original principle is rare."

NEVIL MASKELYNE (Our Magic, 1911): "The difficulty of producing a new magical effect is about equivalent to that of inventing a new proposition in Euclid.... In magic, as in all other directions, the chief source from which inventors derive their inspiration is the work already done...."

SAM SHARPE (Neo-Magic, 1946): "One of the first requirements of the originator is a thorough knowledge of existing feats and methods....invariably consists in producing new combinations.... Nearly all the creations of Hartz, de Kolta, HOUDINI, Devant, and

Maskelyne - to mention but a few of the recognised Masters - can readily be tracked to their predecessors."

Based on those expert statements, it seemed it was very likely that, rather than discovering something completely new, Houdini had improved an existing item. So, I decided my best course of action was to search magical literature in a quest for the roots of Houdini's "test." After further deliberation, I decided there was a way I could narrow down the field of search. Bill Severn had said: "Each trick has two parts: effect and method. The effect is how the trick looks to the audience and the method is how it is done." J.F. Orrin (Put It Over, 1933) stressed: "The effect is by far the more important consideration." So, I decided to look for a similar effect, which hopefully would lead me to the method Houdini had employed.

Houdini's Library

So, where should I look? The answer was in the literature of magic. That sounded easy, but was it? Severn had said: "Many magicians have found old magic books, magazines and dealers catalogues good sources for ideas." The following quotes will give you an idea of what I was now up against:

PROFESSOR HOFFMANN (Later Magic, 1904) wrote: "Magical material has accumulated to such an enormous extent during the last few years as to make it impossible to deal with it adequately within the compass of a single volume." [Yes, an "enormous extent" in 1904!]

CHARLES L. RUFFS: "....the written record of the history of magic is woefully incomplete...magicians, with a bona fide curiosity of the history of their art, express a considerable indecision as to what to seek and where to seek it...as regards 'where to seek', about two-thirds of these works (and these include many of the more valuable references) are now out of print." [That was out of print in 1953!]

ROBERT C. PRUS: "...there is a vast array of material published on magic...Probably there's more written on magic, on conjuring, than any other art form...part of the problem with magic...there is no disciplined way that you can find those things out. These magic books, all this information that is just thrown up into the air, it comes down anywhere...there's so much material, and often material only realizes its significance when the material becomes important to you. You overlook something until that particular bit of information becomes important....There's an assumption that all this information is easily accessible."

DARWIN ORTIZ: "Volumes and volumes of books on card magic sag our shelves...So much has been written on card magic, especially during the last four decades, that it is difficult for many enthusiasts 'to see the forest for the trees'....Many magicians complain of how daunting a task it is to try to study the immense literature of modern card magic."

EARLE J. COLEMAN (Magic: A Reference Guide, 1987): "...the vast literature of conjuring...Because the effectiveness of magic is utterly dependent upon the concealment of its secrets, a good deal of the best magic literature is circulated on a very limited basis....closely guarded writings of small trade publishers...much magic literature is suppressed and circulated only among practicing magicians...most magic literature is distributed by small trade houses or private individuals rather than large lay publishers...publications that are unavailable through public libraries."

JOHN CARNEY: "A fascinating and inspiring feature of magic is that it can never be learned entirely. There is always something that you haven't fully explored."

So, not only was there an almost endless number of books to search, but laying your hands on most of them was nearly impossible! No wonder Houdini's secret had not been discovered.

It seemed like an impossible task. But fortunately there was help at hand. In my early twenties, when I began to get into magic in a serious way, I crossed the Atlantic from Canada to England for just two weeks. I'd seen a reference in a magic book to The Harry Price Library at the University of London, so while in the U.K. I visited it. Now 50 years later I'm still in England, and still reading my way through Price's wonderful collection of magic books. So what has that to do with our Houdini problem?

Just like Harry Price had bequeathed his magic book collection to the University of London, Harry Houdini left his books to the Library of Congress in Washington. If Houdini had improved on an existing trick, there was a strong chance he had obtained the original idea from one of his books or magazines. As the performance had taken place in Houdini's library it would be quite apt if it supplied the answer. I recalled reading a magazine article Houdini had written around the time he performed his "test". The item had been in a box of 'Houdini Material' in the Harry Price Library. In that article Houdini declared that he had assembled the largest magic library in the world. Price had underlined the statement in red pencil and put an exclamation mark and a question mark next to it. If Price's library was almost comparable to Houdini's I could save myself the large expense of moving to Washington. Of course, I'd still have to put in the time researching Price's collection. I began a quest to see how near, in content, the two libraries were.

The April 1904 issue of The Sphinx mentioned the rare English and German magic books in Houdini's library. A dozen years later, in the July 1916 issue, Oscar Teale declared: "The Houdini Library is undoubtedly the greatest accumulation of necromantic literature ever gotten together under one roof anywhere." Houdini's library was frozen in time at the date of his death, 1926, while Price's continued to grow until he died in 1948. So, Price may have obtained earlier works than he had at the time of Houdini's death. Thus trying to compare the two Harry's libraries, book by book was impossible. I decided see if there had been any expert opinions on Houdini's library around the time of his death.

After much page turning and time passing, I discovered that Leo Rullman, the magic book collector/dealer, and noted authority on old magic literature, had looked over Price's library. Rullman had written a column on the "Books of Yesterday" in the leading magic periodical of its day, 'The Sphinx'. In his June 1928 article Rullman wrote of his visit to Harry Price's library saying: "...library of Mr. Price...the wonderful collection of magical psychic literature, that is at once the envy and despair of every collector with similar interests...the treasures of this collection, which in view of the present scarcity of old magical literature, will probably not be duplicated in this generation."

A year later, July 1929, on receiving a copy of Price's printed catalogue, Rullman wrote: "...the collection belonging to the Library of Congress, at Washington recently enriched as it was by the acquisition, through bequest, of the Houdini library of conjuring and psychical literature, ranks well in the forefront of public collections. Nevertheless and notwithstanding, I concede the palm to the Harry Price collection." I like to think that Price on reading that must have thought: "Got you Houdini!" There was also further confirmation.

John Mulholland (Sphinx, Aug. 1929) wrote of Price's catalogue: "...contains more items on the subject than any heretofore published material...Mr. Price's wonderful library...a veritable goldmine of valuable information." Mulholland also wrote a letter that appeared in the 'New York Herald Tribune' Book section for Sunday October 13, 1929. He said: "...You expressed a desire to know how the Price Library compared with the Houdini Library...I separated the Houdini Libraries for the Library of Congress...as to sizes. The Houdini collection of memorabilia was much larger...Price has the largest collection of magic books in the world." There was also further confirmation when Ernst wrote:

"Houdini's collection of material bearing upon magical and psychic topics of all kinds was a fearful and wonderful thing. His purely magical library was of course the finest in the world (with the exception of that owned by Mr. Harry Price)...."

John Mulholland further amplified this (The Sphinx, Oct. 1936) when talking of Houdini's claim to have the largest library of magic. John said Harry included all his manuscripts, photographs, play-bills and other magic memorabilia in his definition of library. When Houdini died, one of the Library of Congress librarians came to his house and picked out the books that the Library wanted. The books in the drama collection did not go to the Library. They were left to Bess. She would have been willing to have someone go over them and remove the magic books to be added to those for the Congressional Library, but there was no one to undertake the mammoth task. So, as Mulholland wrote: "This will explain why, although Houdini claimed and actually had the largest library on magic, the bequest to the Library was not as large as several others, including the magnificent collection of Harry Price of London."

James B. Findlay (Second Collectors Annual, 1950) added two interesting pieces of information. The first was that the Houdini collection of conjuring literature bequeathed to The Library of Congress comprised of 1,620 books on conjuring, 107 volumes of periodicals, and 126 scrapbooks. The second item made my day when I read it: "The late Harry Price commenced his world famous collection in 1889 with a copy of Hoffmann's 'Modern Magic' presented to him by his parents. In 1935 the collection numbered 10,000 items. This is an accumulation rate of over four items per week sustained for more than 45 years."

So, thanks to Harry Price's Herculean efforts I stood a chance of finding the solution here in London, without having to visit Harry Houdini's library in America. I was now sure that searching Price's library would be a near equivalent to searching Houdini's own collection; BUT, it wasn't as easy as it sounded. Price's collection was not segregated into separate categories. All Price's items were shelved and catalogued, in alphabetical order, by author's surname. The books and typescripts that I wanted were mixed in with over 20,000 other items. They included books, manuscripts, letters, scrap-books, handbills, trade-cards, press cuttings, etc., etc. on every bizarre subject you could possibly think of [conjuring, of course, excepted!]. Just some of these subjects were: methods of deception, charlatanism, witchcraft, spiritualism, psychology, occultism, ghosts, superstitions, vampirism, optical illusions, gambler's tricks, lightning calculators, confidence men, psychical research, etc., etc.

My initial thought was that I would only have to search the literature up to the time of the slate performance. That, of course, was completely wrong! I soon realised that many of the almost 'lost' accounts of magic history appear in magazines featuring reminiscences of magicians and their assistants. These are usually published many years later. It can even be after the death of the person relating them, when someone else passes on something that person had said. Naturally, this second hand relating leaves the information open to some loss of accuracy, and even conscious, as well as unconscious, additions to make it a bit more colourful.

Now that I had somewhere to start, I set off on a quest that would consume a large amount of my time and energy for nearly two decades.

Starting To Explore

"Few tricks have been more thoroughly explored than the slate-writing feat"
- Paul Fleming.

Most magicians acquire magic books, tricks, dealers' catalogues, souvenirs, etc., etc. over the years. One of the symptoms of the magic virus appears to be the need to have a closet full of magic debris, and in many cases, a house full. All magic addicts intend to sort out their paraphernalia one day. When you ask them for any information, they are sure they have it but just can't quite seem to find it; but, next week they'll put everything in order, including throwing out what they don't want. I can tell you from my own experience that for some unknown reason next week never seems to come.

Luckily, I had a temporary bout of sanity, early on in my magical pilgrimage. During this hiatus I began constructing a magical information retrieval system. Over the years, while secret searching in Harry Price's vast library, I slowly developed a storage scheme to classify all my precious findings. The system operated along the lines of the one used by public libraries. Currently, the Loomis Legerdemain Library Listing has 26 major magical categories. These are further sub-divided into over 333 sub-categories. (For full details see my now out of print book "The Quest For The Ultimate Secret", 1993) [Isn't it disgusting when authors promote their own work?]

On my first tentative look at what I'd accumulated, in my 'Appearing Messages' file, I found that slates were not the only objects on which words and pictures had magically appeared. Long before Houdini had performed his "test" for Conan Doyle, mysterious data had appeared on/in such items as:

- people's bare forearms [as early as the year 1715].
- empty canvases [spirit paintings].
- empty picture frames.
- developed photographs [spirit photography].
- slips of paper [billets].
- dinner plates by means of soot from a candle.
- business cards.
- glasses and mirrors when breathed upon.
- crystal balls.

The entire appearing message category was far too vast for me to fully examine in the far too short time I had left on this earth. So,

I decided to narrow down the scope of search by restricting it to slates.

To get mentally prepared [Okay, I admit it! To put off starting the hard work for a while] I speculated on what a magic dealer's catalogue advertisement for Houdini's slate effect might say:

THE TRICK THAT BAFFLED SHERLOCK HOLME'S CREATOR

An incredible, baffling mystery. The perfect effect. Approaches the miraculous. Performed under test conditions. An unknown message visibly appears written by an examined cork ball that has been dipped in ink. The ball is propelled by unknown forces across an ordinary slate swinging in the centre of the room. All the props are inspected and handled by the spectators, who hang up the slate and perform all the necessary actions. The magician does not touch or approach any items during the performance. The spectators do everything. There is no apparent reasonable physical causation. Ideal for fooling both magicians and laymen alike. It is both angle proof and spectator proof. So strong an effect that the audience will attribute supernatural powers to the magician. Devilishly clever. Defies analysis. Remarkably ingenious. Price only....

Now if I could only buy one! I began to be sorry I had written that ad. It only made the task ahead seem more impossible. The time for speculation was over. I got down to work. I set about becoming an expert on the performance of "autography", "pschography" or slate-writing. Although slates are an obscure item by today's standards, they were the pen and paper of their day. False Mediums used them because they were an everyday item, and therefore not suspected of involving deception. Every school child had one. Ironically, the only people who seem to use them today are magicians. Most magic dealers sell them. It would appear to negate the original concept, as they are now certainly uncommon items. Surely the average spectator will question their use and wonder why those strange items are being used instead of pen and paper [or even a handheld computer/phone!] So Conan Doyle would have been quite familiar with a slate.

If Houdini was trying to out-do the mediums at their own game I reasoned that a thorough study of their presentations might lead to unravelling his mystery. Right or wrong I had to start somewhere. To give you an idea of what I was up against, Harry Price had written: "Books on fake phenomena and the tricks of the mediums are legion and I suppose that I, personally, must have collected some 5,000 of them." At this stage, I was more interested in effect than method. So, that would help to reduce some of the effort. All I had to do was find a performance that was somewhat similar to Houdini's from a spectator's point of view.

Ernst and Carrington wrote in their book: "Another famous case over which Conan Doyle and Houdini clashed was that of the celebrated medium Slade, who flourished about sixty years ago, and who was famous for his 'slate-writing' tests.... Houdini was most anxious to run everything to earth that he possibly could regarding Slade." So, I started with Slade. Harry Price said that "Dr." Henry Slade was the greatest slate-writing medium, and that his methods were often exposed as tricks. Carrington, in his 1920 book (The Physical Phenomena of Spiritualism), stated that the career of Slade was anything but free from suspicion. Slade was convicted of fraud in London, but fled to Germany. I followed up Slade by studying the other great slate-writing medium Eglinton. Carrington said that Eglinton's whole life-history was clouded over with suspicions and doubts. Especially revealing was his refusal to meet or have a sitting with the Great English magician Maskelyne. It was probably because Maskelyne had testified at Slade's trial exposing his tricks.

To solve Houdini's mystery, I would have to eliminate all the possible deceptive approaches that did not fit the 'plot' from my 'WHAT' section. In setting up his experiment Houdini had eliminated a large portion of those fake methods himself. He had obviously studied the existing techniques of slate trickery and designed his approach to exclude those common approaches, [or

169

at least appear to exclude them]. Most mediums of Houdini's day operated under dark conditions, with the sitters holding hands. This gave plenty of scope for mischief. Houdini did his experiment in full daylight, with no restraints on his spectators. Although Slade had done his writing in daylight he usually held the slates under the table. Houdini eliminated this by hanging his slate in the middle of the room.

But by eliminating those methods used to fake slate writing he was probably at the same time aiding his own chosen technique. On the surface it would appear that he was adding controls to eliminate deception, while all along he was doing the opposite. The other thing Houdini was doing was directing or steering attention away from areas he did not want his observers to notice. What where those areas? I set out to analyse all the possible methods of his day.

Hours, days, and weeks passed, as I studied other slate-writing mediums such as Fred P. Evans, P.L.O.A. Keeler and Mrs. Laura A. Pruden. I learned from Carrington that: "there is no good evidence, in the whole history of spiritualism, for the occurrence of writing on slates by other means than such as might have been produced fraudulently by the medium." Harry Price pointed out: "For some reason I have been unable to fathom, British slate-writing mediums are, and have been, almost non-existent. This particular 'spirit' technique is peculiarly American, and every exponent who consented to be tested scientifically has come to grief."

While searching, I came across fraudulent slate-writing done on both the medium's slates and the sitter's slates. I learned how prepared and unprepared, single and double slates were manipulated, in both the dark and the light. I was becoming quite knowledgeable in the field of appearing messages on slates, but I was not even getting close to a performance mimicking Houdini's. Although I had expended a great amount of energy, I had not discovered a medium producing anything resembling Houdini's test. I was fast approaching the point of abandoning the quest when serendipity suddenly raised its delightful head.

A large amount of the time I had available to devote to magic was being taken up with the Houdini mystery, but at the same time I was editing my Magical Spectators' club's newsletter, 'The Magical Spectator'. One day while checking out a trick source for a newsletter article, an incident happened that changed my search direction. Purely by chance, I noticed a reference to a Mene, Tekel, Upharsin Trick. Somewhere deep in my subconscious a light of recognition flashed on. I remembered Conan Doyle's message had contained those very words!

The Mene Tekel Connection

"Magicians took the slates on stage and refined the presentation and handling to a degree undreamed by mediums. Sleights with slates became an art."
- Al Mann.

Conan Doyle's message that he wrote out on the street was a Biblical quote from Daniel, Chapter 5. During one of King Belshazzar's feasts, the fingers of a human hand suddenly appeared and wrote that message on the palace wall. God had sent the hand. Its message was a warning to the King that his days were numbered.

Magical authors have noted that Houdini was an expert at planting ideas in people's minds. His spectators would later suggest those thoughts believing they had originated them. We will never know if Houdini had hinted at the Bible passage when talking to Conan Doyle, sometime before the performance. The reason for suggesting this possibility will become clear as we progress. The other, and probably more accurate conjecture was that Conan Doyle slipped into his author mode while walking the three blocks to his message writing point. In a classic, Holmes-telling-Watson-what-he-was-thinking-about manner Conan Doyle's mind probably progressed from wondering why the slate was hanging in Houdini's library, to God's warning message as he pondered on what to write.

The Mene Tekel mention I came across referred to a trick of French magician Robert-Houdin. Jean Eugene Robert-Houdin had been young Ehrich Weiss's boyhood hero. The lad had mistakenly thought that by adding the letter "i" to his hero's name, it would mean that he was like Houdin. Harry, in later life, became disillusioned with his hero, and wrote a book denouncing his idol, which he entitled "The Unmasking of Robert-Houdin." Houdini's point was that the French magician had not invented the tricks he claimed to have, but merely improved on the work of others. [Houdini doesn't seem to have realised that his own name was also an "improvement."]

So, in studying Houdin's tricks Houdini would have been familiar with Robert-Houdin's Mene, Tekel, Upharsin Trick. But it was a card trick where three cards from a group in the hands of one spectator passed into those held by another. That effect is still used by many of today's top magicians and is usually called "Cards Across." The bad news here is that only the name of Robert-Houdin's trick had any bearing on my quest. The good news was that finding this connection caused me to alter the aim of my search from mediums to magicians. Magicians had initially been dumbfounded by the "miracles" of the mediums, but it was not long before they were outdoing the mediums in the presentation of pseudo-psychic miracles.

My exploration territory was further greatly extended when, based on the book I wrote explaining my library classification system, I was asked to become a librarian at the wonderful Magic Circle's headquarters in London, here in England. That allowed me to search, not one, but two of the world's great magic libraries. The Magic Circle Library contained over ten thousand items, including the Chris Charlton magazine collection, which was the most extensive in its day. This now permitted me to thoroughly investigate the books that had been published after Price's death.

Later I was able to amplify my search by using the superb 'Ask Alexander' online database of magic, that had originally been set up to research Houdini material. It was a mixed blessing - more information, but a mountain of it to sift through.

After I shifted my investigation from medium's to magician's effects, the weeks of exploration passed into months as I pursed magical performances, once again, more interested in effect than method. I eventually discovered a second Mene Tekel mention. This too was card trick related. It was a special deck of cards, known as The Mene Tekel or Self-Shifting Deck. The deck was said to have been invented by Burling Hull around 1909, but there have been suggestions that it was the brain-child of Donald Holmes. Like Robert-Houdin's card trick, I couldn't see a connection with the handwriting on the wall. I began to believe the title would continue to crop up whenever a magic dealer wanted a mysterious sounding trick name. I wondered if that dealer would actually know it was a warning. [Perhaps to potential customers to save their money!] I made a mental note to ignore any future occurrence of "Mene Tekel." Happily, I then forgot that decision.

The third Mene Tekel reference I came across turned out to be much more in line with what I had been looking for. 'The Magic Wand' (Nov. 1912) stated: "At the Tivoli we had Berol, with the Mene Tekel mystery. This was very well presented, and at once caught on with the audience. A fine thing well done." Now that appeared much more promising. I had to find out about Berol, and what his mystery was. 'The Sphinx' (Nov. 1912) added more in "The London Letter", saying: "'Menetekel,' the clever illusion which was so well presented by William Berol at the Palladium the other week, goes into the provinces next week, and will be seen at the Tivoli Manchester." So, if it was an illusion that was good enough for the Palladium, the top English variety theatre, I had to find out what this "fine thing", "well presented", "clever illusion" was.

Magic Circle Executive Librarian Peter Lane, and Custodian of the Circle's Inner Sanctum, David Hibberd, both kindly contributed to

173

my spectators' newsletter. They also greatly assisted in my search for Berol's Mene Tekel illusion. David was working on a list of magicians, and where they had been performing, starting from the turn of the century. He produced an excellent book in 2003 on the subject (Chronicle of Magic: 1900-1999). The references David supplied saved me hours of searching. Peter came up with several items from his own extensive collection that I could not have found elsewhere. David pointed out that many magicians often changed their names. He also explained that many acts were booked to present "the act as known." Thus everyone knew what the act was so didn't bother to explain it in print. [Would any reader who writes reviews for magic magazines please remember this, and make the life of future magic historians just a little easier by giving full descriptions.]

So, what did I discover? A confusing conundrum, including: a) various names for the illusion such as Mene Tekel, Menetekel and Menetekle; b) various first names of the presenter including Max, William, Felix and Nate; and as well, c) various surnames for the presenter including Berol, Belmonte and Konorah. The first clarification came with the following entry in the "Monthly News and Notes" column of Will Goldston's 'The Magician' magazine (June 20, 1906):

"'Menetekel' an illusion submitted at the leading Halls by Mr. and Mrs. Konorah, is original and effective to a degree. A number of sheets of cartridge paper are suspended on the stage by two wires in such a manner as to prevent any suspicion of trickery. Sheet by sheet the paper is torn away after use as rapidly as the cartoons of the lightning artist. Madame Konorah takes a tiny ball, which has been dipped in a glutinous ink, places it against the cartridge paper, to which it readily adheres, then moves in obedience to the word of command, writing first its own name, then replies to questions from the audience, and finally a spontaneous good-night. The illusion is clever and absolutely inexplicable."

YES, a ball dipped in ink, adheres and writes its own name, Menetekel! Now all I had to do was connect that illusion to

Houdini. The information that I had assembled up to that point was equivalent to having a box of a jigsaw puzzle pieces with no picture on the box, and to make it more difficult, some of the major pieces were missing. Now, suddenly, an item that helped clarify the picture seemed to magically appear. If I didn't know better, I would say someone outside our normal sphere of communion was trying to tell me something. As I entered the Magic Circle Library one morning, Peter Lane said to me: "You know how you've been searching for information on Berol. Well, yesterday I was showing a visitor around the library. I opened this filing cabinet, a yard from where you've been working for a year now, to show the David Devant scrapbooks. I removed a typical one and opened it to illustrate Devant's newspaper clippings. The book fell open at this page, and all I could say was 'Here is Da...Da... Da...!'"

In his hands Peter held one of Devant's many scrap books, that I had helped sort out and put into that filing cabinet. They all contained newspaper clippings of reviews of the Great British magician's performances - just his performances, nothing else. The Centre for the Magical Arts [the home of The Magic Circle] had named one floor of their new building after him. Pasted into the middle of Devant's scrapbook in Peter's hands was a four page brochure of Berol's Second Tour of the World! Not only that, the brochure was for a performance at the Lyceum Theatre in SHANGHAI! It gave many references to Berol performances. I will leave it to an interested reader to find out why it was in a Devant scrapbook that otherwise contained just clippings mentioning his own act. [Possible clue: Devant presented an illusion called "The A.B.C. Fly", in 1913, where an imitation fly crawled around a board containing letters spelling out words.]

The following is a condensed summary of my eventual findings for the background of Berol's Mene Tekel Mystery: The July 1895 issue of 'Mahatma' mentioned in the "From Our Boston Correspondent" column that Prof. Max Berol was playing the summer resorts with Miss Belmonte's new mindreading act. He was apparently German born Max Buldermann and was partnered by Nora "Konorah" Belmonte. By October of that year, Berol and

Belmonte were preparing for an extended tour of the United States. The March 1898 'Mahatma' "Boston Notes" column referred to Berol's Mystegogues saying they were peers in mind reading. It said the great beauty of their work was "originality", which puzzled magicians as well as novices. By this time Max's brother Felix had joined them introducing rapid memory work.

In 1899, Max took his troupe, including his brother William, on a world tour including Europe, U.S.A. and Japan. In 1903, Max Berol-Konorah was in New York City, and joined the Society of American Magicians. In 1904 Berol's American Mystifiers undertook its Second Tour of the World. The tour featured: Madame Konorah, the Modern Witch and Mistress of Mysteries; Max Berol, The Merry Wizard; William Berol, The Jolly Comedian; and Felix Berol, The Living Encyclopedia. At about this point Felix and Max seem to have had a disagreement. Felix stayed in the U.S.A. while Max apparently returned to Germany. Felix took on a young magician named Nate Leipzig as a partner. Leipzig would go on to become a famous magician, and be voted one of the living 10 Card Stars. For a short period Liepzig performed as Nate Berol, which added to the confusion.

The Menetekel illusion (as described above) seems to be first mentioned in the U.K. in early 1906. It was presented by Mr. and Mrs. Konorah, presumably Max and Nora. In late 1906 and early 1907, Mr. and Madam Berol-Konorah presented "Menetekel, the Mystic Ball" in the U.S.A. This is where I found my first link to Houdini. Peter Lane has in his collection a scrap-book containing newspaper clippings of Houdini's performance reviews and publicity. One of those clippings is from the Chicago Examiner for Wednesday, November 21, 1906. It says:

"Two of the most bewildering acts in vaudeville are on exhibition this week at different theaters and though they are far apart in method, each sends a big crowd out of the theater at every performance wondering how it is accomplished. One is the marvellous act of Houdini, 'the handcuff king,' at the Majestic, and the other is 'Menetekel, the Mystic Ball,' at the Haymarket"

When I asked Peter who assembled the scrap-book he said he didn't know, and what's more, someone had unfortunately written all over it, completely ruining it! BUT, I did notice that when Peter said it he seemed to have a twinkle in his eye. Why? Well, as he eventually explained, the person that wrote all over the scrap-book was none other than Harry Houdini himself. This wilful act just happened to convert it from a mere scrap-book to an almost unique magical item - someone's scrap-book annotated by the subject himself. The owner must have shown his work to the master, and had it appraised by him. So, here was proof that Houdini saw the clipping, quoted above, because the item to the immediate right of it had an added comment that was signed by Houdini. And besides he would definitely be aware of who his competition was that week. So, it can definitely be said that Houdini was aware of Berol's Menetekel Mystery by 1906!

Then the trail of the illusion went cold for a few years, but I picked it up again in 1912 when I found a reference to Max Berol-Konorah being in Berlin. He was the manager of Das Program, the publication of the International Artistes Loge, and was instrumental in furthering the equity laws for German actors. During this period while Max was in Germany, William surfaced in the U.K. presenting the Mene Tekel Mystery. It would appear that Max handed over, or sold, the illusion presentation rights to his brother. In the May 1914 issue of 'The Magician Monthly' under the title "William Berol. Menetekel" is the following:

"The long engagement for Russia, which 'Berol', the manipulator of the weird 'Menetekel Mystery,' had made every arrangement for, has been cancelled, owing to the sudden death of his brother. 'Berol' has left London for New York per S.S. George Washington, and he proposes to settle in New York for sometime. A loss to our country of a clever artiste and a novel act! Our condolences to William Berol in his trouble."

Felix Berol had died on April 20, 1914. His timing was unfortunate for his brother. William sailed to America on the eve of the Great

War. At this point I lost the trail completely. Both William and Houdini would have been in New York, but I needed to establish a definite connection between the two. I mulled over what to do, and then had an idea. As an editor of a magical newsletter, I know just how intimidating unfilled blank spaces can be. I'll bet Houdini had the same problem.

In 1917, when Houdini was elected president of the Society of American Magicians he also took over editorship of its bulletin, 'M-U-M'. The title stood for 'Magic Unity and Might'. Although the new editor was semi-illiterate, he was far from being an ignoramus. Others may have polished up his input to the magazine, but the ideas were still his. He was extremely knowledgeable in the ways of magic and magicians, and like his fellow editors he would have used his daily experiences to pad out the paper.

The magazine ceased publication shortly after Houdini's death. Apparently no member had the time or energy to devote to it. I can confirm how much work goes into it. Fortunately it was resurrected again in 1951 and is still being published. Magic collectors consider the first series, from 1911 to 1927, to be scarce. Jim Alfredson and George Daily, the two leading magic magazine experts, said in their book (A Bibliography of Conjuring Periodicals in English, 1986) that the meaning of scarce is twenty-five or less known existing files. Fortunately, one of those files was in the library of The Magic Circle. I started reading the 164 issues printed during Houdini's life.

As I neared the end of the detailed reading of eight years' worth of 'M-U-M', I was becoming downhearted; but, fortunately I picked up the Berol Menetekel trail again. The November 1919 issue contained a note that word had come from Max Berol-Konorah that all the theatres in Germany were prospering. Well, if Max was mentioned hopefully William would soon show up. I returned to the task with renewed enthusiasm, and sure enough eight issues later he appeared. The July 1920 'M-U-M' stated: "Through William Berol we learn that his brother Max Berol-Konorah is seriously ill in Germany." [Max did recover and lived until 1930.]

This was the second confirmation I was seeking. William Berol and Houdini knew each other! Even better news was to come.

In the December 1920 issue Houdini announced that Sir Arthur Conan Doyle would shortly be in America. If it was during the first visit that Houdini performed his test, then he was already planning to perform something. The previous month's issue, November, recorded the events of the annual Ladies Night. Then, as now, Presidents of magic clubs imposed on their friends to perform at various functions as personal favours. In the item was the statement: "....Prof. Berol introduced one of his pupils..." So, William was giving lessons, and Houdini had asked him to supply, and introduce, a performer for the event. This would suggest that Berol, who had performed an effect that was quite similar to Houdini's test, and Houdini himself were close friends, when Houdini was beginning to plan for Conan Doyle's visit. There was further evidence of the closeness of their relationship.

If Houdini presented his test for Conan Doyle in 1922, then a year after the above date Houdini would be hard at work on it. As you'll remember, Houdini said: "Sir Arthur, I have devoted a lot of time and thought to this illusion; I have been working on it, on and off, all winter." In Houdini's Editorial Notes for December 1921 it says: "It is a fact not generally known that Felix Berol, the great memory artist, whose brothers Max and William also are phenomenal memory artists, when he played Philadelphia willed his brain to the Philadelphia Medical Association. After Felix Berol died a man came around with a small black grip and in a most business-like manner entered the room, which he was permitted to do under the terms of the will. When he left he had with him the brain of Felix. This man was a brain expert, and it was only by the closest examination that the operation which was required to remove the cerebrum could be detected." I thought that surely, this came from William Berol, who was possibly working in daily close contact with Houdini, on an illusion that was similar to the Menetekel Mystery.

In Houdini's Editorial Notes for Jan. 1923 was one last, but sad, reference: "William Berol, whose demise we lament in this issue was one of three brothers, who became famous for their super mental qualification. They were each able to recall the date and particulars of any historical event as recorded, instanta. Max B. Berol, 'Kororah,' alone survives..." One third of the front page was devoted to William's obituary, it was written by Houdini and the title, ringed in black, was "William Berol Lamented". Part of the article read:

"I was the last to see him ere he was rolled into the operating room at St. Bartholomew's Hospital. He was a brave man. Looked death in the face without a quiver. No soldier ever paid the supreme sacrifice braver than did William Berol. Coming from a family of super-brains, his mental attitude as he was noiselessly rolled between the awaiting surgeons must have been at a pitch unknown to the ordinary human being.

We made a compact, he and I; he knowing my researches into Spiritualism, knowing my friend, the late Compeer John W. Sargent. We had a secret conversation that no fraud medium could ever guess, and I want to thank the physician who permitted me to have the last private talk with this brave fellow. Tears streamed from his eyes as he bade me farewell - and the next morning after his operation, too weak to talk, he took my hand and telegraphed our secret grip and word to me. His eyes were closed - his soul preparing to meet his God but his superior brain and will-power caused him to will that I should understand that he knew his compact and that he would remember if within the range of soul possibility.

William Berol, I bow my uncovered head to the Will of the Almighty at your Bier. I respected you alive. I revere you in your eternal sleep - for if any mortal went to his Maker upright and unafraid it was you. Slumber well, dear old friend, after life's fitful dream. Your sleep now must be soft and soothing.

You were known as the memory man - a man who never forgot. Those who met you in your travels can assuredly never forget you. I never shall - and will always think of your example of bravery the day you fell asleep."

180

After writing all of the above, I went on to find other connections between Houdini and Berol's Mene Tekel illusion. The February 1906 issue of 'Mahatma' contained an article entitled "Notes From Our Special Correspondent Herr N. Osey." Those 'Notes' had appeared in the magazine from time to time since 1901, and often praised Houdini's performances. This particular 'Note' told readers: "Max Berol has introduced a new act which he has termed 'Menetekel.' In the course of the trick, he suspends a large slate over the stage in full view of the audience and at his command any word, letter or figure appears on it by some mysterious means. The slate is not covered in any way." Herr N. Osey was, of course, a pseudonym. So, who was the 'nosey' scribe? I was able to determine that it was none other than Houdini himself! So, Harry must have seen the illusion as early as 1906 to write that review.

I noticed that although Houdini's description of Max Berol's illusion sounded similar to the trick I was investigating, it didn't mention a ball doing the writing as in Houdini's version. Then I found something in the very first edition of the magazine Houdini edited for several years (The Conjurers' Monthly Magazine, Sept. 1906). It was the statement that Max Berol had been booked to appear in America with his new feat. What was that feat? According to Herr N. Osey, who had moved over to Houdini's magazine, "It is the 'Mene Tenkle' trick, where the blackboard is suspended in the air, and a ball writes any and all things that Herr Introducer wishes."

So, now I had both the hanging slate and the writing ball mentioned by Houdini himself. I dug deeper looking for a complete detailed review of Berol's act. Where did I locate one? That's right, in Houdini's magazine (The Conjurers' Monthly Magazine, Oct. 1907). There, in Herr Ottokar Fischer's Viennese Notes, was a "short description" of the trick:

"When the curtain rises a large wooden frame is seen hanging from two ropes. On this frame are fastened 5 or 6 sheets of white paper. The manipulating lady turns the frame towards the public, showing both sides and proving that nobody is hidden behind it. The attendant then brings an inked ball and by means of a spoon places it on the first sheet of paper, where it mystically remains, without falling down. The lady recalls to the audience the biblical story of King Belshazzar, when suddenly the ball begins to roll over the paper, writing the word 'Menetekel'. When this is done, the assistant removes the ball with a kind of tongs. In this manner the ball, being renewed after each word, writes any words which are called loudly or whispered secretly to the assistant's ear, rolling forwards or backwards, quite how anyone likes. During the time the ball is rolling over the paper, the frame swings to and fro, to show that no magical influence comes from behind the stage."

Yes, even a spoon was used to place the ball onto the paper, and yes, I know it said paper, but in the bits that Houdini wrote he called it a blackboard. So, in his mind it was a blackboard. All the other reviews I managed to locate were similar to the above. They emphasized that "the ball left a trail of words in its path." The act apparently concluded with the ball mysteriously writing the words "Good Bye". I was now very certain that this was where Houdini had obtained his effect to amaze Doyle.

In fact I was now not only sure Houdini had got the idea for his trick from Berol's illusion, but was beginning to think William Berol had some input to it. Then I found further confirmation. In Milbourne Christopher's 1976 book (Houdini: A Pictorial Life) I noticed a description of The Menetekel Mystery and the statement: "After Berol retired, Houdini purchased the equipment." So, was that the end of my quest? Unfortunately not. I was right back to square one!!! Why? Well, at this point it would be tempting to say that Houdini must have presented Berol's illusion, but I won't. The reason will become clear in a moment.

As this section of my opus is supposed to be the "How" [the method], I will explain how Berol's illusion was actually accomplished. I found many guesses in magical literature as to how the Menetekel Mystery was carried out. Those suggestions included electricity, a series of small magnets, and even a trained weasel or ferret. The Sphinx for March 1907 says: "...we all agree that the keen mind and inventive genius of Max Berol actuates the power behind the writing and that, however it may be done, it is well done." Probably the nearest to the real method appeared in Ellis Stanyon's magazine, "Magic."

In the August 1906 "Queries" column, a subscriber asked: "'Menetekel' - This is the title of a trick or illusion recently produced in Manchester: will some reader please offer a solution in this column? Suspended on two 'ropes' from top of stage is a board about 6 by 8 feet, covered with large sheets of white paper. Performer sets the apparatus in swinging motion, places small ball on paper, which adheres, and at command describes any word called for by audience. Board shown back and front. Balls are covered with kind of ink, and travel over paper with a jerky motion. Words written on paper and handed to performer are also produced without anyone speaking. Performer amongst audience. Lady who adjusts the balls remains on stage."

A year later, in the August 1907 issue of "Magic", the editor replied to that query. He wrote: "In the illusion 'Menetekel,' I am given to understand there is a boy (or a small person of light weight with the required intelligence) suspended behind the board manipulating a magnet and by means of which he causes the ball (steel), covered with the ink, to pass over the paper as required. The words called out by the spectators are, of course, heard by the boy behind the board and who then acts accordingly as soon as the lady places the ball on the paper - there is no centre to the board and the ball is, of course, readily attracted to the magnet through the several sheets of paper. The words written on papers and handed, in silence, to the performer in the auditorium, are conveyed to the lady upon the stage (by one or other of the usual methods), who then whispers them to the boy through a small opening in side of board....Boy at rear of board is enclosed in a 'V' shaped box, coloured inside and out dull black; the board, or frame, is also black and it is also hung against a dark background and these arrangements admit the board being turned so far round with the idea of showing there is nothing at the back."

The two hanging ropes prevented the board from being turned far enough to expose the "V" shaped back, allowing the hidden operator to carry out his or her duties undetected. So, although I had satisfactorily solved the question of where Houdini's effect came from, there was no way he could have used Berol's method. So, I was back to the very beginning in searching for a method.

PART 2 - THE METHOD OVERVIEW

The "method" is the secret means by which the magician works an effect.
- Bart Whaley (The Encyclopedic Dictionary of Magic, 2000)

Back To Square One

Although I was certain I had uncovered the source of Houdini's effect, I was still completely ignorant of how he had accomplished it. Why? It was because the method Max Berol used for his stage illusion would not work in a close-up situation. He had cleverly concealed an assistant inside the rear of the board who then used a magnet to write the words backward. The magnet moved a ball with an iron core, to produce the words. I believe Berol based his illusion on a similar one explained in William Robinson's 1898 book (Spirit Slate Writing and Kindred Phenomena). I can even guess at a date when the design of Berol's illusion was commenced. How?

Well, the July 1902 issue of 'Mahatma' included a 'Note' from our friend Herr N. Osey [Houdini] explaining that Max Berol liked to talk. It also mentioned that Chung Ling Soo was performing in London. Soo was actually American William Robinson impersonating a Chinese magician. Osey wrote: "I'll wager that when Robinson and Berol get together in England Berol will talk to Robinson until he will find some Chinese excuse to get away." So, what did they talk about? Probably Robinson's favourite subject - illusion invention. And which one did they discuss? Quite possibly a certain large slate with a ball that spelled out words.

Unfortunately there was no way Houdini could hide someone inside his small slate. Having decided on his ideal presentation, he now had the major problem of generating a flawless concealed method to produce Berol's miracle on a very much smaller scale. From Ernst's description Houdini seems to have managed to keep the overall effect as seen by the spectators, and apparently only reduced the slate size. In fact, this slate reduction could be said to be a great improvement from a spectator's viewpoint. But from a magician's perspective, it would require a completely different technical approach for the secret technique.

Harry's audience was not in front of him here – he was surrounded. He and his team would have to consider many schemes, and resolve many problems, before discovering the best working solution that would have the least impact on the 'effect'. Just some of the variations they would have experimented with were combining new methods with old ideas [and vice versa], replacing mechanical methods with sleights [and vice versa], and replacing both sleights and mechanical apparatus with subtleties and misdirection.

I sought out all I could find on method creation to get an overview. This was the hard work – the design phase. Houdini, and his inner circle of advisors, would have investigated the idea from every conceivable angle, to establish the best approach for producing this theatrical illusion in a non-theatrical setting. The rudimentary 'experiment' would be split into its basic elements, and then provisional methods worked out for each segment. For example, the secret technique for the appearance of the slate message would be chosen from a researched [brainstormed] list of as many possible solutions as could be generated. These would come from several sources - Houdini's experience of performing slate tricks, his wonderful magic library, as well as the deliberations of his team. Just to give you an idea of what would be involved, 'The Sphinx' for Feb. 1922 [around the time of the experiment] states: "there are some fifty ways of executing slate tricks." Patrick Culliton (Houdini – The Key, 2010) quotes a Houdini article in which Harry says, "I know of more than 200 methods of placing bogus spirit messages on slates."

Each approach would be compared to several ideal conditions: It must a) have a minimum skill level, i.e. be basically 'self working' as opposed to being extremely technically difficult, b) need the lowest amount of preparation [minimum 'get ready' time], c) be suitable for his close-up intimate audience i.e. 'worked' totally surrounded, d) not only allow high audience participation, but be completely examinable, e) have an extremely low level of possible failure, f) produce a highly visual impact, and g) need minimum 'clean-up' at the end, i.e. easy to get rid of any incriminating 'dirty work'. The perfect, covert method would fit all of those stipulations; BUT, there is never a perfect or ideal scheme, so trade offs would have to be made between the most direct method and the most practical.

There was one major advantage inherent in Houdini's performance that made the quest for a solution a little bit easier than it usually would have been. The team was able to ignore one of the main conditions for trick design. As Houdini would not be taking this trick on tour, the usual important elements of ease of movement and necessary strength could be ignored. [There's nothing more frustrating than just as you arrive at the venue - the one that will make or break your career - a wheel breaks off your most expensive illusion, and then you discover it's too big to go through the door!] An additional, available bonus was the unique condition of the library. This could possibly be employed to their advantage, or used to disguise the obvious.

After hitting several dead ends and restarting the process, Team Houdini would tentatively agree on the best possible technique. Then I believe they'd create a working script for the performance to build confidence. How can I be sure Houdini would prepare a script for the experiment? Houdini registered two of his set-piece escapes as 'plays' to legally protect them from magical thieves. So I think he most likely wrote a script for this one. It would enable everyone involved to be 'on the same page.' [Yes, he was a frustrated would-be writer, and, yes, I recognise the feeling.]

How do you take a puzzle and turn it into a miracle that blows away your spectators? You need to inject emotion. You must weigh up all the non-technical elements of stagecraft - ranging from blocking out movements [choreography], to devising scene setting 'patter' [talk] - to determine the best way to 'sell' it. This requires yet another skill set. Examples of what I mean would be asking: "What will be the best opening remark?", "How can we add meaning that will draw our observers into our world of make-believe?", "How do we build to an optimum knock-out finish?", and then, for each of the elements of the plot, "Why do it that way?"

Being so close to his spectators would require a totally different presentation technique than Houdini normally employed onstage. The necessary hidden technical movements, sleights, and gimmicks, involved in achieving the sensation climax, would have to be thoroughly explored for a close-up situation. Every component of the 'routine' would need to be gone over in detail to ensure that any sign of deception had been eliminated. All actions had to be justified to keep the integrity of the magic intact, while at the same time, aiming at simplicity of method so there would be less to go wrong. [Remember: 'Simple' does not necessarily mean easy!]

Once a well-constructed working plan had been agreed upon, the group would enter the action [trouble-shooting] phase of the demonstration's design. It was now no longer a theory, but a set of practical problems that had to be ironed out. Developing an effect from a mere inspiration is not an easy task. There is no perfect trick. Every magic trick has a weak spot, a flaw, or a fault. As Houdini's experiment had two major phases, there would be more than one imperfection to cover up. As one fault was eliminated, it would throw up another one somewhere else that would need sorting out. My job was to discover how the team overcame those difficulties?

The trick performance would then be worked on to make it as near to perfection as possible, but the whole process would need to be repeated if the desired result was not up to scratch. A large amount of trial and error was required, as well as the ability to judge whether the notion was completely practical, or, if not, then they needed to back up and make modifications. In other words the performer's reality had to be compared against the false reality being created in the observers' minds. Flashes of inspiration don't usually come without the mind becoming fully attuned to the problem. To make the trick as near perfect as possible, questions would be continuously asked, such as "How can we improve the method/appearance/impact of the effect?", and "Can anything be added/removed to enhance the effect?" Before rejecting any technique, the methods would be expanded, improved, combined, swapped, and adapted, because the outcome had to be an effect that had never been done before [and, as it turned out, has not been done since!].

As well as complete dedication and motivation, you need FAILURE, to inspire creativity and innovation. We learn from our mistakes. Problems offer opportunities for new or better solutions – but to generate them you must overcome your inbuilt mental limitations. Then the result must be thoroughly evaluated as to whether it is worthwhile, and is a realistic alternative. I think the problems involved in Houdini's slate trick may have required the constructing and testing of simple prototypes. Somewhere along the line a trade-off would have been made between the best possible effect and a practical sure fire method for accomplishing it. After checking all the advantages and disadvantages, a decision would be based on which was the more important. Don't forget that the method not only had to be different from existing versions, it had to also completely deceive a very knowledgeable magician in the person of Ernst, while at the same time appearing miraculous. There had to be a lot of thinking outside the box, BUT at the same time risks could not be tolerated - it had to work on the night.

The final step in the process of producing the miracle 'experiment' was to make it as perfect as possible, and as the saying goes: practice makes perfect. The more it was practiced, and the more it became second nature, the more weaknesses would appear along with methods for correcting them. In other words, the design phase would never really be finished. It would merely be moved into the testing and refining stage. Small adjustments would take place right up to the last minute, as the finished polished product was compared against the original envisioned effect.

Testing and Refining

"If this be magic, let it be an art."
- Shakespeare (Winter's Tale)

So, how did Houdini actually 'debug' his 'experiment' in advance, i.e. test out his 'test' before the day of the big test?

Unfortunately, many budding magicians have the desire to show off their new 'material' without adequate rehearsal, with no thought of the impact on their audience. Hence the frequently asked question of magic dealers: "I've got a show tonight. What's the latest miracle?" Those neophytes have not yet learned that trick selection is secondary to the art of proper presentation. A top magician polishes both his act, and performance technique, over a long period of time by trying out new 'effects' where it does not matter if things go slightly wrong, i.e. he finds somewhere to be lousy that won't tarnish his reputation. Unfortunately today there are less and less of these trial and error testing venues ['good places to be bad in']. Typical of the few worthwhile ones still left are shows at nursing homes, and performing for the sick and needy.

The more a magician's tricks are done in public the more they can be fine-tuned. Supposedly impromptu 'bits of business' [biz], 'shtick', and 'deliberate errors' are added and refined. The magician soon discovers what works and what doesn't. Houdini often visited hospitals when performing in new areas. But, in our present case, this public testing technique was not possible, and there was a major constraint - Houdini's experiment had to work perfectly – nothing else was acceptable. So, I speculated on what Houdini would have done to handle the pressure required to not only achieve a flawless performance level, but also to do it within the crucial fixed time limit?

Complete dedication and resolve were required to meet the inflexible deadline of Conan Doyle's visit. To achieve the remarkable level Houdini did attain, without a snag during performance, would have taken many months of brain-numbing planning and rehearsal. How can I be sure Houdini put in that much work? In his day, unlike our modern era of instant gratification, practice was a part of the magic culture. A typical example is Houdini's magic rival, Howard Thurston. Each night, during her husband's performances, his wife would sit in various places in the theatre and make detailed notes. Then after the show the whole cast would assemble and she would read out her evaluations. Any problems noted would be eliminated by meticulous practice before the next show. Thurston's assistants have written how much they hated that inquisition! As Houdini's boyhood hero, Robert-Houdin stated, three things are necessary to become a great magician; they are "PRACTICE-PRACTICE-PRACTICE!"

A further pointer to Houdini being passionate about practice was his brother Hardeen's comment, (The Sphinx, Oct. 1936), "Harry's card work was excellent." You are not born with card handling skills. A classic book of magic written well over 400 years ago explains why. Reginald Scot's 1584 work, The Discoverie of Witchcraft, discloses, "The true art of sleight of hand....can not be mastered without tremendous amounts of practice and dedication." To become a top 'cardician' takes a great deal of time and perseverance. Houdini would have worked on a single card 'move' continuously, hour after hour, until the 'knuckle-busting' sleight became second nature. Still not sure I've proved Houdini would have been totally dedicated? Well, in 1906, in his Conjurers Monthly magazine, Houdini wrote: "when at table I practiced to use the left hand persistently until I could use it almost as easily as the right." So, he was quite used to the self-control necessary to bring his difficult plan for the slate experiment to life.

It would not be easy. In fact, it would be exceedingly demanding, requiring a disciplined, scheduled operation of several phases ['the effect carefully produced']. First, each of the components of the trick would be broken down into manageable parts to physically, repeatedly, practice the technique. [It's the little things that matter.] This is the magician's reality – the method, the tools. Each part would be practiced over, and over, and over, hour after hour, until the mechanics of the 'apparatus' handling, and sleights employed, were 'smooth', and the 'modus operandi' management 'polished' and 'sharp' ['knocking off the rough edges'].

That is the equivalent of a concert pianist practicing for hours each day, until he reaches the level of being able to converse with you while playing his difficult piece. Complete technical mastery is essential so that during the performance the magician's mind can be fully devoted to his dramatic theatrical delivery. Very close monitoring by his team would be indispensable to avoid 'grooving in' imperfect actions. Unfocused, sloppy practice is worse than no practice at all. Only perfect practice makes perfect.

Once this level was attained, [the technical phase mastered] the challenge would shift from 'trick mode' to perfecting the 'effect', i.e. the complete picture ['the whole dynamic']. The distinct individual component parts would be blended into a whole, and the entire operation cloaked by carefully prepared, appropriate misdirection [building the 'routine']. This phase is the spectator's reality, what happens in his mind – the dramatization. Many would-be magi focus too much on the secret complex manipulations, and then have trouble joining the 'moves' together to form a convincing big picture. In other words, they are technically excellent but lack performing capability. Magic is not about the tricks – it's a theatrical experience in which the vehicle just happens to be magic.

Houdini [and his 'invisible' helpers?] would repeatedly rehearse the entire presentation from start to finish with no stopping. That was to simulate an actual performance where you cannot stop and re-do anything [a 'cold practice']. They would be sure to 'dress it' properly, i.e. to wear the clothes and have on the shoes they'd use that crucial day, and do so in the exact location where it was going to be done. Members of the team would act as stand-ins for his guests. Although at this initial stage it was only 'a work in progress', the effect would be performed straight through from beginning to end, just as it would be done for Ernst and Doyle, to get the 'feel' of the routine.

Seeing yourself as others see you [the audience's perspective], according to Robbie Burns, is impossible; so constructive criticism ['supportive feedback'] would be essential. During the long hours of live audience 'run throughs' his team would constantly monitor him to ascertain what was working and what wasn't ['a second set of eyes']. They'd 'tactfully suggest' practical changes, subtleties, and improvements ['rehashing it'], i.e. adding new ideas to make the experiment appear 'beyond manipulation'. [I wrote 'tactfully suggest', because having read about Houdini's huge ego, I imagine there would have been a few fiery, fervent exchanges.] As I pointed out in the 'Who' section, Houdini's greatest gift was the knack of surrounding himself with the exact talented people he needed - those with specialized mechanical and theatrical knowledge – not 'yes men'. He needed guidance, not flattery.

When it comes to criticism, friends are a waste of time; they will only say what they think you want to hear. Their well-meaning mistaken endorsement will only compound your errors. It has been suggested that it is better to have an enemy evaluate your act! When creating his tricks, if Houdini's team members were not familiar with something vital to what they were attempting,

Houdini would go to the most pre-eminent expert on the subject, and then listen very carefully to what he was told. How many of us ask for advice, and then 'really' listen to what we hear?

There is no short cut to magical excellence. A huge amount of work [sweat] was necessary. They had to live with it. It was an evolutionary process. Every moment of the trick had to be thought through. Nothing was too trivial to consider. Why do I say that? Well, as I've pointed out, Harry was an excellent card man. The card man's bible of that era was S. W. Erdnase's book, Artifice Ruse and Subterfuge at the Card Table (1902). That magic classic tells you, "The finished card expert considers nothing too trivial that in any way contributes to his success." So, no practical detail was too trivial to worry about.

It had to work perfectly on the night, so all difficulties had to be surmounted. Anything not fitting Houdini's natural talents as an authoritative lecturer would be reworked and tweaked, with the necessary script adjustment and modification [editing]. Also the timing, tempo and pacing of his delivery [the 'flow'] would be altered to maintain the interest of the two important spectators. During the preparatory phase of the experiment, a large amount of time was used. It would have to be 'tightened'. Anything unnecessary, 'superfluous' or 'inconsequential' would be cut ['the fat trimmed'], while at the same time maintaining the indisputable fairness of the apparatus examination. The enemy here was boredom. Dead spots had to be eliminated. Houdini not only had to build up to the impact of the final surprise ['the grand finale' or 'moment of magic'], but he also had to appear to be doing it for the very first time. A smile here and a laugh there would make it seem new. The necessary energy level required to keep it new, fresh and interesting with repeated rehearsal is far from easy? Practicing spontaneity is as difficult as faking sincerity.

I stated that Houdini probably wrote a script for his effect; it is quite possible that he recorded himself acting it out as well. Today's magicians are advised to video their performance to see how bad they are. I think Houdini may have made an audio recording of his performance. Why? Well, The Magic Circle has a recording of him giving the opening address for his Water Torture Cell illusion, which was recorded several years before the experiment for Doyle. What better way to spot repetitious time filling words and phrases? He definitely took elocution lessons from a fellow magician.

There are no simple rules for attaining trick presentation perfection, but desire and tenacity help. Only an actual performance will show if changes have brought improvement. Houdini's team would evaluate 'blocking', 'framing', 'focusing' and other structure considerations such as prop positioning and crucial sight angles. They would keep asking themselves, "Why do it that way?" "What would happen if we leave out an essential item?" All problem solutions would be tested, and then rejected if they did not add to the deception. What was actually happening had to be completely hidden, and anything not adding to the required perceived illusion eliminated. Any weakness had to be covered.

Crucially, the team had to overcome the natural inclination to resist change after expending much time and energy on an item. Just because they liked a certain bit, or line, unless it enhanced the overall experiment, it was not needed. All the time they had to maintain the positive attitude that they would succeed in their task. They would get stuck, yes, but eventually inspiration would suddenly strike them when they least expected it. They would discover a completely new, better way to do it - one they had not even previously considered.

Houdini's assistants would ensure that all his words and actions were in line with how his two friends were accustomed to seeing him normally act. Consistency was the key. To avoid arousing any suspicion, awkward actions were removed, or reasons constructed for doing them, even if they had nothing to do with any secret. Every movement needed a motivation. [Magicians talk of spectators saying, "It went up his sleeve!" even when the magus is wearing only a t-shirt!] As this was not being presented as a normal trick, but supposedly an 'attempted' experiment, the team members would keep asking what they would do if this was for 'real', i.e. Houdini did nothing to cause it beyond acting as a master of ceremonies - it just miraculously happened. [Houdini's escapes were usually billed as "Attempt to Escape".]

Total commitment was needed to continuously, rigorously examine every detail, in an effort to establish what to accentuate and what to hide, i.e. what worked, and what didn't. All possible choices and options would have their pros and cons weighed. The entire routine would be painstakingly analysed to devise ways of simplifying the stratagems, increasing audience appeal, and yet at the same time build toward the climax. Any hint or clue to the actual meticulous planning involved had to be completely hidden. Every visible action would be checked to ensure that it had a logical reason for being done, and appeared casual and extemporaneous, or involved necessary, natural, spontaneous movements.

It had to appear as if Houdini were almost deciding what to 'attempt' as he went along, and effortlessly ensuring everything was examined. But the 'routine' had to be practiced and learned to such an extent that he could do it on autopilot [unconscious competency]. At the same time he had to avoid reaching a level where the experiment became too mechanical and boring. Once the routine was second nature, peace of mind could be attained. Then he could relax and completely devote himself to his surroundings, and establishing rapport with his spectators. He'd be able to remain fully in the 'present' and reply spontaneously to anything his spectators said or did. In other words, he would stop worrying about being caught out, and become calm and 'confident' enough to adlib and handle any unexpected spectator reaction.

I stress 'confident' because of my many years watching magicians compete in magic contests. I have supplied audiences of non-magicians ('laypeople') to watch, and assist, because magicians themselves make the worst spectators. They don't react properly. They are either attempting to figure out how it's done, or thinking,

"I can do better than that!", or even worse, looking for lines they can steal! Competitors, who presented magic every night for laypeople, with no sign of apprehension, would be shaking before appearing before their peers, to be judged on their performance. Here Houdini had to avoid any first live performance 'jitters'. As he performed the observers would subconsciously pick up his thoughts. Houdini's guests would notice any sign of nervousness, or anxiety, and become distracted wondering what his problem was. Confidence inspires confidence. The correct tone of voice, as well as body stance and posture, facial expression, and eye contact are necessary to be persuasive. A confident performing persona can create miracles. As with everything else here, he had to, at the same time, avoid becoming too cocky. There is a fine line between being a self-assured presenter and a smug show-off. Empathy between magician and spectator is the objective.

The level Houdini had to achieve was to actually believe he was doing what he claimed, i.e. had to completely enter into the fictitious part. Then any secret 'moves' or the surreptitious operating of special apparatus would be done subconsciously, i.e. it's the presentation that counts, not the props. The conscious part of Houdini's mind would be concentrating on his guests. His body language and reactions [nonverbal communication] would subliminally cause them to accept the false reality they were observing as genuine. Those 'silent cues' are quite similar to the way a ventriloquist functions. If he believes his dummy is real, then you will as well. It is often hard for beginners in magic to forget the sleights and gimmicks, and understand that it's what they say that counts. They don't grasp that they should initially walk through the effect many times, as if they were really able to do it magically, to get the correct feel that spectators pick up on. In other words, you have to live the illusion to make others do the same.

Outs

As it had to work perfectly, Houdini's team would also have spent a great amount of time assessing where things could go wrong.

196

These potential setbacks would be divided into causes 'within their control', and those 'outside their control'. They would probably classify these latent faults into how they would affect the outcome of the experiment, using a scale having 'complete failure' at one end, with 'a minor hiccup' at the other. Typical examples for those 'outside their control' would be: a) a devastating effect on the outcome if one of the guests became seriously ill [action: abort the experiment], b) in the middle of the scale, a major stoppage would be a long-term power failure [i.e. an unplanned all evening blackout] [the answer: have candles ready], c) at the other end of the scale, the need for one of the observers to go the men's room would only hold up proceedings [answer: make sure they go there beforehand!]. For the potential problems 'within their control' they would consider every possible thing that could go wrong with their 'method', and the covering misdirection, and assess what they could do to reduce or eliminate the problem. This would range from completely changing a risky method to having a back-up plan in place.

As for the completely unexpected, Team Houdini's experience, gained from years of facing different challenges each night while doing the escape act, would not only enable them to develop and build in multiple 'outs', and 'wriggle' room, for any possible incident they considered could happen, but also judge how to handle the completely unplanned occurrences. His guests did not know exactly what Houdini was going to do. They would not only have a plan A, but a plan B, C, and D; but no matter how much contingency practice and rehearsal they did, there was no way of telling exactly what Doyle and Ernst would actually say and do.

As in everyday life, things don't always go as planned. It was a 'given' that something unexpected would arise – a 'glitch'. At that point Houdini's vast experience of audience handling ['working a crowd'] would kick in, and he could go 'off-script' for a few moments, and then, when the problem was handled, return to the set plan. This seamlessly changing the technique as he went along would cause his audience to not even be aware that something unexpected had happened. I like to call this 'The Swan Principle', which derives from a swan gliding along effortlessly on the surface, while underneath his feet are paddling like mad.

I also think that Houdini's team members would be involved in any emergency action. They would be partners here, not mere assistants. They had to adapt to any circumstance to ensure that the 'boss' would appear to be a superpowered magus. They would definitely not accept defeat! I'm quite sure of that. Why? Because I'm talking here about fellows who were known to 'accidentally' knock out anyone who got too vociferous in escape challenges. My father, who grew up in Houdini's era, was an excellent checker player, BUT he used to say if all else failed you 'accidentally' tipped over the board! I think that, if all else failed, Houdini's boys would create an electric failure by turning out the building's lights, and then relight them after the crisis was handled.

So, how do I know that Houdini would go to all the trouble necessary to design plans for something that quite probably would not even happen? Well, his fellow magician and associate, Fulton Oursler [see 'WHO' section for his particulars], described a mysterious Houdini 'feat' in his autobiography (Behold This Dreamer!, 1964). During discussion after completing the 'challenge', Houdini stated that he definitely knew his business, and had anticipated any outcome by taking "into account everything that might happen." In fact, Harry was amazed that Oursler would think that he hadn't gone to all the trouble he did. And, that's why I say that he most certainly would have done so in this case.

The sign of a great magician is his/her ability to handle the unexpected, i.e. to 'think on his feet', improvise, be creative and get out of trouble while under pressure in an emergency. The other side of 'living in the moment' is looking out for, and then capitalising on any lucky coincidences that arise. Houdini had certainly developed the intuitive understanding of human nature and psychology, along with the showmanship, and nerve, needed to spot and grasp any possible opportunity, and then use it to heighten the overall effect of the experiment ['milk it for all it's worth']. He looked on problems as 'a window of opportunity' to manipulate human perception. His confidence, poise and assurance convinced observers that an astonishing miracle had taken place. His skill at audience management was always the ultimate 'out', i.e. 'if all else fails then "wing" it'.

There is a final 'unexpected happening' that I think Houdini would have included in his performance. It's the sort of thing a great showman like Houdini would delight in doing. Many great performers build problems into their acts to make people think they are seeing something unique that others wouldn't have witnessed. Often it is something that has actually happened to them during a performance, and got such a great reception when overcome, that it is added to the routine. To make Houdini's experiment appear as if it was completely spontaneous a minor problem would be incorporated to cause a supposed temporary embarrassment. Then a clever quick remedy, apparently thought up on the spur of the moment, would resolve the setback. I imagine a typical incident of this type could be finding that the wires used to hang the slate were too short to reach the walls. A quick rummage in a draw would produce a roll of longer wire, and save the day. This would subconsciously underline the fact that he had obviously not tried out the experiment in this room before.

As well as being thoroughly routined, scripted, and rehearsed, Houdini's experiment also needed to be very well organised. A list of props and pre-performance checks would have been established. Every single item would be ticked off just before Ernst and Doyle arrived. Houdini's team could not afford to leave out a single crucial item. So, how do I know they prepared such a list to organise the props? Well, Kenneth Silverman's 1996 book, Houdini!!!, describes Houdini's meticulous handwritten lists of the contents of his London warehouse. He must have compiled the detailed fifteen pages himself because they are in his distinctive spelling. As well as major items of escape apparatus, like barrels and boxes, he'd listed such mundane things as "old J[ock] straps"! Not only that, Houdini kept a large number of scrapbooks and notebooks of trick ideas. Not having a comprehensive prop list for the experiment would be completely out of character.

So, how could Houdini be completely sure that it would work as envisioned? In other words, how did he road test the 'test'? Well, when it was finally considered ready, and the time for the actual performance was rapidly approaching, the other team members, who had not been initially involved in the experiment, would be employed. Two at a time, they would be invited to see the experiment, just like Ernst and Doyle would, and then evaluate it. [Yes, I can't resist saying that if they didn't like the slate trick they would 'slate' it.] That would be the final, ultimate test of the 'test'.

So, what was the bottom line for all this self-disciplined, dedicated, commitment to persistent practice and rehearsal? What was Team Houdini aiming at – what was their target? They were not trying to perform a magic trick, BUT taking the two observers on an emotional journey - creating an amazing theatrical experience – one that would so overload both Ernst and Doyle's trained minds, that when they tried to rationalize what had happened, they could not even begin to explain it. Then, and only then, would the desired moment of 'pure astonishment' happen! Yes, a mental scream of "Impossible!"

Lifting the Secret Curtain

To allow you to fully understand my quest for a solution to Houdini's magic miracle, I'm now going to reveal a major bit of magic theory. BUT before I do, I want to disclose the problem you face. Your dilemma is that as soon as a magicians' puzzle is solved the magic ceases to exist. In order to discover how Houdini accomplished his 'test' you must destroy the impossible nature of it. Once you have satisfied your curiosity you will feel a sense of disappointment because you have ruined something of great intrigue. So, please remember that you cannot unlearn the secret. To gain the knowledge you must kill the mystery. If you do not want to be de-mystified or disillusioned then please do not read any further, just give this book to someone else. I will applaud your willpower. Still here? Okay, then don't forget I warned you.

Most serious books devoted to the performance of the art of magic quote the famous dictum of Houdini's childhood hero, Robert-Houdin. [Yes, Houdini 'borrowed' his name.] Robert-Houdin stressed that a magician is an actor playing the part of a wonder worker – someone possessing magic powers. As magic is a performing branch of the theatre, this is correct; in fact, each trick is a complete miniature play. For most productions on stage, film or TV, the script is sacrosanct. You do not deviate from it. So, when a play does not go over well many actors will tell you that the fault was the author's not theirs! What most magic books don't tell you is how magic in the situation we are looking at here differs from normal theatrical acting.

The major difference between an actor in a play and a stage magician is the imaginary theatrical fourth wall at the front of the stage. While watching a play, spectators merely observe the actors through this transparent wall. That wall does not exist for the magician. A magician is more like a performer in the variety arts who directly engages the audience. Instead of the spectators seeing actors communicating only with each other from a side view [i.e. no eye contact], the magus faces the audience, and directly addresses them. [Yes, actors do it sideways, while magicians face you!] But magic is also different from the rest of the variety arts: none of the others touch the mind in the way magic does.

The major point in common between magic and the theatre is that magic is also a play. Magicians are asking the spectators to suspend their disbelief, and enter an imaginary world where anything is possible. Most theatregoers will suspend their disbelief as soon as the lights dim down and the curtain goes up. Unless they are in the 'game', they usually don't start thinking about where they last saw the actors who appear before them, but wonder about what the people they portray are going to do. When a magician comes onstage many spectators are on their guard. They are aware

201

that he will attempt to fool them. So, the magician's first job is to get the audience on his side by overcoming this reluctance to accept his playful world.

Houdini's experiment for his two guests was something else again. He was completely out of his normal comfort zone. He was not on the stage of a music hall or vaudeville house. He was not projecting his powerful stage presence across the footlights to an assembled crowd. He might be an expert on knowing which area of the stage is most emotionally powerful, and how to move about it with maximum impact, but in the intimate setting of his 'test' the spectators were as close as it is possible to get. In fact, his two guests were not observers at all - they were participants - they were unscripted fellow actors. So, part of my task would be to discover what he did to control [direct] them?

The trick itself would have to be designed for that audience. In Houdini's day the two main performance areas were stage and parlour (or living room). Today close-up magic done under your nose is one of the main sources of income for magicians. In Houdini's day close-up was only performed impromptu for friends. It would not be until the 1930s when close-up began to become an acknowledged source of income. So Houdini would be designing his trick for a performance in an average living room or parlour. This would mean that he could not get away with some things, such as angles, that he could normally do on a stage.

The other performance area of his day, parlour, grew up in the days before radio and television. On Saturday night the family would all gather in the parlour, and then each person in turn would entertain the others with their speciality. This would stretch from piano playing to poetry reading, with the odd magical performance thrown in [and based on my own childhood, some of them were probably quite odd].

I also wondered if Houdini would be a bit apprehensive performing if he were not onstage. Today a large percent of magicians earn their money doing close-up magic in venues like restaurants, parties and tradeshows. In Houdini's day, doing magic at close quarters was not considered a paying venue. But many magicians did load their vests or waistcoats with small tricks to amuse their friends or possible future employers. At the same time, many did not. They considered themselves to be stage performers only.

So, I wondered if Houdini were an all-rounder. If he were, he'd have little trouble entertaining his guests. I found my answer in a book written by Ernst's legal partner, Melville Cane. Non-magician Cane wrote (in The First Firefly, 1974) that a visit to his office by Houdini would mean a general suspension of work until he left. It seems the master magus needed very little coaxing to put on an act with whatever was at hand. Houdini was obviously an expert at 'impromptu magic'. [The word 'impromptu' does not mean 'no practice'. It merely gives the impression of spontaneity. We'll see later that the magic was probably planned in great detail well before his visit.]

Now, getting down to secrets – as I said, modern magic is a form of theatre [a performance art] that creates the impossible. Its practitioners pretend to do things they really aren't doing. In other words, there is a dual reality taking place. The magician has to successfully hide the huge gulf between what his observers think is happening and what is actually taking place. The spectators must be convinced they have seen everything that has happened. The principles and techniques that create magic go back more than 5,000 years. So that you can grasp what actually happened during Houdini's experiment, I will touch on the relevant ones here; BUT I won't gratuitously expose any secrets that are not directly related to the task in hand. For example I'm not going to tell you how magicians take rabbits out of hats. Oh all right! They take them out by the nape of the neck - never by the ears. Now, maybe you get the idea. To think magically, you should NOT be asking, 'How are rabbits taken out of hats?' You should be speculating on how they are surreptitiously put into the hat in the first place.

BUT my main reason for not explaining unrelated secrets is to prevent spoiling your enjoyment the next time you watch a magician. The unfortunate truth is once you know how a magic effect is actually done, you cannot relive the wonder and awe of seeing something you are definitely sure is impossible. You will lose the excitement of the "Wow" factor. So, I won't expose too much here. I'll just give you enough information to grasp and appreciate how much effort actually goes into the theatrical art that makes the magic occur in your mind and heart.

The specific branch of magic Houdini performed for his guests is known as mental magic. It is the hardest of all to succeed at. Typical of the hidden 'methods' used that I would have to consider are: specially constructed or mechanical props, the use of scientific methods to produce messages; as well as other principles, such as physical manipulation or sleight of hand, and mental manipulation or control through sneaky ruses and subtle ploys. A large percentage of completely baffling magic tricks use more than one of those techniques, as well as other devices. This employing of multiple secrets tends to deceive most people, who assume that there is only one secret involved. So, my first assumption was that there had to be more than one secret technique at work here or the answer would have been guessed a long time ago.

The fact that Houdini employed multiple secret techniques was confirmed in a covert manuscript written by Houdini's good friend, magician John Mulholland, for the Central Intelligence Agency [C.I.A.] in 1954 (reprinted in Genii, Aug. 2003). John explained that there was no overall secret in magic, and that magicians chose the best one to use under the circumstances of their performances. What example did Mulholland give? He said that people still wondered about Houdini's secret that allowed him to escape from any restraint. The fact was that he used a different method for each type of escape. So, as I said, there were likely several secrets involved in Houdini's test.

There is another major weapon in the conjuror's arsenal. It's the biggest secret of all – the fact that the secret is a very small part of the overall performance. Most magic "gurus" will tell you the actual "hidden method" or secret is only between 10 and 25 percent of the trick. The larger 75 to 90 percent is the technique used to hide the device, gimmick or sleight employed. In fact, there can be no magic without what is usually referred to as 'misdirection'. It's the psychological attention diverting technique that attracts the spectator's attention to the wrong spot at the right time. The fact is that the mind is always actively processing information. There is never a time when it is dormant. So it has to be distracted from what the magician does not want it to perceive. Shooting off a gun would definitely work, but it would be far too obvious. It has to be accomplished so subtly that the spectators do not even suspect it has been employed. By a thorough understanding of human behaviour, and the assumptions people make, wrong suppositions are created. What do I mean by that?

Well, to greatly oversimplify an extremely complex psychological process, the magic takes place in the spectator's head. Magic does not fool the eye - it fools the brain. The whole key to creating the impression of magic is the viewer's perception faculty. He must be left with only one possible explanation of what has happened. He normally makes sense of the world by creating hypothesises based on the comparison of incoming sensual data with learned knowledge and experiences. The spectator's mind continuously acts on all the input it receives from his senses. When it interprets the sensations it picks up, it can create entirely false impressions. The magician cannot alter the input to the mind but can directly influence the way it is comprehended. Based on the laws of habit and association, along with the nature of perception and consciousness, the mind can be led to fill in the gaps and imagine something that it did not really see. So, the magician sets out to disrupt the spectator's judgment causing him to misinterpret what he sees.

The magician's job then is to determine, for any given situation, which stimuli will best allow him to completely control, and direct the spectators' attention. The goal is to induce passivity so as to retard deduction, i.e. direct the audience away from the 'method' and at the same time toward the 'effect'. Typically, the mind can only devote its entire attention to one thing, or idea, at a time. The magician capitalises on this by minimizing certain details and stressing others. Something dramatic or novel will attract and hold people's interest, as will a magician's actions and gestures, as well as the magician asking a direct question. So, distraction of attention ['misdirection'] can be accomplished with an object, an action, or speech, but is strongest if done with all at the same time. It is not what you do in magic, but how you do it. The quickness of the hand will not distract a spectators' attention, he will be aware that something has happened, but a dramatic pseudo-scientific setting and suitable patter will nicely sidetrack him.

Another useful approach is to stimulate the spectator's imagination in a different direction by playing on his fixed mental habits, or preconceived opinions that will create a vivid expectation, i.e. arouse associations and feelings to influence the perception of his senses. The example here is Houdini's use of a slate for the appearing message, just like Doyle often saw in the séances he attended. Part of his mind would be recalling examples of those past events. As well, fake mediums pretend to evoke spirits in the dark – you couldn't ask for a better setting to influence a spectator! You can get away with murder in the dark, as Houdini proved with the daylight séance part of his stage act. Houdini would blindfold a spectator on the stage and have him hold Harry's hands and feet while he acted as a fake medium. The sightless spectator's mind interpreted Houdini's actions completely differently from the rest of the observers. That onstage spectator's mind had its senses limited so it created a completely false impression when compared to those who were able to clearly see what Houdini was doing.

If a magician uses the simplest and most natural psychological misdirection there will be no possible discernible link between the initial condition and the final one. In the case we are looking at here the misdirection was so well hidden that no trace of it remains. Unfortunately, there is no universal technique. Each ruse, dodge, or stratagem must be devised specifically for the particular trick. So, my best approach here would be to come up with a potential secret method, and then see if the misdirection it needed would fit in with the recorded performance.

Finally, how do I know Houdini employed misdirection? Well in his 1924 book (A Magician Among the Spirits) he advises his readers "not to be led astray by the glib-tongued medium's misdirection."

The Search Problem

In trying to narrow down my search area, I decided that the hidden technique used in the slate experiment would have to fit Houdini's skill set. I looked to see if I could eliminate anything that he was not comfortable with, i.e. I looked at his strengths and weaknesses. I knew that Houdini was quite adept at demonstrating magical illusions/escapes effectively. He certainly had the necessary presentational/social skills to hide the secret workings of magical devices, but I needed to establish whether Houdini also had the motor skills to deceptively employ sleight of hand. If he did not possess the latter, I could limit my search to devices only, and eliminate hand skills.

Like most things in life, nothing is ever easy. I found that when Houdini was younger he billed himself "The King of Kards", [yes "cards"] and was also quite skilled at coin magic. There is also a third area of magic that is not usually considered when evaluating magicians. Houdini was also very accomplished at that. What is it? It's the psychological aspect of magic. Houdini was said to be able to introduce a topic into a conversation in such a manner that a person would later raise the point thinking that he had originally thought of it. So, this attempt at limiting my search was a disappointment. I had to suspect everything.

Another major problem I faced in solving the mystery is that there are often too many ways to perform individual magic tricks. Although a spectator can see two different magicians perform what appears to be an identical trick, one magician might be completely fooled by the technique used by the other. The library of the most prestigious club in magic, The Magic Circle, has over 10,000 books dedicated to the subject. Try naming another hobby that has such a vast literature. One trick alone, The Rising Cards, has many hundreds of different published techniques for doing what appears to the onlooker to be the same thing!

Unhappily there is no easy way of finding information in the world of magic's thousands upon thousands of books and magazines. Most major magic libraries merely file their books under the author's surname. There is no Dewey Decimal System in magic. In fact, there is only one single number in the Dewey System allocated to the subject of conjuring. In June 1930, Clement de Lion wrote (in The Sphinx) that there had been a book-writing epidemic, and a thorough knowledge of the art could not be obtained as the literature was so "planlessly" arranged. The information was "scattered to the winds" so one could only gain a surface knowledge. So, if the past was a problem, then what about keeping up with current output of the magic press? Well, the editor of The Sphinx wrote, away back in Aug. 1948, that there was "no possibility of reading and digesting all the books and magazines on magic currently published around the world."

Over the years, while trying to solve Houdini's experiment, I devised a system of filing all the magic information I came across. It consisted of 26 major categories, broken down into many sub-categories. The Magic Circle Executive Librarian, Peter Lane, liked my idea so much he used a very simplified version of it to catalogue their books. Then because of my work, The Magic Circle very kindly made me an Honorary Member, as well as a librarian.

Although my booklet explaining the system was a very specialized work for magicians only, and is long out of print, it still does massage the ego by reaching more than its original price on internet auction sites when it occasionally appears. Sadly The Magic Circle Library eventually had a problem with my filing system. They found that the members did not replace the books into their proper categories. The librarians, quite rightly, got so fed up searching for lost books that they re-filed them into author surname order! Fortunately for me, my system worked a treat in my own home research library. I managed to acquire a book for each sub-category in the system, and amassed what I considered to be one of the best research libraries in magic. As far as it went, it was excellent in giving me an overall grasp of magic, but it did not give a thorough grounding in any one area. That would take a very much greater magic library than my some 1,400 books and 100s upon 100s of magazines.

The problem with locating the great number of variations for each individual trick in magic is that they are spread in no particular order throughout the vast literature. To show you how difficult it is to find variations on a trick, often as a Magic Circle Librarian, after I have carried out an extended trawl through magical literature, to uncover a specific item for a magician, I'm told, "Oh, I have that book at home!" The urge to kill often arises.

Why are there so many secret methods/alterations for many individual magic tricks? The reason is very complex. Just a few examples will give you an indication of why. First there are the ego driven motives involving things like "Mine is the best method!", or "I've published a treatise on '25 Ways To.....'". Of course, you also have to define the word "best". For example, is it the best because it eliminates knuckle-busting sleights, or is it the best because it is more visual? Then there are performance considerations, such as being able to do it surrounded, or repeat it immediately afterward using a different hidden technique to discourage anyone close to guessing the first method. The secret behind Houdini's experiment was performance driven – it had to work, but in addition it had to fool both a non-magician and a knowledgeable magician! So, I had to put myself into his mind set, and eliminate anything I found that did not fit that condition.

If I was going to successfully 'reverse engineer' Houdini's experiment, then I would have to initially look for places where things did not quite appear natural, and actions not carried out in a straightforward manner. This, of course, is what Ernst would have done repeatedly over the years. So, I was quite sure it wasn't going to be easy. If the experiment was definitely a magic trick, then there had to be an action or a device that was out of the ordinary, but one that had been adequately hidden or covered with a natural seeming reason, or explanation, otherwise Ernst would have spotted it. Houdini, of course, was a master at working on two levels at once. One level was what you saw, the other you didn't. This later one was practiced to such an extent that the magician himself believed he was doing what he claimed. All the great magicians believe in their illusions. This ability caused Ernst to discount the irregularities, and not report them to us. So, I would have to read between the lines if I was going to discover what was missing.

Another thing that helped Houdini obscure the secret techniques was the fact that he was a master showman. He had the ability of all great artists to make you more interested in them than in what they are doing. His commanding, persuasive personality could keep you focused on what he chose. His likeable performance character, along with the deep understanding of human nature he had developed over the years, allowed him to take something that was inherently simple, and build it up to an emotional level that would lure his spectators into believing they had witnessed a miracle. In our case not only a unique miracle but one the spectators remembered the rest of their lives.

Coupled with this was Houdini's perfect mastery of the sense of timing. He knew how to build up tension until it reached a peak. Typically, he would rapidly escape from being locked into a dangerous looking, water filled container, and then read a newspaper behind the curtain. When he felt the audience had worked themselves up to the point of maximum anxiety for his safety, he would splash a bit of water on himself, and then appear to stumble out exhausted from behind the curtain.

In the circumstances we are investigating, he had a further advantage. Unlike most magic performances, he knew his intended audience extremely well. There would be no 'problem spectator' here. He would be interacting with his audience before the experiment to 'soften' them up. He was familiar with their attitudes, reactions, interests, and especially how they perceived reality, and what it would take to amaze them. Based on that knowledge, he had decided that maximum impact would be obtained by assuming a pseudo-scientific lecture presentation style of demonstrating an occult phenomenon to his friends, which is why I have called it an experiment.

The First Cut

Very few illusions are based on a single principle. A single trick can involve three or more techniques. Instead of trying to work out all the possible approaches to Houdini's experiment, I decided to initially limit myself to certain effects, and then gather and thoroughly investigate all the methods to accomplish them. So, what were those categories? Well, firstly I divided it into two phases: indoor and outdoor. I initially ignored the outdoor phase, and turned to analysing the indoor part of the experiment. I saw it as an animation [the cork ball movement], an appearance [the message on the slate], and a divination [the discovering of Doyle's message].

I decided to separate the cork from the message based on my use of pen and ink in school as a lad. You had to continuously dip the pen in the ink as it quickly dried out. Houdini's ball was similar to modern ballpoint pens, but they carry their own supply of ink in the barrel of the pen. There is no mention in Ernst's description of Houdini having to re-ink the ball. AND besides, it would completely kill the dramatic moment if he had to stop to dip the ball in the ink. They wouldn't take the chance of it running out of ink. So, I had my parameters. Now all I had to do was become a world expert in them!

It would involve a huge amount of hard work, over many years, to both read and file away anything relevant I came across in the thousands of upon thousands of magic books, magazines and catalogues. Okay, I admit it. I love to read magic books, and enjoy the thrill of discovering something important. I eventually managed to give all the ten thousand books in The Magic Circle Library a cursory once over, and was left with a twenty-five page list of books to meticulously go over in detail. I also read all the major magazines, cover to cover, that had been produced in Houdini's era. But that wasn't all. In case a later publication had anything that might be applicable, I was also forced to read everything that had ever been produced on the art of magic.

My subconscious worked on all that great mass of input and occasionally would produce moments of insight and inspiration, but usually it was the correct assembling of just a few of the jigsaw pieces that produced the 'eureka' moment. I'll give you a short example now of the last type, which, although not directly related to the experiment, provided a great insight into Houdini's creative approach to the performance of miracle magic.

Ernst's legal partner, and celebrated poet, Melville Henry Cane gave an example of an incomprehensible, perplexing Houdini mystery in his book (The First Firefly, 1974). It seems that one day, while Houdini was visiting their law office, a stenographer challenged him to open the huge office safe. He half-heartedly walked over to it, inspected it, and said he was not too sure he could do so because it was a genuine antique. Cane agreed with him, as they had purchased it second-hand, and it probably should have been in a museum. Cane said he could never remember the combination, as it had to be twirled four times, left and right, to the necessary numbers. Houdini reluctantly agreed to have a go at it. They all gathered around him as he set to work. Without anything but his dexterous fingers he twiddled the dial for some time, and then, when it looked like he had failed, he triumphantly pulled open the doors!

Yes, another Houdini miracle. Surely no one could open a safe with just his fingertips, even 'Hollywood' burglars need stethoscopes. Much later I had the great luck of finding two other related items, and my subconscious managed to put all three

212

together to come up with the answer. Ernst, when talking about Houdini's escapes from jails, mentioned that when visiting anywhere Houdini would carefully memorize all the locks there and later note them down in his many notebooks. Then on a subsequent visit he'd be ready to open any lock when challenged. As Ernst said, "It was easy to have someone suggest that he show his skill on any occasion." BUT, that didn't explain how he opened the office safe without any apparent keys, instruments or gimmicks. And then I hit it lucky again!

Ernst described (The Sphinx, Oct. 1936) how Houdini had become angry at him for not being amazed when Harry had opened a locked door at Ernst's office. So, Houdini decided to show him how great he really was by opening Ernst's office safe. Ernst made sure the six feet high by four feet wide safe was definitely closed and locked, and then was told to leave the room. In only a minute Houdini called Ernst back in and turned the dial, using the correct combination, to open the safe. When Ernst this time positively showed astonishment, Houdini, uncharacteristically showed him the incredible, delicate 'gimmick' he carried in a special bag down his trouser leg. It was based on several principles and had indicating needles on its face. Ernst did not give its full details to prevent the knowledge falling into criminal hands and rendering ordinary office safes useless. That information would have made acetylene torches, and other burglar's tools obsolete.

So, there you have it. It was not the impromptu miracle it had appeared to be. In fact, it had taken at least three visits to the office to set it up. The first visit he secretly noted the make and type of safe, and then checked it out at home. The next time he opened the safe, unobserved, to impress Ernst; and the third visit he finally turned the memorized combination into a miracle, that totally astonished the rest of the people in the office. Yes, you might be tempted to say, "Easy when you know how!", BUT it involved three vital points that only a master of magic like Houdini could successfully accomplish: a) the determined, long range, detailed planning to carry it out, b) the supreme mastery of locks required to open the safe the first time, and finally, c) on the third visit, the outstanding showmanship to pull off the miracle that left Cane and his staff wondering for the rest of their lives how Houdini had done it. A similarly detailed approach must have been used on the slate test. Could I work out what it was?

PART 3 - THE METHOD INDOORS

Inventors and Magical Inventing

"...it has been my life work to invent and publicly present problems, the secrets of which not even the members of the magical profession have been able to discover."
-Houdini.

It was not going to be easy discovering how Houdini fooled Doyle and Ernst. [I can't resist it – it would take a Sherlock Holmes to solve it. Now, back to reality.] All the conjectures by others of how it was done, that I looked at later, took the simple approach, but when thoroughly examined unfortunately would not work in the exact situation Ernst described. Those investigators had either altered Ernst's description to fit their theories, or left out a vital part of the narrative. As Ernst had said, when Harry went into a thing he did it thoroughly, nothing was too much trouble. So, I would also have to go to a great deal of trouble to find the answer. I decided to begin by looking at the constraints Harry faced.

The technically complex aspect of Houdini's 'experiment' was that it was not an unannounced happening, such as when a favourite uncle suddenly produces a coin from behind his nephew's ear. What we had here was a specific series of events leading up to a predictable outcome that was nonetheless impossible. So, each step along the way had to be meticulously planned to eliminate anything that was in any way unusual. All actions had to take place under seemingly "fair" conditions that counteracted any idea of the real cause, and as well did not cause either guest to suspect any possible underhanded methods. If this were achieved then, even if the observers did not 'suspend their disbelief', the outcome would still appear to be impossible.

The one thing in my favour was that during the experiment Houdini could not take the time to contradict every conceivable method, as boredom would rapidly set in. So, he was forced to only eliminate the most important ones. This gave me a starting place. I would look to see what positively couldn't be the secret method, and then take the attitude that it just might be it after all.

So, based on that, even though Houdini's guests closely examined his apparatus, and helped arrange them, were his 'props' really completely free of trickery? Because Houdini created the strong conviction that they were normal, most investigators assumed they really were innocent. Perhaps I could get further along in my search then others did by assuming the opposite. I had learned the overriding rule of magic investigation the hard way - "assume nothing!" The other major 'law' in magic that seemed applicable here was, "if you can't get away with hiding something, then paint it red and hang it in full view." So, I decided to assume that the items used were NOT necessarily normal.

If Houdini had really been supernatural, as Doyle assumed, then why would he supply the slate and the cork ball? If I wanted to prove that I was really enchanted, I would have my guests bring a slate and cork ball with them. That way there would be no possible way I could be said to employ tricky props. So, my first supposition was that the props were perhaps not quite what they appeared to be. Okay, okay, I admit it. My declaration that spectator supplied devices would eliminate trickery may also be a bit suspect. During my investigating I came across an instance of Houdini's magical hero, the Great Harry Kellar, sending an assistant out to buy one of every type of slate available in a town to swap for the spectator supplied one. Yes, don't believe anything a magician ever tells you. [Of course, that doesn't apply to me! Well, mostly.]

215

To dispel any thoughts of trickery, Houdini had his spectators examine everything. There are generally two schools of thought in magic about handing things [props] out for examination. Those against doing so say that it slows down the action. They also declare that if you just treat the items you are using as normal, so will your observers. In other words, "Don't run when no one is chasing!" The other side of the question is that once everything is examined you can guarantee that your observers will not be able to say, "If I could have examined the things he used, I'm sure I'd have spotted something!" In other words, you validate the impossibility of the experiment.

BUT there is another major advantage here. In having his spectators examine the items used, Houdini was able to completely involve Ernst and Doyle in the experiment. Active audience participation means spectators don't have time to wonder about anything else. It becomes a personal experience. It also allowed Houdini to use the audience management skills he had developed while handling challengers during his escape act. His guests were now his helpers. Although they might think they were able to inspect everything, they were doing exactly what he wanted them to do, and when he wanted them to do it. They were following his script, not independently examining all the items at their own pace. Although they were completely unaware of it, he was in control by focusing their attention.

This is backed up by Houdini's writings (A Magician Among the Spirits, 1924) when he stated: "Investigations under conditions favourable to the medium cannot be termed 'investigations.' They are nothing more than a demonstration of the medium's power to divert attention, carrying it at will to any place they wish and numbing the subconscious mind. Under such conditions they are not only able to delude the innocent and simple-minded but also men whose accomplishments have proven their intellects to be above average."

This is a very powerful psychological tool in magic. Magicians often talk about using misdirection to hide something, i.e. by diverting the observer's attention somewhere else. But as I just described, the use of 'direction' is even more powerful. Houdini was managing the investigation of the items used. People make assumptions. Ernst and Doyle would believe they were responsible for examining everything, but, for example, Houdini could easily do something to the already examined objects while Ernst and Doyle were looking over the next ones. The result of properly applied 'direction' is that people make false assumptions, which then become reality to them. The only sticking point here was that Ernst would be quite aware of 'misdirection' and 'direction'. So Houdini's use of those principles would have to be extremely subtle, and as near to the real thing as possible to get away with it. But for someone who was a master at creating the illusion that he was risking his life every night, when he wasn't usually doing so, this experiment would be much easier to handle.

If Houdini's props were in fact tricky then did he invent something completely new? What was magic creativity like around the time of Houdini's experiment? At a Closed Meeting of the World's Most Prestigious Magic Club, The Magic Circle (reported in The Magic Circular, July 1924), Will Blyth presented a paper entitled "New Effects." Blyth stated that often what appeared to be an absolutely new magical effect in principle or effect was merely an elaboration of an old effect. The presentation was usually much more artistic, but was often just the reconstruction of an old idea. So, I set out to locate everything I could on slate tricks, to see if Harry's miracle was merely an old principle in a new 'dressing'.

I had found the source of Houdini's effect, Berol's stage illusion, but for all I knew Conan Doyle could have been right about the method Houdini used to do it. If Houdini had performed the effect today, I'd be looking into thin, radio operated, computer-driven display units and electronic surveillance techniques, but his miracle demonstration occurred in the early 1920s. To give you an idea of what I was now up against, Milbourne Christopher, in his 1973 book "The Illustrated History of Magic", explained a trick invented in 1574, and then revealed that there were now more than 400 different methods to do it. [That was 400 methods back in 1973!] It puts into proper perspective the conclusion that most non-magicians come to when they discover how a trick is done. They think they now know everything there is to know about the trick. That is why watching trick exposing TV programs and reading exposing type books is often a waste of time. The sign of a non-magician is a person asking how a trick is done. Most magicians are into variations on a theme. At this point I was into a modification of a method. How did Houdini take Berol's stage effect - an effect that could not be done close-up – and then alter it to become close-up performable?

At this point I decided to return to where I began the search for Houdini's effect. I turned again to my Inventions file to see how magicians invent methods once they have settled on an effect. Here are just a few of the writings I found:

HENNING NELMS: "Once you have decided what you want to do, you are half way to doing it....In order to create your own illusions, you will need familiarity with the standard devices for deception and a knowledge of the proper procedures....Difficult and even insolvable problems can arise..."

BILL SEVERN: "...the more a magician knows about what has been done the better equipped he is to explore the creative possibilities of what can be done."

PAVEL: "Before one sets about such a task there must be, as a background, an extensive magical knowledge....a knowledgeable magician, using a logical approach, can ultimately discover the means used to create that effect."

PETER WILKER: "...do not for one moment think you can invent something by just following rules! What you need is experience, hard thinking, a bit of luck and, finally inspiration...There is a background to all creativity viz. a sound knowledge of the subject...Never stop reading!...had to play for hours with [object] till I found the right way to do it."

MICKY HADES: "How does one go about inventing a magical effect? Unfortunately, there is no simple answer because there are a number of elusive factors involved. These factors depend largely on the inventor's general aptitude, imagination, awareness, personal requirements and knowledge of magical principles."

DARIEL FITZKEE: "...common solution... is a laborious and tedious search... catalogues, textbook... other magi scouted... magic shops visited... depends on luck and inspiration... look at ways of accomplishing it."

TOMMY WONDER: "When working on a method, there is surely much calculation and weighing of possibilities. A lot of consideration of course goes into what is practical, economic and effective. This lies within the domain of craftsmanship, which entails technique, knowledge and experimentation... the time, the knowledge, the talent or creative spark...put in some very hard work... wasn't a short or easy search...Eliminate all moves that could even be remotely seen as questionable... determination and imagination."

SAM SHARPE: "The true artist works under self-imposed conditions and willingly chooses the most difficult road if there be merit in so doing...nothing can come from nothing and even a conjurer's brain cannot work without raw material... a trick should always be adjusted to the effect.. not the effect to the trick."

NEVIL MASKELYNE: "...perfecting of minor details is the most tedious and trying..."

ERIC C. LEWIS: "...good creative thinking is hard work. That is why there are so many imitators and so few original performers... enthusiasm and zest... toil and determination... gathering data... tackle problems one at a time... comparing, drawing from the well of memory, linking, developing and associating the various impressions... We try method after method, principle after principle. We persist in the continual re-arrangement of our knowledge. We cull all those hidden ideas that have long since sunken into the recess of our memories. We probe, re-mould, rebuild, adapt. We keep on until we strike a suitable combination of ideas; a series of thoughts so combined that the solution to our problem is formed without altering the original conception in the least..."

J.F. ORRIN: "...there is no royal road...calls for any amount of patience... capacity for taking pains...must be prepared to see many carefully-prepared schemes fall to pieces... a consuming desire... patience and tenacity... tedious business... a bleak and dreary prospect... a good deal of chance... aim should be to discover the simplest method...a matter of training and research. Abandon the indifferent or hopeless efforts and look for a more promising clue to follow up."

From the above comments it's easy to see that Houdini expended much time and effort on the method of converting Berol's illusion from stage to close-up presentation. I feel that he not only spent the previous winter on it, as he said, but the previous year as well, because he first published the announcement that Conan Doyle was going to visit America at least sixteen months before the performance of the trick. Houdini also altered the presentation of the Menetekel Mystery. Berol's version was a two person performance, as far as the audience was concerned, and actually involved a third hidden assistant. As far as Conan Doyle and Ernst knew Houdini was the only one involved the illusion.

But was Houdini the sole inventor of this method for presenting Berol's Menetekel Illusion? After reading the William Berol eulogy Houdini had written, I felt that at the very least Berol must have contributed toward the trick method. Here is what Will Goldston had to say about magical inventors in his book, Great Tricks Revealed (1935):

"The real makers of magic are seldom heard of. They are the men who invent, those mechanical geniuses whom the public never meet....Generally speaking, performers are not inventors. They are the showmen, the demonstrators on whom the spotlight of publicity is incessantly focused. The men who make this possible for them are hidden away from the public gaze in work-rooms and tool-sheds. They are there, working patiently, year in year out...There could be no such thing as magic were it not for these inventors. In my lifetime, I have met many scores of them, and have never ceased to be amazed at the patience and modesty that so often characterizes them and their work. Many of the best are now unfortunately dead, and not a few of them are quite forgotten."

Was Houdini one of the few magicians who invented their own tricks, or did he have a group of "back room boys" to develop the method for his close-up version of the Menetekel Mystery? Who was the best person to tell us how Houdini created his effects? It was Ernst! Houdini had willed his private notebooks and memoranda to him. My first query had to be, "Why hadn't Ernst found out how Houdini had accomplished the trick from the notes?" Here is what Ernst wrote: "The notes which Houdini left...were intended primarily for his own reference. Methods that were already built or in operation did not require written description; in fact, Houdini made it a practice not to set them down in writing..." It must have been very frustrating for Ernst when he found the notes Houdini left didn't contain the solution to the trick that had been troubling him all those years.

Ernst gave us an insight into Houdini's inventive ability in the two prefaces he wrote for Walter B. Gibson's books. Houdini hired Gibson to ghost write a series of simple trick books for him, but died before the project could be started. Ernst gave Houdini's notes to Gibson, who then used them to write two books, "Houdini's Escapes" and "Houdini's Magic." Here are extracts from Ernst's introductions to the two books:

"The reader will be amazed at the simplicity in some cases and at the complexity in others of the devices and methods employed or originated by the master of escapes...The artfulness of any deception lies in introducing simplicity where people look for complexity, and this is evident in many of Houdini's methods...Some are the outgrowth of suggestions given to Houdini; others are improvements or additions to older methods...He relied on research and hard work as much as inspiration...It is evident from his notes that he relied on accepted methods, but increased their effectiveness by improving or disguising them...he frequently chose the simplest and most direct way to obtain the results he desired, then depended on his showmanship and his ability as a performer...."

"Houdini's attitude toward magic...He raised a barrier of permanent silence where his own escapes were concerned...When magic became his chief aim, Houdini adopted a different attitude...He exchanged ideas with those who knew the principles of magical deception. He was receptive to the suggestions of those well versed in magic...He sought to adopt old ideas to new uses, to discover methods that would produce startling and unusual effects...He frequently took chances with tricks that involved the danger of failure...He gained many excellent ideas from his associations with other magicians...It must be remembered that Houdini was a great collector of magical literature and data regarding magic..."

So, other magical experts were most likely involved in the creation of the method I was seeking. This meant that, if all else failed, I should trace down all of Houdini's known associates and read what they had published. An interesting note was that the method was possibly an old one dressed up so that it was not recognisable.

The time had come to stop basking in the glory of discovering where Houdini had obtained his effect and get on with finding how he had actually done it.

Accumulating Methods

"You know my method. It is founded upon the observation of trifles."
-Conan Doyle (The Boscombe Valley Mystery)

I resigned myself to a long investigation, and set about gathering all the trick slate writing methods I could lay my hands on. I won't bore you by explaining all the techniques I came across. They would fill a book bigger than this one. I split them into methods devised before Houdini's performance, and those in general use at the time of Houdini's test for Doyle and Ernst? I had accumulated fifty years' worth of slate writing methods to examine in detail. Should I start with Houdini or the medium Slade? I used a scientific technique to decide....

Okay, I admit it! I flipped a coin. Houdini won! Somehow it was appropriate. What better way to begin with than with the man in question? I turned to chapter VII in Houdini's 1924 book, "A Magician Among The Spirits." Houdini had entitled that chapter "Slate Writing And Other Methods." Knowing Houdini's penchant for keeping the secrets of his own tricks, I really didn't expect to find anything resembling what I was looking for. My assumption was correct. There were many effective techniques, but nothing giving a clue as to how the trick in question was accomplished. The closest method involved words appearing on the inside of two slates that had been fastened together. The writing came apparently from spirits using a slate pencil that had been placed between them. That clever method actually involved the use of a specially constructed slate pencil that was magnetically attracted. A strong magnet, on the outside of the slates, was used to trace the words in backward writing. Yes, just like Berol's illusion.

Houdini had written: "A remarkably large number of methods have been used at one time and another by the numerous mediums of lesser repute then Slade who prospered on slate writing..." I can tell you, from experience, that Houdini was absolutely correct about the "remarkably large number of methods." After countless months, I was beginning to drown in slate writing techniques. I was waking up at three in the morning and realising I had been dreaming about slates. I had almost completed my research of the fifty years of slate methods, but wasn't even getting close to a solution. The only answer was to somehow classify what I had found. That way hopefully I would spot a clue, but I couldn't work out how to arrange my findings. I was too close to the situation and couldn't see an easy way to do it. Fortunately Professor Hoffmann came to my rescue before I conceded defeat.

Professor Hoffmann was the pen-name of barrister Angelo John Lewis, M.A. He wrote the classic magic text, "Modern Magic," in 1876. Hoffmann had the ability to not just explain magic, as most of his predecessors had, but to teach it. Some magic authorities consider him the greatest writer on magic who ever lived. "Modern Magic" was a milestone in magic. It summarised all the tricks that had been devised up until the time of its publication. Frustratingly, the one trick absent from the book was the slate writing trick.

The reason for this lack of inclusion was because it was only as the book was being published that Slade was making the test popular. If the trick wasn't in the book, then how did Hoffmann come to my rescue? Well, in the "Journal of the Society for Psychical Research" for August, 1886 I found an article entitled "How And What To Observe In Relation To Slate-Writing Phenomena." None other than Angelo J. Lewis had written it. He said: "...I have been requested (as an expert, and in a quasi-professional capacity) to read and criticise a series of reports...of sittings with Mr. Eglinton." [Eglinton was the slate writing medium who followed on from Slade.]

Hoffmann wrote that he would be offering investigators a little practical counsel on slate writing by calling attention to possible means of deception. The crucial part of his article for me was:

"In the case of slate-writing produced by trickery there are five alternatives, which practically cover the whole ground.
1. The writing may be then and there executed by the medium.
2. A slate, on which writing already exists, may be substituted for the one first shown.
3. The slate used may already have writing upon it, but at the outset invisible, and rendered visible either by application of some chemical re-agent...
4. A slate may be used with a movable face, which may be discarded at pleasure...
5. The characters may be 'printed' by the medium from some prepared surface...."

It was just what I needed. I added a sixth category "various" to cover the techniques that were conceived between Hoffmann's writing and Houdini's death. A typical item in this new category would be the one from Houdini's book that I explained above, using a slate pencil that was attracted to a magnet. I cheerfully set about filing my findings under Hoffmann's groups. I also included the items gathered over the years in my Appearing Messages file. When I finally finished I scrutinised the results. What did I discover? Not one item seemed to answer the question: "How did Houdini do it?" Nothing even came close to Houdini's hands-off, ball writing effect.

I went back to read what Hoffmann had said about the categories: "It will be observed that the four last alternatives are dependent upon previous preparation, and these may, therefore, be disregarded where an answer...of a given written word...on the spur of the moment. In such cases, therefore, the whole vigilance of the spectator may be directed to one point, viz., to ensure that the characters are not then and there written by the medium himself." He followed this up with a warning about slates being placed under the table. [This was a common practice at that time.] He mentioned firmly attaching the slates with clamps. The next sentence referred to that method, but if we substitute the hanging of Houdini's slate it is very applicable: "The slate should be attached...by the investigator himself, and the question to be answered or word to be written should not be stated until the slate is actually attached." This is exactly what Houdini had Conan Doyle do! So, the message was produced under seemingly impossible conditions.

Based on my findings so far, I felt I had all the methods of producing slate writing that I would need to solve Houdini's test. I had organised them into an ordered structure. Now, what I needed was a method for analysing the data I had accumulated to spot the discrepancy. Somehow it was beginning to look like a hopeless case. The only answer was to go back to the beginning.

I returned to the "What?" category and re-read Ernst's description of Houdini's test. There did not seem to be anything there that would help. As it was rather late, I gave up and went to bed. The next morning my fresh mind [okay, it took a cold shower and a hot coffee to get it going] suggested a new approach. I had located the source of Houdini's effect, but was unable to discover the method. Possibly the answer lay in going back to the effect and breaking it down into its constituent parts. I had been looking at only one part of the overall effect - the slate writing.

I opened Sam Sharpe's classic text on magic theory, "Neo-Magic." In it Sharpe had written: "Complex effects are those formed by using two or more feats in conjunction to form a complete whole, which cannot be added to or have any part removed without loss of unity."

I mentally stood back and studied Ernst's description trying to visualise the various sub-effects. Using Sharpe's "Primary Magical Plots," I came up with four sub-effects. I then listed them in what seemed to be the easiest order to determine the method:

1. Attraction - Mysterious adhesion. Gravity is overcome when the ball sticks to the slate. This is not Anti-gravity which is unsupported floating of an item, such as a ball or lady. It more resembles magnetism – in our case pseudo magnetism.

226

2. Animation - Movement is mysteriously imparted to an inanimate object. The ball is moved with no visible means of accomplishing it.

3. Production - Mind over the inanimate. A definite message is produced on the slate. It goes from not being to being. There is a gradual visible appearance.

4. Identification - Specific discovery of an identity – the unknown message. Possible telepathy or mind/thought reading of Doyle's note. Extra Sensory Perception, unspoken thought passing from one person to another, or an unknown entity.

During the time I was pondering how to break down Ernst's description into sub-effects, I was still helping catalogue the Magic Circle's books. One book struck me as different from the others. Most magic books tell you, quite rightly, to devise your own tricks and not to attempt to discover how others effects are achieved. Nelson C. Hahne and Joe Berg's 1930 tome, "Here's Magic" was different. In the section entitled "Method Of Analysis," Hahne states: "If it is possible to evolve a method for an effect, it must be possible to detect the method used in an existing effect by following the same process. Of prime importance is a knowledge of the general principles of the art. Certain things must be recognized at the start. It will be found, usually, that most baffling problems are accomplished by surprisingly simple means."

The system of analysis the book explained consisted of first outlining the problem with every known condition. Then you collected all the ideas of methods for accomplishing the effect. The next step was discarding all the obviously impossible ones. Then all impractical ideas were rejected. After this process of elimination, the remaining idea must be the true one even though it might be very unusual. Hahne also explained: "...remember that in conjunction with his apparatus he can utilize the many laws of psychology. In this manner, it will be evident that the conditions do not have to be fool-proof or too exacting." Hahne's idea sounded very much like the modern idea generating system known as brainstorming, although it is usually carried out in groups. The only differences were that brainstorming stresses suspending judgement in the initial phase, especially on crazy ideas, and Hahne's last statement said that the remaining idea must be the true one even if unusual. I decided to give it a try, if for no other reason than that it was a break from searching magic literature.

The Cork Ball

"...when you have eliminated the impossible, whatever remains, however improbable, must be the truth."
-Sherlock Holmes

I wondered if Nelson Hahne had read that quotation?

In line with the above method, I looked at what appeared to be the easiest sub-effect to solve, "Attraction." To begin, I re-read what Ernst had written about it. Ignoring all the rest, he said: "Upon Sir Arthur's return, Houdini requested him to stir up the cork ball once more in the white ink, and then to lift it, by means of the spoon, and hold it up against the suspended slate. He did so, and the cork ball stuck there, seemingly of its own volition!....The cork ball then dropped to the floor, and Houdini invited Sir Arthur to take it home with him, if he so desired."

Then I wrote down all the ideas I could possibly think of [whether they were completely silly or not] for how the ball could have stuck to the slate in a pseudo-magnetic fashion. [Okay, I admit it! I cheated, but just a little bit. I turned to the two best idea generators in magic, Maskelyne & Devant's "Our Magic" and Fitzkee's "The Trick Brain." - Hey, magicians cheat all the time, why can't spectators do it as well?] When I had all my [and their] ideas listed, I took out three more pieces of paper. The first one I labelled "Impossible", the second I titled "Improbable" and the third I headed "Possible Except For...." Returning to my original list of ideas I deleted the definitely silly ones [like invisible tiny leprechauns] and then transferred the remainder to the appropriately headed papers. Here is what I was left with:

1. Impossible:
a) Velcro - Not yet invented.
b) Rubber Sucker - Conan Doyle would surely have seen it.
c) Suction or Air Pressure - Too noisy and unwieldy.

2. Improbable:
a) Adhesion - Glue, or wax etc. would probably have stuck to the spoon as well, and sliding glue had not yet been invented.
b) Invisible Support - Wire, thread, etc. would have been seen by Conan Doyle, and definitely suspected by Ernst.
c) Concealed Support - A hidden pin, mechanical arm, etc. would have to be a very special means of actuation that the onlookers would not see.

3. Possible Except For....:
a) Magnet – the facts against a magnet were:
   i) The spoon would have been attracted as well.
   ii) The ball was apparently non-magnetic.
   iii) The ball fell off the slate, evidently of its own volition.

Well if Sherlock Holmes and Nelson C. Hahne were right, and I had executed my part in the proceedings correctly, it wasn't pseudo magnetism - it really was magnetism.

A magnet would make sense as Berol's Illusion had used one, and Houdini's team would likely have started with Berol's method, then adapted it to suit their requirements. It was conceivably possible for a magnet to be concealed in a false hollow slate. Hahne had stated that: "...he can utilize the many laws of psychology." I didn't immediately see how psychology could overcome the above three objections, but decided to see if it was possible.

My first restriction was that a magnet would also attract the spoon holding the cork ball. [These days you could use a plastic spoon.]

Would a normal metal spoon give the game away? This was the easiest one to test out. So, after a bit of searching I located a magnet and headed for the kitchen. [All right, I admit it! I gave up looking for one and went to the kitchen to drown my sorrows in a cup of coffee. As I opened the refrigerator to get the milk, what did I find? Yes, a magnet holding down a note on the door!] Now, all I had to do was lower the magnet into the cutlery drawer. So, what happened? As I had expected, spoons stuck to it; BUT, the exciting thing was that some of them didn't! So, Houdini could have given Conan Doyle a spoon that was not attracted to a magnet. This opened up a whole new avenue of investigation. Perhaps both Hahne and Holmes were right!

I moved on to the second uncertainty I had listed. It was the fact that the ball was supposedly non-magnetic. After a bit of deliberation, I reasoned that Houdini could possibly have switched the ball for one with a core of magnetically attracted material. He would have had to distract Ernst and Conan Doyle to do it. Houdini would most likely have switched the container as well. [Otherwise it would have been too difficult to avoid getting ink on his fingers.] A duplicate inkwell and ball could have been conveniently hidden nearby.

I recognised at this point that I had to prove my conjectures, and not make unfounded assumptions as others had done in the past, but I decided to run with the idea a little bit more to see where it led. The switching back of a special [gimmicked] ball for a normal one, once the message had appeared, could easily have been done psychologically, as Hahne suggested. You obviously don't give a man a ball covered in ink to take home. You first dry it off. For a magician, as skilled at sleight of hand as Houdini was, switching the ball under cover of a towel would be ridiculously easy.

The last problem I'd listed for the magnet theory would take a bit of research. Somehow the magnetic power would have to be removed to make the ball drop from the slate. Was it possible to do this? The answer was yes! Professor Hoffmann had the solution. In his classic 1876 book, "Modern Magic," he wrote: "Some of the most mysterious of the stage tricks are performed by means of electricity, or, to speak more correctly, of electro-magnetism...nearly all attributable to the inventive genius of Robert-Houdin...In the case of the ordinary magnet this attractive force is permanent, but in that of the electro-magnet it may be produced or destroyed at pleasure. The electro-magnet consists of a short piece of soft iron, (either straight, or bent into a horseshoe form), with copper wire (covered with silk or cotton) wound round and round it nearly to the ends. If a current of electricity from a galvanic battery is made to pass through this wire, the iron core becomes powerfully magnetic, the attractive force, however, ceasing as soon as the current is interrupted." The mention of Robert-Houdin reminded me that he was Houdini's boyhood hero, and that Houdini had thoroughly investigated his contributions to magic.

That sounded feasible, but was there definite proof that Houdini was aware of the use of electro-magnets? Yes. In his 1950 book, Sixty Years of Psychical Research, Houdini's great friend, Joseph F. Rinn, explained that he begged Houdini to help him devise a method of opening a safe in the dark, to include in a play he was writing. Houdini said he did not want to publicise the real method of safe opening so suggested a fictitious technique. It involved the use of an electro-magnet under the floor, near the safe, operating a magnet placed in the combination lock. The enticing thing about this event is that it took place at about the time of Houdini's performance for Ernst and Doyle.

So, was that the third objection solved? Well, not quite. There was still one very major obstacle to overcome. Where did the electricity come from to power an electro-magnet? A decade before Houdini performed his test, Maskelyne and Devant had written in "Our Magic": "According to our present knowledge, it would appear that there is but one specific principle upon which magical apparatus embodying an electro-magnetic...has ever been constructed. That is the principle of concealing, within the appliance...an electro-magnet to which the current is conveyed through suspending wires." What did Ernst tell us?

231

"Houdini produced what appeared to be an ordinary slate, some eighteen inches long by fifteen inches high. In two corners of this slate holes had been bored, and through these holes wires had been passed. These wires were several feet in length and hooks had been fastened to the other ends of the wires...."

So it appears that the supporting wires were used to conduct the electricity to the electro-magnet, at least it does until you read what else Ernst had to say:

"Houdini passed the slate to Sir Arthur for examination. He was then requested to suspend the slate in the middle of the room, by means of the wires and hooks, leaving it free to swing in space, several feet distant from anything. In order to eliminate the possibility of electrical connections of any kind, Sir Arthur was asked to fasten the hooks over anything in the room which would hold them. He hooked one over the edge of a picture-frame, and the other on a large book, on a shelf in Houdini's library. The slate thus swung free in space, in the centre of the room, being supported by the two wires passing through the holes in its upper corners. The slate was inspected and cleaned."

This would appear to negate the use of electricity, which Ernst definitely seems to have considered. I once more returned to Hahne's statement: "...he can utilize the many laws of psychology." So how could Houdini use psychology to surmount this seeming impossibility? To find out, I first established what Houdini knew about using connecting cables to conduct electricity. Kenneth Silverman's book "Houdini!!!," explains that Houdini had a replica of Robert-Houdin's Crystal Casket constructed at least seven years before doing the test for Conan Doyle. [It would appear that Houdini had a love/hate relationship with Robert-Houdin.] When performed, the Crystal Casket is usually suspended from cords - not wires; BUT they were far from normal cords. As Professor Hoffmann explained, they had wires running down their centres.

If electricity were the medium of operation then it was essential to hide the fact from his audience. So, what did Houdini do? Harry stated in his 1924 book, A Magician Among The Spirits, that he firmly believed in the workings of the subconscious mind. So, he employed the old conjuring maxim, "If you can't hide it then paint it red!" He hung the slate in plain view! If Houdini had used the traditional cord, or ribbon, with a wire in the centre, a knowledgeable conjuror like Ernst would have suspected it. By Houdini boldly using a bare wire, Ernst would have initially suspected it, BUT then discount it completely because of the seemingly fair method used to hang the wires.

The genius of Houdini's presentation was to let his spectators decide where to hang the slate. Did this ruse plus the use of bare wires work? Yes. Ernst declared that Houdini allowed Doyle to suspend the slate from anything which could hold it, "In order to eliminate the possibility of electrical connections of any kind..." This stratagem not only fooled his spectators, but also apparently all the others who read Ernst's description of the proceedings. No one else seems to have thought of the possibility of an electrified slate.

So, if my theory is correct, that still leaves one major obstacle to overcome. How did Houdini manage to connect the source of electricity to the wires that someone else had hung up? I believe he employed a typical form of conjurors' limited, or restricted, choice. What do I mean by that?

Dingwall's book How to go to a Medium, 1927, explained, the word 'control' referred to the methods used to restrain a medium from using 'normal' methods to produce the phenomena. The important thing to remember here is that it was Houdini who made the conditions under which the mystery was produced - not the spectators. This was not a formal organized demonstration. It was virtually useless as proof of Houdini's ability as a medium, but Conan Doyle chose to ignore this. This was something Houdini was doing under the circumstances he chose. Doyle and Ernst were

233

not investigators but merely guests/viewers. They were relying solely on their observational abilities to detect trickery. They might have been able to make choices, but it was Houdini who restricted the limits of those choices. Dingwall advises you to distrust elaborate mechanical controls. So, my question was: "Why did Houdini hang up the slate, and not just leave it on a table?"

The photograph of Houdini's library [that I discuss in the WHERE section] gave me the answer. It showed Houdini leaning on cupboards that stick out at least twice as far as the book shelves above them. Those cupboards extended from his waist downward toward the floor. Above them were six shelves of books. The bookcase/cupboard unit extended in sections continuously all the way along the visible wall. When compared to Houdini's body, each section or bay of shelves appeared to be about four feet in length. There were several inches between each of those bays. Those spaces were filled in with vertical boards and framed pictures hung from them.

What objects existed at the required level to support the hooks? From the photograph it is evident that the only conceivable place a hook could be hung from was a picture or, if one of the doors enclosing the shelves was opened, on a book. This was the first limitation to what, on the surface, would appear to be a free choice. The next constraint was Houdini restricting the placement of the slate to the centre of the room. That limited the number of hanging places to those above chest height. It would restrict it vertically to the top three shelves and top three pictures. By keeping the length of the wires short it would also cut down on the number of places horizontally to hang the slate. This probably limited the placement of the wires to only one bay and two sets of pictures.

This psychological forcing technique is a form of "conjurer's choice." Although it would seem to the participants that they had unlimited choice, Houdini had drastically reduced the available area. His spectators thought they were in charge, but in fact he was.

This still left me with several electrical connection problems. Neither books nor picture frames usually conduct electricity. What did Houdini do? The first area I looked at was how the wire hung over a picture between the book shelves could be coupled to the electrical supply. Silverman's book explains that Collins, Houdini's assistant, was an accomplished carpenter who also made bookcases for his boss. So, the bookcases could have been constructed specifically for this trick, or easily modified by the fellow who made them in the first place. I suspect the picture hanging wires were supported on long nails, that passed completely through the boards they were nailed to. Further wires could then have been fixed to the internal ends of those extended nails to connect them to the electrical source. The length of nails was a definite Houdini ploy. He was known to replace long nails with short ones in packing cases to make his escapes easier.

What I was not happy with was the fact that the electrical circuit was still not complete. A separate wire was needed to connect the hook hung over the picture frame, to the wire supporting the picture. I decided to take my own advice, that I mentioned when discussing the creation of new magic tricks, I stopped thinking about it and let my sub-conscious ponder over the difficulty. While sleeping, the mind is not bombarded by all the daily data it has to process. It can concentrate completely on the problem pondered over before falling asleep. After sifting through all the knowledge it possesses, the brain often comes up with the answer by looking at parallel situations.

In my case it must have done exactly that. Why? Well, because when I woke up one morning the first thing I thought of, after "What did I do with my slippers last night?", was the solution to the problem [no, not where are my slippers]! A connecting wire would not be needed if a metal picture frame was used instead of a wooden one. Yes, in magic the rule is "Assume Nothing!" I had assumed Houdini's pictures all had wooden frames. Metal ones would solve the problem nicely. I like to think that Houdini, or his assistants, had the same revelation that I did. As an aside, I later came across a reference (The Sphinx, Oct. 1922) to David P. Abbot inventing a "Talking Picture Holder" that answered people's questions. Did it give the Houdini team the idea?

I also noticed a very tenuous link in John Mulholland's 1932 book, Quicker Than the Eye. Mulholland, a very close friend of Houdini's, wrote about a 'running gag' Houdini would play on him. John had admired a painting of a magician on Houdini's wall, and each time John was in the house Houdini mentioned he'd taken precautions to make sure John didn't make it vanish. At one point Houdini said that one of those precautions was "that he'd put stronger wire on the frame". Had Houdini actually been putting stronger wire on his pictures, but for a completely different purpose altogether – to carry electric current?

So the pictures could already be electrically connected well before the day of the test. That appeared to be the wire hung over the picture sorted; BUT, the slate supporting wire at the other end, which Doyle had hung over "a large book", was something else. It would not only have to be handled completely differently, but also after the slate had been hung in the middle of the room. For Doyle to connect the slate support wire to the book he would have had to hook it over the spine of a book and down between the pages, i.e. like you would place a bookmark in a book. If it were only hung over the spine of the book the weight of the slate might have damaged the book, and possibly torn itself out of the book. The best answer I could come up with was to run a wire from the electric supply along the back of the three upper shelves well before the test. It would then only need a short jumper from that wire to the hanging hook to complete the circuit. The jumper would be hidden in the book itself. Yes, quite a great amount of speculation, and a major problem to overcome!

The obvious difficulty was, "How did Houdini surreptitiously connect the jumper wire to the hook in the book after Doyle put it there?" Again Professor Hoffmann supplied a possible solution. In his article on slate writing phenomena, he wrote: "Another point which strikes an expert in conjuring as suspicious is the request to sitters to talk of indifferent matters, and not specially to fix their minds on the work in hand...the greater part of a conjurer's power lies in the misdirection of attention, and if the object were to divert the notice of the sitters from any personal manoeuvres of the medium, the request to talk and think about indifferent matters would be readily intelligible." So how did Houdini misdirect a fellow conjurer familiar with that technique? Was I grasping at straws here to bolster my theory, or was I about to make a significant contribution toward a solution?

Eric Dingwall gave me an important clue here in his book How to go to a Medium, 1927. He wrote: "Pay no attention when you are told that a message was obtained upon a slate 'which never left the sitter's hands for an instant', remember that the probabilities are that the slate left his hands for several minutes whilst the message was being prepared upon it. Malobservation of this sort has been proved to occur in many cases with intelligent and experienced sitters, and it is unlikely that you will be an exception to the general rule." Dingwall later added: "always remember that some simple normal explanation will probably account for the facts."

Dingwall also mentioned that "if the sitting takes place at the medium's house, and a confederate is used to produce the phenomena, the 'medium' merely acts as a decoy to occupy the attention of the controller, since the actual phenomena are being produced by a person whose very existence is unsuspected by the sitters."

So, was an unsuspected accomplice employed? Well, it would have been extremely impolite of Houdini and Ernst not to accompany their honoured guest, Conan Doyle, to the door when he left to write his message. That would have been all the opportunity Houdini needed. Houdini would know what method to use to distract his dearest friend from returning to the library. Whether it was Houdini's latest magical acquisition, or a non-prohibition drink, or one of a dozen other things we will never know. Ernst wrote: "...Meanwhile, Houdini had kept Mr. Ernst with him in order to see that he did not leave the house." Ernst spelled out that Houdini was doing the keeping. He was in charge. This was the normal employer/employee or mentor/pupil relationship between the two men.

The other important factor to note is that Ernst wrote "the house" and not "the library." If Houdini had failed to distract Ernst, and he had wanted to return to the library, then Houdini would certainly have had a back-up contingency plan, such as having Bess suddenly appear and require the help of both of them. And, of course, once they helped they had to have a cup of coffee, or something much stronger! I decided to look into this part later and carry on to see if the technique would be feasible.

Once Ernst was out of the library, a hidden assistant could quickly switch the ball and ink container, and then add the jumper between the book and the shelf wire. So, where did this assistant hide? The average magus just does a set routine of tricks. One of the key techniques used by Masters of advanced magic is to assess their surroundings and then use them to advantage. I went back to the notes I had collected under my "Where" section, and went over in detail the area in which Houdini had performed his miracle. What were the major areas of the room that could be used to advantage? Ruth Brandon's book, The Life and Many Deaths of Harry Houdini (1993), gave me a clue. She wrote of Houdini's mahogany bookcases and asked what was hidden in their extra-deep bases. It doesn't take much stretch of the imagination to guess that one of Houdini's trusted assistants could have been the answer.

It's my feeling that Houdini had originally intended to substitute ['switch'] the gimmicked cork ball for the examined one by sleight of hand. Of course, that is just the sort of thing Ernst would be looking for. Professionals don't take risks, so I think that once the idea of using a hidden assistant to switch the slate was decided upon it was realized that the ball could be exchanged as well. This fits in with the old magic adage of paring away until you get the simplest technique that will still maintain the mystery. It would also take the pressure off Houdini to do a 'clean' sleight, and allow him to be more in the moment, as he then had less to worry about.

It was time to take stock of where I was. Although the above explanation seemed on the surface to be reasonably feasible, I did not want to move on to the other sub-effects and continue building upon a possibly false base. So, I looked for further evidence to support my electro-magnet hypothesis. I returned to Robert-Houdin's trick. Although Houdini had a replica of Robert-Houdin's Crystal Casket constructed, I wanted to learn what he actually thought of the principle of using connecting cords as conductors. Many magicians buy a trick on the spur of the moment because the method appeals to them. Once they find the effect doesn't suit their performing personality it goes into a cupboard and is never seen again. This was not so in Houdini's case. Silverman says Houdini used the Crystal Casket to open his 1925-26 magic show. He certainly thought the trick strong enough to impress his audience, and therefore certainly have approved of the hidden electrical connection technique in support wires.

My next line of inquiry was to see if Houdini had shown any other interest in electrical trick methods. Harry Price answered this question. In his wonderful collection is an article written by Houdini. It was probably sent to Price by Houdini himself. The article appeared on pages 100 to 107 of the October 1922 issue of "Popular Radio." It was entitled: "Ghosts that Talk - by Radio." In the article Houdini wrote: "Magicians have used the radio telephone in their performances for several years - long before radio was generally known to the public." This article must have been written about the time Houdini performed his test for Conan Doyle. So, Houdini was very familiar with the use of both electricity and radio by magicians.

Finally, I wanted to find out if Houdini would actually go to all the effort and trouble required to wire up his house for a single magic trick [and, more importantly, would Bess have allowed him to do it!] I came across T.H. Chislett's 1949 book, Spirits in the House, which described how Chislett had run cables all over his house. At

239

around the same time Houdini was preparing his trick, Chislett had installed several different electrical circuits, each for a different trick. Did I find any proof to support my conjecture that Houdini had done the same? Yes! In Kellock's biography he wrote: "...the Houdini home in New York was a trick house from cellar to roof. It had an intricate nerve-system of signalling apparatus." This was further confirmed by Brandon's saying that Houdini had the house wired so he could eavesdrop on conversations while he was absent from the room.

I was feeling fairly confident that I had sorted out the 'Attraction' part of Houdini's test, BUT then I had the chat with Sidney Radner that I mentioned in the "Where" section of this book. As I said there:

"I was able to talk to Sid then, and asked him about Houdini's library. Without me prompting, he said it had a bookcase on one side but the other wall was plain....So, there you have it - books on one side, and pictures on the other, with the slate swinging between them."

Yes, a plain wall! The bookcase side was obviously the one that had the hook over the book, but the slate's hook on the picture was on a plain wall. Short of a channel being dug out of the wall to install a wire, along with a complete redecorating job to hide it, I couldn't see how my theory was any longer valid. I decided to temporarily shelve it and look elsewhere for a solution.

The Problem

I wasn't entirely convinced that Houdini would go to all the trouble of having major alterations done to his walls for a mere magic trick. Much later, while looking at speculations on the internet of how it was done, I discovered that people could not believe Houdini would have expended major effort to carry out his tricks. On the other hand, when I looked into the subject of magicians fooling their fellow magi, I discovered they loved to fool each other. They often went to great expense and effort to 'blow them away'.

So, why do they do that? Well, in the short term it greatly massages their egos, but in the long term it can greatly enhance their reputations. As proof of why magi will go to great lengths to create an unforgettable experience, I am now adding to their reputations in this book by mentioning them, long after they have gone! So, would Houdini have gone to all the trouble and expense to hide wires in the walls of his house? Well, his hero, Harry Kellar, wired up his house to amaze guests. Kellar referred (The Sphinx, Oct. 1922) to this type of trick as a "house-mystery."

I came across several instances of magicians a decade later rigging up their homes to deceive knowledgeable friends, but what about magi of the era I was investigating? The answer was in the obituary of "well-known illusionist Carl Hertz." Although born of German parents in California, he died in England in March 1924. His death notice (in The Magic Circular, April 1924) said, "Hertz lived quietly in a small flat in the West End when in London, which flat he had 'faked' in various ways so as to amuse his friends by the sudden disappearance of furniture, and other magical effects." Disappearing furniture sounded like he had gone to a lot of expense and trouble just to fool a few fellows. This seems to be a part of the magical psyche. People are less suspicious of theatrical devices, like trap doors, in someone's home, so magicians take advantage of it. I wondered if Houdini was aware of the mysteries in Hertz's flat, and, after a bit of searching, discovered that while Houdini was President of The Magicians' Club in London, in 1914, Carl Hertz was one of the Vice-Presidents. So, there was a very strong chance Houdini had visited the "small flat".

By the way, don't let the "small flat" description above make you think Hertz had died nearly penniless, like sadly many magicians do. He had used the large salary he commanded to "acquire numerous old buildings in 'Frisco and New York, which he demolished, replacing them with residential flats which steadily

241

increased his income." He was believed to be worth a quarter of a million pounds sterling at his death. This was at a time when the average wage was about three pounds a week.

What about Houdini's worth? Well, in 1920 he is said to have earned seven hundred pounds a week for a two week engagement at the London Palladium. The average variety performer at that time could get as much as ten pounds a week. So, how many thousands did Houdini leave when he died two and a half years after Hertz [1926]? Believe it or not, the answer is, "None!!!" Yes, his estate was insolvent! There's a whole book to be written about why it was, and how he really died – perhaps I'll get around to it one day. But for now, back to our present quest, and the answer to whether Houdini had created a "house-mystery."

Walter B. Gibson's 1977 book (The Original Houdini Scrapbook) describes his c.1920 visit to Houdini's house, along with Chicago magic dealer Arthur Felsman. Felsman told Gibson that he suspected Houdini had wired up his house like fake mediums do, so that they can listen in to what their clients say. Gibson divulged that he later learned the rooms were "bugged" so Houdini could secretly listen in to conversations. This adds a whole new dimension to the Society of American Magicians committee meetings held in Houdini's library. What better way for the President to really find out what his committee thinks of him than to leave the room and eavesdrop on them during his absence?

Milbourne Christopher's 1969 book (Houdini: The Untold Story) tells of Houdini doing a thought transference trick for distinguished guests in his home in 1925. Although locked in a box upstairs, Houdini was able to demonstrate that he could read their minds. Christopher says the secret was that Houdini's undercover man, Amedeo Vacca, had wired up the house on 113th Street. Houdini's brother Hardeen, who was with the guests downstairs, repeated the chosen words out loud to "fix them in the minds of those present." While he was doing so Houdini heard them on a receiver that was ingeniously concealed in the box he was in.

A similar Houdini mind reading trick, devised by Amedeo Vacca, was discussed by Bruce Reynolds (The Linking Ring, Dec. 1947). Several newspaper men were in Houdini's living room while others were outside with Harry. Those inside talked on any subject they chose while Harry was guarded by those outside. On going back in, Houdini was able to tell them about everything they had discussed. The newspaper men were allowed to thoroughly examine the house but found nothing suspicious. The event made headlines in all the papers. Richard J. Weibel (M-U-M, July 1982) confirms that Vacca had wired the walls of Houdini's house.

I had come across Amedeo Vacca while checking out a reference for my spectator club's newsletter on the subject of his Human Volcano Act. Frank Garcia and George Schindler's 1974 book (Amedeo's Continental Magic) says Vacca and a stenographer were in the basement listening to the newspaper men's voices. The book maintained that the plaster walls of the house still had the wiring installed by Vacca. William Kalush and Larry Sloman's 2006 book (The Secret Life of Houdini) completed the picture. It described how Harry's house was wired with an elaborate system of hidden wires, including induction coils under carpets, and a series of hidden "Dictaphones". [Kenneth Silverman's 1996 book, Houdini!!!, says a "dictograph" was a primitive bugging device with a buttonlike transmitter.] A secret electric induction belt and a hidden telephone receiver in his sleeve, allowed Houdini to hear what was transmitted to him. A sound surveillance system originally installed by Louis C. Kraus, a nephew of Houdini's, had been rewired and upgraded by Amedeo Vacca.

I presumed that part of Vacca's upgrading work included the wiring for Houdini's slate test, but needed to find confirmation. Fortunately, I was able to locate it in the very magazine Houdini had edited. The M-U-M for Aug. 1957 contained a report of Amedeo's visit to the Stamford Assembly No. 33. It ended by saying that, although it was not generally known, Amedeo was the man who set up the effects in Houdini's house, enabling Houdini to do the spirit effects that amazed A. Conan Doyle. It added that Amedeo had documentary evidence to back this up. So, there it was, proof that part of the secret of the slate test was electrical wiring.

A further rider to this section throws some question on the statement made that Bess Houdini was unaware of Vacca's exact activities. John Booth described (in The Linking Ring, Nov. 1941) a visit to Bess in California, a decade and a half after Harry's death. While chatting to Bess, Booth was amazed to hear mysterious voices from an unidentifiable source apparently floating into the room. He then recognised them as his telephone conversation with Bess the previous day. He said the entire house was wired. So, perhaps Bess knew a thing or two about wiring up houses after all, and just might have been involved in setting up the slate test.

Returning to Houdini's library, the few bits of wire in a bookcase certainly wouldn't have been any trouble compared to installing wiring in the plaster walls and ceilings. The shortest route for the slate test would have been to run a wire down from the ceiling inside the wall, and then have it branch off to be soldered to the nails of several pictures in the middle of the room.

Why do I say the wires were soldered to the nails supporting the pictures on the walls? Well, Vacca is quoted (in The Linking Ring, Dec. 1947) as saying he could point out where he had wired up the walls and ceilings. How do you find a specific spot on a wall? Simple, just look for the nails. I believe the wires were soldered because, as a lad in Electricity Class in High School, I spent many frustrating hours soldering nails together! A matrix of many nails was first hammered into a board, and then wires were soldered between each nail. To test out our soldering ability, the teacher would then take a hammer and whack the wires to see if they came loose. So, from hard experience, I believe the wires were soldered to the nails, and then the wires were plastered over to conceal them.

At this point I decided to definitely run with my electrical hypothesis. The test for it would be if it held up when combined with the methods I worked out for the other sub-effects. Before I moved on to the second sub-effect though, I did have one final deliberation. I wondered whether Amadeo's induction coils could have been used to supply the power to the slate's electro-magnet. That way the connecting wires wouldn't need to be used, but decided against it. If it had been done that way then why use wires on the slate? Ribbons or ropes would have done quite nicely.

Another reason for eliminating induction was that if the slate contained an electro-magnet, it would need to be thicker than normal. This would necessitate a substitution of the examined slate for the replacement one by a hidden assistant. So, if you were going to exchange the slate Conan Doyle had examined for a fake one, as well as switch the ball, you might as well also connect the book hook to the electric supply. Both slates would, of course, have a slight imperfection in exactly the same place so that the well-trained eye of Ernst would not fail to notice it.

Animation

Having resurrected my electric theory, I decided to move on to my second sub-effect, 'Animation', to see what I could discover about it. I had defined it as: "Movement is mysteriously imparted to an inanimate object. The ball is moved with no visible means of accomplishing it." This did not include the writing of the message. I delayed thinking about that troublesome area until I had a reasonable conjecture for how the movement of the ball was accomplished. For now I was just concerned with getting the ball to move across the slate, the writing part would come later. After a bit of reflection, I decided that if I were to see Houdini's test today, I would probably expect the ball to move up and down while the message was being written. This is because we use ballpoint pens. They did not exist in Houdini's day. So, I concluded that just moving the ball across the slate, while the message appeared under it, would be quite magical in the early 1920s.

Ernst had written: "...the cork ball stuck there, seemingly of its own volition! It then proceeded to roll across the surface of the slate, leaving a white track as it did so. As the ball rolled, it was seen to be spelling words." Ernst seems to agree with my conjecture that the ball just rolls across. Doing this would helpfully limit the complexity of the hidden movement mechanism. As Hahne told us: "It will be found, usually that most baffling problems are accomplished by surprisingly simple means...remember that in conjunction with his apparatus he can utilize the many laws of psychology. In this manner, it will be evident that the conditions do not have to be fool-proof or too exacting." I think that psychologically all it would have taken was for Houdini to exclaim: "Look it's writing something!"

So, once I had limited the ball's movement to only horizontal across the slate – not up and down - my next objective was to determine how a sideways movement could be accomplished. Beginning from what I had already established, an electrically connected slate with an electro-magnet inside, I started my investigation. Were there available methods in magic? In Maskelyne and Devant's book (Our Magic) under the principle of "Trigger Action by Electric Current" they explained: "The principle consists in the use of an electro-magnet for releasing a motive power already stored up in a piece of apparatus. Thus any form of clockwork may be started or stopped, by moving its detent electrically. A supply of compressed air may be turned on and off, a spring released, or a weight allowed to fall. In short, there are a thousand and one operations in which trigger-action is used, that may be most conveniently controlled by an electro-magnet. There is also a great advantage in the fact that the magnet need have no contact with the device it moves. Its attraction will pass through all substances save those which are themselves magnetic."

So, discounting the compressed air, any of the above methods could have been used. Applying the electric power to the slate would have energised the electro-magnet inside it, which in turn would have started the mechanism to move it along horizontally inside the double slate. When the electro-magnet reached the end of its travel, it would move beyond the electric rail. That would break the electrical circuit, disconnecting it from the power source, and cause the ball to drop off the slate just as Ernst had described.

This type of mechanical slate would be relatively simple to construct when compared to the complexity of some of the automatons that Houdini had written about in his book "The Unmasking of Robert-Houdin." Elastic, springs, and wind-up mechanical devices were all in use in the era's automata. We will never be sure which was used, but failure was not an option. A failsafe method was needed so the rule was to simplify. Whichever technique was employed it had to work on the night, and the movement had to be uniform. I think many hours of experimenting were required until they were completely happy.

I decided that this theory for the animation of the cork ball fitted in nicely with the previous sub-effect. So I temporarily left it and turned my thoughts toward the third sub-effect. It was the one I had started with in the first place. Then, as usual, I ran into trouble again!

An Electrifying Appearance

I had defined the third sub-effect above as: "Production - Mind over the inanimate. A definite message is produced on the slate. It goes from not being there to appearing. There is a gradual visible appearance." I had to start somewhere, so I theorised that if the first two sub-effects, Attraction and Animation, could be done by electricity, then possibly the third could as well. It was worth seeing if it could. I returned to the slate writing categories Professor Hoffmann had devised. The only category that looked remotely promising was the extra one I had added to his list - "various". I looked over the items I had gathered in that category, but didn't expect to find anything. The fact that I had managed to devise a reasonably feasible explanation for the first two sub-effects kept me going.

Initially I found nothing remotely resembling what I wanted, but then I spotted something that I didn't believe at first. It was an entry in a 1920 book written by Ernst's co-author Hereward Carrington, "The Physical Phenomena of Spiritualism." He stated:

"A very elaborate and ingenious method of obtaining writing on a specially prepared slate, by means of electricity, I shall not now stop to consider. The explanation may be found in Mr. Hopkins's Twentieth Century Magic"

It would appear that Carrington had the answer under his nose all the time but had just not seen it - neither had I. I had that very book in my own home library!

Two books containing conjuring effects written by two gentlemen named Hopkins, were published in 1898. The first is a classic, Albert A. Hopkins "Magic: Stage Illusions and Scientific Diversions, including Trick Photography." The second, "Twentieth Century Magic" by Nevil Monroe Hopkins, is not considered to be a classic at all. In fact, the second book is mentioned several times in magic literature as an example of an author using over-elaborate methods to bring about an effect, i.e. using a sledge hammer to crack a simple nut. Its author, amateur magician, Nevil Hopkins was a chemist and a teacher, who had written several technical monographs. His magic book was subtitled "A Treatise On The Construction And Introduction Of Scientific Magical Apparatus." It seems this book was aimed more at the home craftsman than the magician. The section of Nevil Monroe Hopkins' book Carrington referred to had appeared in serial form in "The American Electrician."

Hopkins' book was probably the last one any modern magician would think of looking in. It had been published more than 20 years before Houdini's performance for Ernst and Conan Doyle. During that time the magic world had written it off as full of unworkable daydreams. I purchased my second hand copy of the book from one of the world's most well-versed magicians in the

1960s. He told me, "You don't want that, it's full of rubbish!" He was mostly right but that was exactly why I wanted it - as an example of what not to do.

What did I find so exciting when I looked up Carrington's referenced method in Hopkins' book? In the section entitled "Electrical Magic" were details for the construction of an "electric slate" - a slate wound internally with wire heating coils that were used to cause the appearance of a message previously written in a chemical solution. The slate's supporting ribbons contained secret wires, which ran to innocent-looking hooks. The circuit had a switch, which was operated by an assistant hidden behind the scenes. Hopkins wrote that the slate required about 30 seconds to get piping hot and accomplish the spirit work. He advised numerous trials before exhibiting the trick to an outsider.

Would Houdini have looked at a book other conjurers had discounted? I believe the answer is yes for at least two reasons. The "Electrical Magic" chapter of Hopkins' book included two other items that would have attracted Houdini. One was The Obedient Padlock - a lock designed to open in the normal manner, or by means of a secret pair of electro-magnets. How could the World's Greatest Escapologist and Master of Locks not fail to be intrigued by this item? [And yes, it sounds very much like the idea Houdini gave Rinn for opening the safe in his play that I've already mentioned.] Also described was The Spiritualistic Cash Box. It was a version of Robert-Houdin's greatest electrical trick - The Light and Heavy Chest. Surely Houdini would have consulted it while writing his debunking book on the French magician.

As with everything else on this quest, this was not the final answer. There were several major differences between Hopkins' slate and Houdini's. The first difference was that Hopkins hid the connecting wires in the supporting ribbons on which the slate was hung, while Houdini boldly displayed them. Why did Houdini not hide them from view as Hopkins had? The answer strangely [as I've already noted] is that Ernst would have been suspicious if Houdini had! Ernst would have been familiar with the Electrical

Tricks section in Professor Hoffmann's "Modern Magic." This describes three devices using the technique of concealing electric wires in supporting ribbons, namely The Magic Bell, The Crystal Cash Box, and The Magic Drum. As I wrote above, Houdini used The Crystal Cash Box or Casket to open his magic show. Professor Hoffmann explained that Robert-Houdin's trick used fine platinum wire, which being a bad conductor heated up and severed a cotton thread to actuate the apparatus.

The second key difference between Hopkins' slate and Houdini's was the message appearance. It materialized directly on Houdini's slate. Hopkins had the message appear on a piece of paper stuck to the slate. A message had been written on the paper using a solution of diluted sulphuric acid and allowed to dry. The heat produced black characters similar to India ink. Hopkins suggested experimenting to get the correct strength of acid. To prevent the message appearing a bit at a time a scarf was thrown over Hopkins' slate.

The third difference between Hopkins' slate and Houdini's was the size. Hopkins says his ordinary school slate measured 7 inches by 11 inches, excluding the wooden frame. So, if we add an inch all the way around for the frame, that makes the slate 9 inches high by 13 inches wide. Ernst says the slate Houdini employed was 15 inches high by 18 inches long. Allowing for the passage of time between Ernst's seeing the slate and recounting the details, we have approximately 6 extra inches in each direction on Houdini's slate. This could be accounted for by the space required for the electro-magnet's sliding contact and the means of locomotion.

Unlike Hopkins' manifestation, Houdini's message appeared as the ball moved along. So, I decided that the only part of Harry's slate that was heated was the area the ball passed over. This could be done by having the moving electro-magnet attached to a sliding contact, which connected electric power to only the part of the heating coil that it passed over. It would work in a similar manner to a variable resistor. One end of the electrical power supply would be connected to the end of the heating coil, with the other end fastened to the sliding contact. The electrical power, and thus the heat, would be applied to the coiled heating wire gradually, not all at once.

Would the ink on the cork ball obscure the letters being formed by the heated chemicals? No, because the heat from the board would quickly cause the ink on the cork to dry. This would be a definite bonus. On the outside of the slate it would appear as if the ball was writing the message. Of course, a fair amount of experimenting would have to be done to produce the illusion of the ball doing the writing, but the movement of the ball across the slate would nicely cover up any variation in the heating as the individual coils warmed up.

Was there any other detail that would not seem quite right for my electric slate theory? Yes. Ernst wrote: "In two corners of this slate holes had been bored, and through these holes wires had been passed." The support wires passing through the bored holes in the corners of the slate would seem to be in contact with the wooden frame only. Wood is a non-conductor of electricity. Hopkins got around this difficulty by using screw-eyes screwed into the upper sides of the slate that were long enough to pass through the frame to act as electrical terminals. [Similar to my long nails holding up the pictures.] Houdini presumably wanted to have the slate support fastenings appear non-conducting, so as to, once again, allay any suspicion of electrical usage. I think he had the holes in the frame drilled very slightly larger than the support/power wires, and then inserted internal metal bushings that would be in electrical contact with the inner heating wire at one end and the electro-magnet's sliding contact's channel or rail at the other.

Now I had a device that could theoretically do the job, I wondered if Houdini had the ability to construct it. Was he a Maskelyne [an original inventor] or more like his hero Keller [a man who allegedly hired Maskelyne's assistant to discover how an illusion was accomplished]? Some of the most innovative illusions Houdini presented he purchased from others. Examples are Morritt's Disappearing Donkey and Josolyne's [probably Selbit's]

251

Walking Thru a Wall. Bart Whaley's Who's Who In Magic (1990), says Harry's Milk Can Escape was jointly invented with his assistants Kukol and Vickery. Will Goldston, Houdini's friend, wrote (Who's Who In Magic, 1934), that Harry did not invent all the illusions attributed to him. Hopkins impresses on his readers the importance of neat and careful work in constructing his slate, and suggests employing a carpenter. Did Houdini know one? Yes. Brandon (The Life and Many Deaths of Harry Houdini, 1993) points out that Harry's assistant Jim Collins, a master mechanic and cabinet-maker, was able to embody Houdini's wildest ideas in solid form. If Collins, or someone else, constructed the slate for Houdini to Hopkins' specifications there was still a problem with the chemical writing on the slate.

The trouble here was that, unlike Hopkins, Houdini's message appeared directly on the slate, and was presumably white like one normally written in chalk would be. Did Houdini have that necessary chemical experience, or did he need the help of someone with a detailed chemical knowledge? In the index of Silverman's book is a list of tricks that Houdini performed. It is a page and a half long. None of those tricks seem to employ chemicals. Houdini did not mention the use of chemicals in the slate section of his 1924 book, but that would be in keeping with the times. In that era, magicians' books exposed the secrets of their competitors, not their own.

I eventually found my answer to the question of Houdini's knowledge of invisible inks in the magazine Houdini edited. The April 1908 issue of his Conjurers' Monthly Magazine contained an article on The Art of Cryptography written by Harry himself. Under the heading of "Imperceptible Inks" was the statement that by "applying heat" invisible inks can be made to appear. Houdini said that he had "found by investigation that it is best to experiment yourself."

The way Houdini's message appeared, as described by Ernst, completely fits the use of chemicals. So, discounting a unique lost method, I concluded that Harry used what was currently available to him, and didn't waste time inventing something he didn't need. Instead he put his energy into concealing the fact from Ernst that he was using chemicals.

Traditionally, the message that mysteriously appears is written in a chemical that vanishes when it dries. To make it re-appear two methods are used - either chemical or heat. Houdini would have been aware of the chemical technique. How do I know? Well, I came across an advertisement Houdini had placed in the Sept. 1904 issue of Mahatma. It had no bearing on this topic; he was seeking copies of an early magic magazine. BUT the item above it said: "Spirit Slate Writing. I want genuine secret for producing writing by the acid or chemical method. Must have been tried with success...." Houdini would have noticed the advertisement above his and found out what the fellow had discovered. To keep ahead of competitors, he had to have the latest magical knowledge.

I found that William E. Robinson's 1898 book, Spirit Slate Writing and Kindred Phenomena, split the chemical methods for producing messages into three classes: 1) chemicals that appeared when exposed to light, 2) those that were developed by a second chemical [reagent], and 3) those that became visible when heated. So, which version did Harry choose? The imprecise nature of the light exposure method would have ruled it out. The second method seemed like a good candidate. It would be easy to assume the cork ball was dipped into a reagent, masquerading as ink, which then developed the message as it traversed the board. The obstacle to using it is that only a small portion of the ball is in contact with the board at any one time, similar to a ball-point pen. This would mean the method of animating the cork would have had to be extremely accurate. Although perhaps possible with today's high-tech methods, it would have been too complex for Harry's time.

It is possible Houdini tried the chemical developing technique first only to abandon it, but retained the cork ball as an excellent piece of misdirection. As I was already speculating on electricity being used to move the ball, I decided initially to stick with it. The more you simplify a magic secret, the less there is to go wrong. So, I temporarily dropped chemical actuation, and concentrated on electrical heating. I also looked to see if there were other heating methods in magic. The other major technique was a heat lamp hidden in a table. I eliminated this because the slate was hanging in space, not resting on a table. This ideal method of heating would allow Houdini to be well away from the slate, while the slate itself was as far away as possible from any surrounding furniture. So I decided now to concentrate only on the electrical heating technique to activate the chemical message.

I next checked to see if the use of chemicals in magic was relatively easy, and wished I hadn't! The two classic works written on 'mental magic' gave me the answer. Corinda's 1958 work "13 Steps To Mentalism" declared: "I recommend that you do not involve yourself with chemical techniques unless you enjoy performing troubles." Ted Annemann wrote in his magazine Jinx (No. 138): "Too often we find articles and tricks which refer to a certain chemical way of doing something, and, upon trial discover that it just won't work. Of course, it all could work itself out if someone sincerely wouldn't print such tripe unless he had given it a try." A final problem came to light when I took a look through my "Appearing Messages" file. It would seem that the use of chemicals at close quarters, such as Houdini's library, would have been a dead giveaway due to the smell of the chemicals.

So it looked like an expert was needed to help Houdini convert Hopkins' method into the effect that was more like Berol's Menetekel Illusion. I wondered if Houdini had known such a person, and fortunately discovered that he had! This I learned by looking again at Professor Hoffmann's slate categories. His third category was: "3. The slate used may already have writing upon it, but at the outsct invisible, and rendered visible either by application of some chemical re-agent..." I went through all the chemical information I had accumulated under that heading and discovered that one of the first magical experts on the chemical method of message appearance was a friend of Houdini's.

Houdini's pal, Joseph Rinn's 1950 book, "Sixty Years of Psychical Research", tells how Herrmann The Great's assistant, Billy Robinson, discovered that the false medium Slade had been using a chemical slate writing method. Robinson wrote what is probably the first book devoted to a single magic trick. In his "Spirit Slate Writing and Kindred Phenomena," published in 1898, he listed sixteen chemical formulas for "Inks that Appear through Heat." It is important to note here that, as in Hopkins' slate trick, the messages all appeared on paper, not on the slate itself.

Houdini and Robinson were friends. If not in America, they definitely were in England. Legend has it that Houdini immediately hit the big time by escaping from Scotland Yard. While I was attending the Davenport Magic Company's 100th Anniversary Convention, I noticed a unique handbill displayed amongst their incredible collection of magicana. It listed both Robinson, in the guise of Chung Ling Soo, and Houdini on the same bill. Although both were to become subsequently world famous, neither was top of that bill. I am certain Robinson would have leapt to the challenge of solving Houdini's chemical problem for him. Unfortunately I discovered that he probably did not! Why? Because, while performing as the pseudo-Chinese Chung Ling Soo, Robinson was tragically fatally wounded doing the dreaded Bullet Catch Trick. That was at least four years before Houdini's test for Conan Doyle.

Ernst had said that Houdini turned to others when he needed help. So, I looked to see if there was another candidate who could have helped solve the problem of a chemical message appearing, in white, on a slate without an obvious smell.

A Helping Hand

So, who else could help Houdini solve his chemical problem? If, as Joseph Rinn had written, Slade had used a chemical slate writing method, then all you had to do was figure out what he had done – not an easy task.

After much searching and consideration, I began to suspect Robert H. Gysel, "Houdini's undercover man" [see "Who" section for details] had been closely involved in the development of the slate trick.

Bart Whaley (Who's Who In Magic, 1990) says Bob Gysel worked for Harry for five years. So, I had to find out if those years covered the period when the trick was performed. There is very little mention of Gysel in the literature of magic, including many Houdini biographies. So I talked to the late David E. Price who had lectured to magic collectors on Gysel, and was probably the world's greatest living authority on him. [Note: David was the U.K. David Price, and not the U.S. one.] David said he began his quest for knowledge on Gysel after acquiring a series of letters Gysel had written to Henry Sara in England. They were a very, very revealing series of letters, from one magical eccentric to another. David said Gysel stated he had worked as Houdini's "dirty-tricks man" from the time of Harry's mother's death to the time of Houdini's own death. This would be more like thirteen years and adequately cover the period of the performance. As well as being extremely knowledgeable in the areas of lock picking and fake spirit mediums, Gysel was very well informed chemically and electrically.

I also managed to pick up something that tended to point toward Gysel being part of Houdini's team. In a Mar. 1924 Sphinx article, Gysel stated, "In all of Houdini's work, he positively does not use any faked slates that you find in magic stores, etc., as, for instance, Alexander, who makes use of the Dr. Q. slates in his act." So, how did Gysel know "positively" that Houdini employed only specially constructed slates unless he was, in fact, intimately involved in their construction?

Harlan Tarbell, the creator of the classic magic course, The Tarbell Course In Magic, is quoted in Volume 6 as saying that Gysel was "a magical inventor in a million." I discovered that Gysel had both the electrical and chemical background knowledge necessary to develop the trick slate used to fool Doyle. How could I be sure? Well, Will Goldston's 1931 book, Great Magicians' Tricks, contained an electrical trick of Gysel's involving the use of wires and batteries. Additionally, there was a Gysel trick in the October 1945 issue of The Conjurors' Magazine, using magnets made by winding coils of wire. The magazine [Houdini's brother Hardeen was Editor Emeritus] quoted Gysel as saying: "Please remember – too many turns will make the magnet weak – too few will make it hot. You will have to experiment." Gysel had obviously experimented with electrically operated magnets, and knew how to produce heat with the same wires.

As for Gysel's chemical knowledge, Goldston described Gysel as "a qualified chemist." Oswald Rae (in The Demon Telegraph, Oct. 1947) says Bob "studied Pharmacy and for a time held a State Licence, but I understand he gave up his medical studies after a year or so." In The Jinx No. 23 (Aug. 1936) editor Ted Annemann, a close friend of Gysel's, reported the death of Bob Gysel's father. Annemann stated: "He was the oldest druggist in the state of Ohio, and much of Bob's unique knowledge came from their close association." A Gysel letter to Henry Sara (Aug. 1, 1930) [from David E. Price's collection] states: "I could tell you things that you would not believe, when Houdini was living, and my dad was helping us out in the chemical game." Unfortunately, he doesn't explain what that chemical help was used for, but I like to believe it was for the slate trick. Try to find an alternate trick of Houdini's that would fit the bill. I couldn't.

But perhaps the best clue of all to Gysel contributing to the project was in Burling Hull's 1929 book, Original Slate Secrets. He says, "For many years past magicians have tried to achieve the ideal of a slate writing method operated by a chemical action." Hull gave a reference to someone who had solved the problem. It was none other than Bob Gysel's magazine, Psychic Fakeries, which Bob published around the time of Houdini's test for Doyle and Ernst.

So, what experimentation would Gysel have carried out on the slate for Houdini? What did they need to convert Hopkins' electric slate into the one Ernst described? Electrically it would involve the use of the electro-magnet for the ball animation, and the means of gradually heating the slate. Chemically there was even more to do. The message appearing formulae that Robinson and Hopkins had described were for use on paper, and not on the slate itself. Even simple items like the method of writing the message to be vanished, and then revealed, had to be considered. Did you use a brush or a glass rod? Did you print or write the message? Did you write the message before hanging up the slate so the liquid would not run down the slate?

The amount of experimental effort required is shown by Houdini's comment to Doyle and Ernst after the trick. Harry explained that he had been working on the method, on and off, all winter. Can I be sure Gysel did the work for Houdini? Well, if Houdini needed an expert on chemicals and electricity, and wanted to keep his method secret, he'd be rather foolish not to use the expert who already worked for him. Harry was many things, but one thing he was not, was foolish. In fact far from it.

If my theory of an electrically operated slate, coupled with a chemical message appearance, was right then I was certain Gysel had been involved in at least the chemical side of it. But what I was not entirely certain about was whether Bob had actually constructed the final special slate used for Houdini's test. I couldn't seem to find proof that Gysel was an expert at apparatus constructing. So I looked to see if there were other candidates who might have been involved.

I uncovered several possible suspects. My first candidate came from Houdini's niece, Marie Hinson Blood. In Kenneth Silverman's Houdini!!!, (1996) she revealed that Harry himself had a workshop in his basement for creating tricks and illusions. So, it was possible that because he wanted to keep the gimmicked slate a very close secret, Houdini and his trusty assistant Jim

Collins constructed it. BUT that did not fit in with Houdini's tendency to go to the best experts he could find, especially when the device had to work perfectly the first time it was used. There would be no second chance. This was supported by H. J. Burlingame's 1891 book, Leaves From Conjurers' Scrap Books. It revealed that very few professionals invented their own illusions, but depended on "persons who make that a speciality."

One of those persons was Houdini's brother-in-law, John A. Hinson, who was a qualified carpenter and cabinet maker. According to his daughter Marie, John would often meet with Houdini and Jim Collins to discuss tricks they wanted him to build. Using John would definitely keep the secret in the family, but was Hinson familiar with electric wiring? Someone who fitted the bill, both electrically and mechanically, was Rudolph S. Schlosser, the gifted New York eccentric magic prop builder. Tad Ware (Magicol, Feb. 1995) calls Schlosser "one of Houdini's favourite builders," and lists several items he constructed for Harry. One of those was "Houdini's Lighted Lamp to Flowers." An electric lamp would have needed wiring as well as mechanical input; but, just in case it was actually an old fashioned oil lamp, Schlosser also built another illusion, The Light Bulb Cabinet, for The Great Leon, which again required electrical/mechanical input. So, I was on the point of voting for Schlosser as the slate builder, when I discovered G. G. Laurens.

It is very difficult to find anything about Gustave G. Laurens in magic literature. That, of course, is just the kind of person Houdini would have used as a hidden assistant/accomplice. There are practically no pictures of him. The main one I located (in the June 1969 issue of M-U-M) was labelled "A Rare Houdini Photo Taken Around 1920." It showed eight of the top magic personalities of the day. Four were seated and four standing. Directly above a seated Houdini was a standing Laurens. On Laurens' left was Houdini's brother Hardeen. Is that my only connection of Laurens to Houdini? No.

259

Laurens was one of the hard working behind the scenes people of the Society of American Magicians [S.A.M.]. He not only performed, and was master of ceremonies on many of their shows, he was also on various committees, and the council. He was made Secretary in 1915, and became Second Vice-President in 1917. At that time the President was none other than Houdini.

When Houdini died in 1926 nearly 200 magicians from all parts of the country attended the funeral. But it was G. G. Laurens who delivered the eulogy. Then Laurens nominated Bernard M. L. Ernst to replace Houdini as the Most Illustrious President of the S.A.M. So, he was definitely a close associate of Houdini, but what has that to do with constructing the slate?

Well, I first noticed that he was without doubt a craftsman while reading the minutes of the Oct. 1916 S.A.M. meeting. It said two beautiful plaques were presented to the Society. They were the gift, and the work of Laurens. It was said that his cleverness along such lines had only been known to a few. A further item, in the minutes of the January 1919 S.A.M. meeting, added to this. "Laurens exhibited the delicate mechanism which made the Magic Clock possible (this antedates the clock of Robert-Houdin) and was worked in conjunction with the pendulum of a Dutch Clock and an electro-magnet." When I read "electro-magnet" I decided Laurens needed further investigation. It led to a very interesting find.

The November 1911 issue of M-U-M [the magic magazine Houdini would edit a few years later] contained a special four-page supplement written by Frenchman G. G. Laurens. Entitled Conjuring By Electricity, it was the paper he had read at the November 1911 meeting. I consider Laurens' article to be an excellent summary of the use of electricity, in the early part of the twentieth century. He wrote that Houdini's boyhood hero Robert-Houdin had employed electricity to operate several of his illusions. By opening and closing electric circuits 19th century magicians operated tricks like The Spirit Drum, Spirit Rappings, and The Magic Bell.

Here, extracted from Laurens' paper, are just a few of the relevant items that apply to the present quest:

- Magnetism is the basis of all electrical results, and magnetism was exploited for conjuring purposes as soon as its properties were observed.
- During the last half century, electrical devices have been the secret of many conjuring effects.
- Electro-magnets may be designed in most any shape, long and narrow, short and thick, straight, curved, square, etc., and that the desired "pull" may be obtained by proportioning the parts.
- Electric motors constitute excellent substitutes for clock mechanisms…motors can be designed in most any shape; the writer succeeded in constructing flat motors equivalent to 1/8 H.P., which can be concealed within a board measuring six inches square and one inch thick[!!!]
- Electricity is in its infancy, yet the devices and contrivances one can design or procure are innumerable.

So, based on the above I can't help thinking that one of the devices Laurens designed was Houdini's slate. What did other magicians of the era think about electricity?

Five years after Laurens' article, electrician and magician, Justus Eck, gave a lecture entitled 'Electricity and Magic' to the Magic Circle on June 7, 1916. A review of his talk (The Magic Circular, July 1916) gave the most important magical applications as: a) the development of secret writing, b) magnetism, and c) telephony for conveying secret messages. The relevance of each of them to the task in hand was beginning to look more and more certain. Four years later, Stanley Witcher talked to The Magic Circle members on "Electricity in Magic." The Magic Circular, June 1920, reported that he gave an example of the effects as "the revelation of secret writing." He also said, "It might be inferred that some of the more impressive effects ascribed to spiritualism could well be produced by the use of electricity."

Laurens' M-U-M (Nov. 1911) article on employing electricity in conjuring describes one use I've not mentioned so far. It is the hiding of the contacts to operate the device. Laurens was not in favour of an assistant controlling a push button, as it took the control away from the magician. He advised a hidden metallic spring under the carpet that could be stepped on by the magus at the correct "psychological moment." After careful consideration, I suspect Houdini used his hidden assistant to do the electrical actuation. It would have been something less for him to worry about, and allow him to be fully in the moment wondering what would happen.

So, as Doyle approached the slate carrying the ball the electro-magnet/heating was operated. The assistant would have to be fully aware of what was going on. Houdini would verbally cue him in his directions to Conan Doyle. All he would need to say was: "Place the spoon against the slate, in the upper left hand corner." The timing would be crucial because the invisible message would start to appear prematurely if the board heated up too early, and if the power was switched on too late the ball would not stick to the slate. To be absolutely certain of hearing, I suspect the assistant was connected to the electrical eavesdropping system in the room that various authors have mentioned. [Then again, Houdini operating the system would be the safest....yes, I'll leave it to you to decide who was the operator.]

The Weak Point

Every trick has a weak point that must be overcome or the trick will fail. If my theory for the first part of the slate trick is correct then it too has a very weak point. Everything hinges on Houdini's ability to entice Ernst out of the library for an extended period, and especially doing it without raising any hint of suspicion. This is the key to the whole trick. Team Houdini would have developed many possible methods to achieve it.

Back in the WHO section I mentioned Walter Gibson saying that Harry had a genius for finding out people's weakness and using it on them. I mentioned the army of spies he used against mediums, but Ernst and Carrington's book refers to the files he also had on his fellow magicians. They contained things people thought no one else knew. So it appears Houdini's spying was not limited to mediums. It would also include investigating both of his audience members for our slate test. This performance was not just for any audience. This was for a precise pair of men. He would be able to control their observation and judgment by exploiting what he had learned about their natural human biases. This means Houdini would have easily been able to entice Ernst out of the room, while Conan Doyle was away from the house.

Ernst would have begun to relax his vigil thinking a natural break had occurred, and that nothing could be done until Doyle returned. Houdini would not have rushed to get Ernst out of the room either. During the time Doyle was walking the three blocks to the place of doing his writing, boredom, and a resultant lapse of attention, would set in, allowing Houdini to suggest an alternate place containing something that would appeal to Ernst.

Monotony was an effective tool here, as the largest part of the test was taken up by Doyle not only walking the three blocks away, but as well the three blocks back. Houdini would also have created multiple methods or 'outs' if a simple suggestion didn't persuade Ernst to move from the room. I speculated on what typical tactics would be:

a) Bess arriving to drag them away to have a cup of coffee with Mrs. Conan Doyle.

b) Showing Ernst Houdini's latest magic acquisition, which just happened to be something that Ernst was very interested in.

c) Having legal papers that Ernst wanted Houdini to sign, ones that Harry had not quite got around to looking at yet, or Houdini would have told Ernst to bring them with him.

d) Sampling something a little stronger than tea or coffee. [Remember this was during prohibition.]

The most effective one would be for Ernst to suggest it himself. Houdini was an expert at planting a suggestion in conversation in such a way that the person would later bring it up thinking he'd originated it. If Ernst himself had proposed it, he'd completely discount the time spent away from the room, and not even bother to tell us about it. Of course, Houdini would make out that he was not too happy to leave the equipment behind. So, he would have to lock the door to make sure nobody interfered with the apparatus.

The key to the room would probably be given to Ernst for safekeeping. Besides how could Houdini get up to mischief if he didn't have the faintest idea what Doyle was writing blocks away, and he'd be in plain sight at all times. On Doyle's return, when they met Sir Arthur at the door, he would never know they'd been out of the room for some time during his absence. Alternately, Houdini and Ernst could return to the room before Doyle's arrival, after Houdini was signalled that the coast was clear, and someone else let Sir Arthur into the house. This would definitely confirm to Doyle that they had not left the room.

My question then was what could Houdini do to get Ernst to suggest they leave the room for the period Doyle was outside? One way would be to start several days before the performance. Magicians often employ 'preliminary work' in their tricks. Houdini could have contacted Ernst about a special document that he urgently required. A typical document would be his will. He revised his will every time he had a falling out with someone, which was quite often. Houdini could then have told Ernst to bring it with him on the day of Doyle's visit, and that they could go over it if they got time.

So, once Houdini and Ernst had seen Conan Doyle off at the door, Houdini could ask what they should do to fill in the time. This was Ernst's cue to suggest the document. Houdini would probably recommend they do it somewhere more comfortable, and with an accompanying drink. He'd then suggest they lock the library door, just in case. [Yes, to help put Ernst's mind at ease, BUT also to ensure Harry's invisible helper was hidden again when he heard the key in the door.]

If that ruse did not work Houdini's team would have several other scenarios ready for execution. I think offering Ernst a drink of something strong would be an effective enticement. Why? Well, this was in the middle of prohibition, and I'm sure Ernst would accept. How can I be sure? Well, if you check out the WHO section you'll see that I described a liquid trick Ernst performed that originally had me fooled, until I realized that he had produced a certain type of liquid to be sampled by all [during prohibition]. "All" did include Houdini. Harry was supposed to be completely temperate, but in the WHO section I describe Houdini being apparently drunk! It has also been suggested that Bess was on her way to becoming an alcoholic after Houdini's death, before kind friends set her up with a new manager/confident. Alcohol was definitely available to Houdini during "the great dry period." So, you can see why I think it played a part in getting Ernst out of the library. Yes, a human weakness helping to cover the weakness in Houdini's trick.

So, I think my conjecture that Houdini enticed Ernst out of the room is feasible, but is my 'hidden accomplice' part of the theory realistic. In Houdini's day, mediums had been caught many times during séances, using accomplices who had secretly gained access to the room, or cabinet. Ernst's report does not mention the room being thoroughly searched before or after Houdini's 'test', so it's safe to assume it wasn't. Would you insist your host lets you thoroughly search his house? Typical means of secretly entering rooms used by unprincipled mediums were windows, panelled ceilings, and floors containing trap doors. Access had also been gained by removing hinge pins to open doors.

In our case, a cupboard in the room, locked from the inside once the accomplice was in it, would have done just as well. [It is interesting to note that magician Chislett (as described in Spirits in the House, 1949) also wired up his own house at about the same time, and hid his assistant in a cupboard under the stairs.] Doyle's walking six blocks [three each way] would have allowed ample time for Houdini and Ernst to settle down outside the room. Then one or more of Harry's co-conspirators would come out of hiding, do the substitutions, connect the jumper wires, and chemically do the writing. [How they knew what to write was going to be my next big problem.] The only down side with my conjecture is that Ernst did not tell us the room had been unattended at any time. It's my feeling that Ernst considered it safe enough, and establishing this bias, with the decay of memory over time, eliminated it from his report. [Besides, would you have mentioned that you and Houdini had broken the law by having a quick illegal libation while Doyle was absent?]

At this point, I decided to turn my attention to the other major problem – the outdoor part - to see if it would fit in with my speculation so far.

PART 4 - THE METHOD OUTDOORS

As a Magician I think anything is possible and
there's always a method or scientific explanation.
- David Blaine

Magicians are like blood-hounds: when they start on a trail
they don't stop till they get "there".
- Eddie Joseph

Introduction

Now for the most challenging part of the problem - as Ernst and Carrington put it: "The miracle of the writing was one thing; how Houdini had managed to obtain a knowledge of the contents of the written message was another. The conditions seemed fraud-proof." Attempting to solve the outdoor part of Houdini's 'experiment'

266

was the most difficult phase of the investigation. The challenge was a double one. As well as discovering how Houdini secretly obtained Conan Doyle's written words, I had to uncover how he covertly got them to the hidden assistant in the library. Over the many years, when I came across possible ideas and clues, I collected them in an "Outdoors" file. Slowly connections between those items began to emerge. What follows is an overview of the many different approaches I took in solving the conundrum.

Part of the solution lay in reading between the lines. A magician presents so many details during a performance that it is impossible to observe everything. As William L. Gresham's 1954 book Monster Midway explained, Houdini was a master at misdirecting his spectators' attention away from the parts he did not want them to think about. Magicians are well aware that observers can only concentrate on the things they consider important, and are forced to ignore the rest. The secret to Houdini's trick lay in those insignificant, rejected trivial items. The problem I faced was that they would not be in Ernst's report because he would have dismissed them. So, how could I reconstruct those missing details?

Ernst's detailed description of Houdini's presentation had three major break points. I analysed each of them for possible omissions. Eventually I decided that if Ernst thought something was important he would have described it in more detail. To gain an overview, I decided to make a timeline of the test. I checked Ernst's account for the length of time the performance had lasted, versus how much he had written about it. I decided that the more he wrote about what happened, the less I would initially concentrate on it. Conversely the less he described something, the more I would suspect that something undetected had happened. So, here is my breakdown of the performance:

Initial Stage – Here Houdini set the scene by having the corks and slate examined. He then cut up one cork while placing another in the ink. Finally the slate was hung from the places chosen by the spectators. Ernst used 65% of his description on this phase. The elapse time would have been about 10 to 15 minutes.

Outdoor Stage – This is where Conan Doyle walked three blocks to where he wrote his message, and then three blocks back again. Ernst gave us very little on this activity - only 10%. The most important thing here is that Ernst made no mention of what he and Houdini were doing for at least the 30 to 45 minutes this stage took, which was more than twice the time taken for the other two sections of the presentation.

Grand Finale – This is the mysterious production of the message on the slate. Ernst used 25% of his account on this part. The elapse time would have been about 5 minutes.

Taking my maximum estimated figures for the elapse times, it gave me:

Initial Description 65% for 23% of the time.
Outdoor Description 10% for 69% of the time.
Finale Description 25% for 8% of the time.

So, from the very minor importance Ernst placed on it, it would appear that the second, outdoor phase was where much of the dirty work was accomplished. The major question the timeline seemed to produce was what were Houdini and Ernst doing while Doyle was absent. Also why waste so much effort [more than half of the overall time] going so far away when Doyle could have merely gone into the next room? As I had nothing written to go on, I was forced to reconstruct as much of this stage as I could from basic magic principles.

As this is the 'HOW' section, an important 'how' to ask was, "How is it possible to solve this part of the slate trick nearly a century after it occurred?" The answer is to not ask "How?", but to ask several "Whys?" First, why write down the message that was to appear, when Doyle could merely have thought of it? The obvious response is that writing it gave Harry, or his covert accomplices, a chance to surreptitiously see it. The usual excuse for doing the writing is that it helps concentrate the subject's mind, if his thoughts are being 'read' by the magician, or it 'assists the spirits' so they can reproduce it. And as well, quite logically, the medium/magician/mindreader wants proof so that the person will not deny what he actually thought, or change his mind.

The second 'Why' to ask is, "Why would Conan Doyle have to walk for three blocks to write a message he could have written in the next room?" The answer is that Houdini needed the time for his hidden assistants to exchange the slate and the cork ball, and then to write the message on the slate. I wrote assistants because I envisage two of them. My reason is because there could only be one attempt at getting it right. If one of them was suddenly taken ill, then the other could carry on. As well, two people would hopefully be quicker than one, and crucially able to check that each had done his job correctly. Although changing the slate and cork could be done as soon as the room was empty, the amount of time available to add the message to the slate was restricted to the last half of the time Doyle was away, i.e. his return journey. So, the further away Sir Arthur went the better it would be for carrying out the necessary 'dirty work'.

The critical question then was, once Sir Arthur set off on his walk, how could Harry obtain Doyle's written message? On the surface, it would appear that there was very little he could do because Ernst remained with Houdini all the time. But, there are two clues to what Harry possibly did. First, Houdini explained to Ernst and Doyle that he had spent most of the winter preparing for that moment, so it must have involved a great amount of groundwork. Second Houdini's trusted assistants Collins and Vickery, not to mention Bess, and his team of undercover agents, were conspicuously absent from Ernst's description. I think it's fairly safe to say that one or more, if not all of them, were involved in finding out what Sir Arthur wrote. So what exactly did they do to learn Conan Doyle's message?

As Houdini must have done, I spent a very long time studying every conceivable technique for secretly gaining knowledge of written information. My many years of investigating the wonderful

Harry Price Library paid off. Once I was fairly clued-up on the subject, I turned to Houdini's own writings. So, why didn't I start with him? Surely it would have saved me a lot of trouble? The answer is no, it wouldn't have! Often when writing their books, magicians of Houdini's era left out the methods they employed, and concentrated on revealing their competitors' secrets! When I finally got around to Houdini, I found that his friend Joseph Dunninger had written a book (Houdini's Spirit Exposes, 1934) based on Harry's own manuscripts. It contained a section on "Methods of Getting Information". Although most of those methods were only applicable to séance rooms, there were two techniques that could have been employed in our case. They fitted in with what I had already found from other sources. The methods were using a pickpocket, and following victims to observe their actions.

Pickpocketing

The use of a pickpocket at first sounded feasible. In fact, most of the existing theories of how Houdini accomplished his slate mystery had someone pick Doyle's pocket. Harry even mentioned the subject in his 1906 book (The Right Way To Do Wrong), when he wrote, "Among the most interesting classes of thieves is the pickpocket..." As any magician will tell you, the public credits a magus with the skills of the pickpocket. People invariably think they are being original when they say, "Hang onto your wallet, he's a magician!" But, there is a vast difference between the entertainer and the thief. The misdirection used by magicians onstage is totally different from that employed by the "dip" in public. A magician can usually get away with the odd mistake in the name of entertainment. A cannon/dip/fingersmith's mistakes are not laughed off!

Ricki Dunn (The Professional Stage Pickpocket, 2006) says three things are necessary to pick a pocket. He lists them as: a reason to get close to the victim, a reason to touch the victim, and a logical reason to divert the attention away from the pocket to be picked. Mark Raffles (The Pickpocket Secrets of Mark Raffles, 1982) states that top criminal pickpockets work in teams, as distinguished from the lone opportunist thief, who takes advantage of a victim's carelessness. A typical team would consist of at least someone to spot the appropriate pocket, someone to distract the victim, the pickpocketer, someone that he quickly hands the item to, and someone to intervene if the pickpocket is caught in the act.

Eddie Joseph's manual on pocket picking for entertainment purposes only (How To Pick Pockets, 1940), explains that nobody ever pickpocketed out in the "wide open spaces". Eddie says it can't be done. It is usually carried out in a crowd, with some ruse like the light-fingered thief accidentally colliding with the victim. The pocket thief has to work under cover of some action. He cannot just walk up to someone and 'snatch' what he wants. Like the magician, he needs misdirection. Raffles says a typical method of misdirection employed by a team is having a pretty young lady drop her handbag in front of the victim. The magician performing stage pickpocketing usually does his removing while having his victim help him in a magic trick. That person is manoeuvred into the best position to help the magician get what he is after. The criminal has to 'case' the scene looking for the best victim to be his 'target'. So, it would have been very difficult for someone to steal the piece of paper from a specific target like Doyle, without him being aware that something was going on.

There is another major problem with picking Sir Arthur's pocket, in addition to the pocket being an inside one [as Ernst explained], once the paper was read it had to be replaced without him being aware it had temporarily left him. Criminal pickpockets do NOT practice replacing items they have removed. Although magicians have loaded spectators' pockets for centuries, the environment is once again totally different from that of the thief. Their 'loading' is done as part of a magic routine. They, like the thieves, do not replace something they have previously removed. Magicians are able to choose the person they wish to work with, the same is true of the pickpocket. Both look for the most suitable candidate. Here Houdini's team would be forced to both 'pluck', and then replace the paper, from someone who was not of their choosing.

Another problem with picking Doyle's pocket was that it would cut down on the time for the message to be added to the slate. A convenient time, and location, for the necessary misdirection to cover the 'lifting' would have to be found as he was walking back. Then the paper would have to be secretly replaced before the message appeared on the slate. The replacement would require a completely different misdirection scenario. After much consideration, I decided that it would be much better to have the necessary 'work' done when Doyle was writing the message. That would maximize the time available for adding it to the slate. Another reason against pickpocketing was that it would be the obvious method the creator of a master detective would be looking for.

Based on all those facts I decided to initially rule out pickpocketing as the main method of obtaining Doyle's written message. But I decided not to eliminate it entirely. Houdini may have kept it as a final 'out' if everything else had failed. If he did, it would be used only as a very last resort because it had to work - there could be no failure. If Sir Arthur even slightly suspected either the act of extracting the paper, or its replacement, then the trick would be a failure. After eliminating pickpocketing as the main information gathering method, I concentrated on the other relevant technique mentioned by Houdini (in Dunninger's book Houdini's Spirit Exposes, 1934), which was following victims to observe their actions.

A Surveillance Team

Observing Sir Arthur had major problems as well. The initial difficulty was that Houdini was with Ernst all the time Doyle was outside. Using this technique would force Harry to completely rely on others to secretly discover Doyle's message. The trouble this raised for me was that many magicians are 'control freaks' ['one-man bands'] due to the secret culture of the magic art. Unlike the theatre, where there are authors, directors, stage crews, and even understudies for the main performers, many magi attempt to do everything themselves. So, I had to see if Houdini was willing to risk the whole outcome of the experiment, by placing the outdoor part entirely into the hands of others. Great artists tend to take chances. Was Harry confident enough to fully trust others? Could he hand over control? Could he let go of the reins? Was he willing to do whatever was necessary to win? I found my answer in Fulton Oursler's autobiography.

Oursler was a member of Houdini's Secret Army [see the "WHO" section for more details]. In his book (Behold This Dreamer, 1964) he described Houdini's appearance at a public hearing of a bill to ban fortune tellers. When asked to testify, Harry challenged any mind reader to do anything he could not duplicate there and then. He held up ten thousand dollars to give them if they could beat him. A society lady accepted Houdini's challenge. She explained that she had taken an out of town, visiting friend to a palmist, who told the lady's husband's name and many other details. That friend was also in the room, and took the stand to challenge Houdini. Harry forced his way through the crowd to the front to face the test, and then handed his money to the committee to hold.

Houdini declared that if he were a faker or swindler he'd pretend to go into a trance and roll his eyes and talk in a hushed voice. But he was not a fraud, so he would look the lady square in the eye and tell her what she wanted to know. He called out her name, her husband's name, where she came from, and her husband's job, just as the palmist had done! The lady burst into tears and admitted that Houdini was completely correct. So how did he accomplish this miracle?

When an astonished Oursler asked Houdini how he had done it, Harry grew angry and said that he wouldn't have waved all that money in the air without taking into account everything that might happen. [This is a key statement! - No pun on handcuffs intended....okay, maybe just a bit.] He explained that he'd engaged three men who knew everyone in the city, and posted each one in a different part of the room. When the challenge came, he looked at his three covert assistants, and got the signal that one of them knew who the lady was. Only then did he accept the challenge. On the way to the front of the room, he 'accidentally' stumbled and fell next to his assistant. As the man helped Harry up, he whispered the information into his ear. [The important parts to me were Houdini 'taking everything into account' and the 'convenient' accident.]

Oursler's story convinced me that Houdini was willing to completely trust others to do the cloak-and-dagger work on which his reputation depended. If you are going to reach the top in your profession you have to take risks, and it seems Houdini was quite willing to do so. But, the most intriguing thing about Oursler's story was that Houdini hired not one, not two, BUT three men, and then placed them in different locations. As he only had one 'shot' at getting it right, he was ready for any eventuality. Once again he was showing his resourcefulness. I believe he used the same technique in the case we are looking at. The street contained inconspicuous bystanders, who were, in fact, his secret army.

So, who were the secret citizens Houdini placed on the street? Houdini's undercover team member Joseph Rinn (Sixty Years of Psychical Research, 1950) gave us a clue to the range of people Harry might have enlisted. Rinn describes mediums using anyone, from a 12 year old child to an old lady, to pump victims for information. If you think about it, it could be anyone who would normally be on the street. Typical ones would be street cleaners, shoe shine boys, and newspaper sellers. They would be stationed inconspicuously along the way. [Of course, a pretty girl, as Harry often used, would certainly be helped out of any predicament by a gentleman like Doyle.]

Finally, as I mentioned in the 'WHO' section, Patrick Culliton (in Walter B. Gibson's The Original Houdini Scrapbook, 1977) revealed that Houdini's number two assistant, James Vickery, often appeared as a police detective, an insane asylum attendant, or whatever official-looking character was needed. So, who better to employ in this undercover role? But Houdini would not just have relied on a single individual. As he said, he took everything into account.

To me, William L. Gresham's 1954 book Monster Midway confirmed this attitude. It revealed several things about Houdini's technique when it came to devising a solution to a magic problem. Although Gresham was referring to escapes, the same logical approach would have been applied to our current puzzle:

1) He was not a man to let a chance go by.
2) He had every possible angle covered.
3) He was a master of misdirection.
4) His technique would be as varied as the circumstances demanded.

Using the Police

It was Conan Doyle himself who gave me a hint to who some of Houdini's clandestine observers could be. Sir Arthur's 1923 book recounted the events of his second visit to America (Our Second American Adventure). In it, he said, "the police seem as smart as ever, but otherwise there is great and obvious deterioration in the city." It seems that within the space of merely a year there was no longer a young New York cop standing on every corner. So what had caused this abrupt change? Surely all the conspicuous law enforcement officers Doyle had noted on his earlier visit weren't there just because of him? [Then again, maybe they were!]

In their book, Ernst and Carrington tell us that Harry always worked hand-in-glove with the police, and they availed themselves of his expert knowledge on more than one occasion. Houdini's police connection was confirmed in a July 4, 1925 letter he wrote to fellow psychic researcher Harry Price. The letter (from the files of The Harry Price Library at The University of London) states:

"You know I am instructor here to the Police Academy to about one hundred and fifty detectives."

So, what better field exercise than to place some of your student detectives on the street to deceive the creator of the fictional detective who regularly made fools of the police! Did Houdini give us other clues that he might have employed the shadowing method? Yes. His 1924 book (A Magician Among the Spirits) has a chapter entitled, "How Mediums Obtain Information". It explains, "As the person leaves the building he is followed by one of the medium's confederates who gathers enough information about him to make the medium's powers convincing when the séance is held." Houdini's boyhood pal, and sometime undercover agent for Harry, Joseph Rinn, confirmed this fake medium strategy (in Sixty Years of Psychical Research, 1950) when he wrote, "Persons who regularly attend spiritualistic séances or meetings are trailed, after they leave, by employees of the medium, who manage to acquire information about them."

Okay, the thought of police detectives helping Houdini outfox the creator of the fictional private detective is a delightful idea, but surely the police are too busy chasing criminals to engage in such foolish activities. I discovered the answer is often they are not! After years of critically observing myself, I've concluded that it's human nature to engage in anything that is interesting and fun, instead of what you are supposed to be doing, especially if it's a little bit naughty, but not illegal. It definitely applies to me. To confirm it you only have to ask my wife, but the following shows that others are also that way inclined.

While the writer T. E. B. Clarke was creating the script for the classic British film 'The Lavender Hill Mob', he approached a Bank of England official for advice on how to steal its gold. Expecting a rebuff, he was completely surprised when a committee was set up to devise the best method. All right, all right, perhaps the Bank staff might play ball, but surely not the New York police of Houdini's day? Well, amateur magician, and Houdini friend, famous novelist Sax Rohmer discovered the answer a few years after Houdini had performed his slate experiment. Cay Van Ash and Elizabeth Sax Rohmer's 1972 biography of Sax Rohmer (Master of Villainy) explained what happened. In May 1935, Rohmer planned to make a quick study of New York crime and police methods, presumably for one of his many Fu Manchu novels. He wasn't quite sure what reaction he would get when he asked the New York Police Department, but it co-operated with "boisterous enthusiasm". Detectives showed up at his hotel and whisked him off to show him the secret life of their Chinatown.

I wondered if this relationship between magicians and the law in New York could still exist today. I guessed the police would consider magicians to be benevolent con men. By their very title, magicians tell you they are going to fool you, and then do so. They take your money up front by selling you a ticket, or pass the hat after a street corner performance. Con men do not warn you. They unlawfully purloin your money, and certainly do not entertain you. From what I've been able to gauge, police officers still enjoy magic. This was substantiated by a Chris Capehart article about his days of doing 'street magic' in New York (Genii, Dec. 2008). He eventually became 'streetwise' when he argued over a prime 'spot' with another magician, and although he was apparently in the right, the cops chased him! The police took the side of the other magician because he "did shows for the cops." Somehow Chris's anecdote reminded me of Houdini.

My hypothesis of Houdini's using police detectives was further strengthened by several examples in Kenneth Silverman's book (Houdini!!!, 1996). Silverman said Houdini cultivated lawmen and stayed abreast of their affairs. He bought tickets to the Policeman's Ball; and, as President of the Society of American Magicians, he arranged a benefit dinner for the widows and orphans of slain policemen. The Commissioner of Police attended that meal. Houdini even owned a New York City Police Department pass that authorized him to cross "all police lines". My favourite quote from Silverman is the statement: "He of course knew his way around police and other law enforcement agencies and was able to enlist their help." [Yes, "enlist their help"!]

277

Here is just a very small sample of many other reports of Harry's link with the police that I came across. Raymond Fitzsimons (Death and the Magician, 1980) says Houdini's 1906 book (The Right Way To Do Wrong) was a disclosure of the methods of criminals, and a public relations exercise to show that Harry was firmly on the side of law and order. 'The Sphinx' reported that Harry Houdini, the King of Handcuffs, was the feature entertainer at the police field day, August 28, 1920, which was held for the benefit of the New York Police Hospital Fund. Bruce Cervon & Keith Burns wrote (Dai Vernon A Magical Life, Vol. 4, 1992), "Houdini's good friend was the Police Commissioner of New York". 'The Sphinx' (July 1925) stated: "Houdini is an instructor at the Police Academy in New York City, giving a three months' series of lectures and demonstrations enlightening the men on how to detect fraudulent mediums and has in his class one hundred and fifty detectives and rookies." William Kalush and Larry Sloman (The Secret Life of Houdini, 2006) even suggested that Houdini acted as an operative for early American and British intelligence agencies.

Potential Problems

Once Houdini, and his 'backroom boys', considered sending Doyle outside, it created a whole list of planning problems. The first would be resource allocation, i.e. how many people to employ on a surveillance team. I wondered if Harry used the easiest and most direct method. Did he have the police cordon off the area so that the only people on the street were in his employment? Although it would make the job of discovering Doyle's message easier, I don't think he did. The main reason is that Harry always used people who would not overact, and who would not talk about their role afterward. [I've mentioned several of them in the "WHO" section.] I believe Houdini used a small, highly trained, elite group of mobile police detectives, backed up by several members of his trusted secret army already located along the route.

All of them would be appropriately dressed for the part they were playing. To avoid an over-zealous 'normal' police officer arresting one of his spies, or stopping one of his vehicles, he would have informed the other policemen near his home that he was mounting an exercise that day.

As I've already pointed out, one of the major problems was the time taken to get the message back to be written on the slate. That's why Doyle was sent three blocks away. Later, when Houdini did a similar mental magic trick for newspaper men [without the slate] he merely went outside the house himself (as described in The Linking Ring, Dec. 1947, and Frank Garcia and George Schindler's Amedeo's Continental Magic, 1974). The great distance Doyle walked was to allow time for the message to be retrieved and written on the slate before Sir Arthur returned.

If Doyle stopped too quickly, the outside team would immediately spring into action, but hopefully he'd follow instructions, and go quite far away. If he returned too quickly, he would need to be delayed to allow time for the message to be added to the slate. Something like a 'real' English cup of tea, before going into the library, would do the trick. The only thing to worry about was creating a false start when he stopped at each corner to cross the road. The obvious answer was to put a policeman on each corner, as Doyle himself had described. I suspect that Houdini tried out this technique by having his police stand on the corners near Doyle's hotel, in the days before the visit to Harry's house. It would certainly have given the undercover assistants practice under live conditions, and made them slowly vanish from Doyle's attention. [One of the major principles of magic is that what you are used to seeing becomes invisible when you accept it as normal.]

One thing Houdini's team must have worried about was inclement weather. Rain, wind and heat would have been on their minds from the start. I grew up in Toronto, Canada. Over the years while investigating this problem, I compared the weather in New York to Toronto, and concluded that the conditions were quite similar.

If the experiment took place on Doyle's first visit in the Spring, then it would not have been too hot. It was late May before we could fry an egg on the Toronto City Hall steps!

As for rain, when I came to England in the early 1960s I found that it did nothing but continuously drizzle. Then it began to change in the mid-1970s. These days the U.K. weather pattern has altered considerably. Whether it's due to the Clean Air Act, global warming, or long-range weather patterns, I'll leave you to decide. As a lad, I remember that it only bucketed down rain in Toronto for a short time and then stopped. The British carried umbrellas, but we locals didn't. If you were caught out in the rain without shelter, you got soaked. I even had a wristwatch, under a coat and shirt, ruined by rainwater. So, Houdini must have stocked up with umbrellas for Doyle, and prayed for sun. What other contingencies they devised we will never know; but, if the weather had been too bad, the option of doing it on another day, with all its logistic problems, must have been considered.

There is one other major thing that Doyle might have accidentally done while outside that would have completely ruined the experiment! What was it? Well, being an Englishman in New York, he had the traffic to contend with. At first that might sound silly because London is a very large cosmopolitan city as well; but, the problem is not the size of the traffic, it's the direction of vehicle flow. The British drive on the other side of the road to North Americans. I became very much aware of it after a near mishap, shortly after arriving in London from Canada in the early 1960s. I quickly learned to look both ways before stepping off the curb. Houdini performed for many years in England, and his Chief Assistant was English, so they too would be well aware of the problem.

Think I'm beginning to overwork my imagination yet again? Well, less than a decade later, another Sir - Sir Winston Churchill - was hit by a car while looking the wrong way when crossing 5th Avenue, and spent eight days in a New York hospital! Now, see why I raised the point? I suspect that this could be another reason why they positioned a policeman on each street corner? Of course, who better to handle any inconvenience, like an obnoxious drunk, than a policeman? [Yes, that drunk who bothered Doyle at the crucial moment just might have been working undercover for Houdini!]

Methods of Detection

I spent a long time pondering over exactly how Houdini might have deployed his surveillance team on the street. Just as I was concluding that I'd have to go to New York to walk Sir Arthur's route, I discovered that I could do it on my computer - thanks to Google. This helped tremendously in visualizing what Doyle had done. [See the "WHERE" section for full details.]

My first question was whether Houdini's outdoor shadowing team had to cover both directions, i.e. right and left of the house. Ernst quoted Houdini as saying, "Sir Arthur, I want you to go out of the house, walk anywhere you like, as far as you like in any direction...". Giving apparent freedom of choice to Doyle would greatly strengthened the view that nothing could possibly have been prearranged. But, was there some way Houdini could subliminally influence Doyle to go a certain way, and thus cut down on the number of people involved? Ernst says that Houdini did not request Doyle to walk in a specific direction, but it was Houdini that sent Doyle out of the house. He was giving the directions. Harry was in charge. He stated (A Magician Among The Spirits, 1924) that he firmly believed in the workings of the subconscious mind. He was a master at subliminal forcing, and would have loved doing it to the creator of the detective who was supposedly a master at detecting it.

As Houdini told his friend Oursler, he never left anything to chance. Just hoping that a right-handed person would go to the right was far too risky. Of course, if the local New York public works department were digging up the sidewalk on the left hand

281

side it would also make setting off on the right much easier than going out into traffic to go around the construction! Magicians, and pseudo-mediums, have done much more devious things than this in the past as psychological forces. I think Harry would have accompanied Sir Arthur to the bottom of the steps and subtlety ushered him in a specific direction. I suspect Houdini told Conan Doyle, as an afterthought, that he did not want anyone accusing him of using a telescope to see his writing, so to go at least 3 blocks away and then go around a corner. While saying this Harry could have pointed in a specific direction to subconsciously control the route. He could also have told Sir Arthur to take himself well out of range of Harry being able to read his mind.

Houdini would also have other subtle ways of forcing Doyle to go in a specific direction. A typical one is that he could only go three blocks in one specific direction [as explained in the "WHERE" section]. Houdini would also have a backup plan in case all those techniques failed, and Doyle insisted on going the opposite way. The people initially following him would be all right. They would just change direction. The problem was with those already planted in fixed positions. I suspect Houdini would cover the first block in both directions, and then quickly transport the other people around the block by car to cover the next blocks if needed.

In the end, I gave up trying to discover exactly what the complete surveillance system was. I grasped that although Hollywood makes it appear easy, surveillance is a very advanced investigative technique that takes a long time to perfect. There would be a great amount of trial and error needed to set up a satisfactory scheme. I also concluded that the experts at undetected monitoring and tracking of others were police detectives. So I decided that Houdini must have challenged his class of detectives to devise the best failsafe, robust, surveillance scheme to fit his requirements. Their goal for allocating their manpower was threefold: first, not to lose sight of Conan Doyle; second, not to let him even suspect he was being followed, and three, to secretly obtain the information that Sir Arthur wrote. The detectives would then have thoroughly scouted the potential route, noting all possible ways Doyle could go, as well as looking for potential problems. Then they would have devised a plan for the most efficient allocation of both their fixed and mobile manpower resources. Their major advantage was that they were on their own patch, i.e. in the city where they normally operated, and not on a lonely road in the country where they would be easily spotted.

Yes, Harry would have repeatedly thoroughly tested their surveillance system by employing others to discover whether they were being followed. If you want to determine whether you are being followed ['flush a tail'] suddenly do something unexpected and illogical, like turning and going in the opposite direction, especially just after you've turned a corner. Having studied detectives' 'tailing/shadowing' methods [okay, okay, after watching too many B films] I can tell you that their tactics would have included, as a minimum, following Doyle on foot using a sophisticated rotating plain-clothes surveillance team. It in turn would be backed up by police in uniforms on each street corner, and as well, be supported by non-conspicuous stationary male/female 'operatives' staked out at regular intervals along the way.

I suspect Houdini augmented those operatives with mobile delivery people who would normally be on the street. Typical vehicle users in that era would be milkmen and breadmen. When I was a lad in Toronto, in the 1950s, we still had our milk delivered by a horse drawn wagon. So, Harry would have both horse and cars to choose from, and probably used both. Typical other mobile people of that era were telegram delivery boys on bicycles. All of those movable operatives, as well as police cars, would be available to return the message to Houdini's house.

The above mobile operatives would also be used in conjunction with door-to-door delivery people who would walk down the street at a regular pace, such as mailmen. Everyone involved would wear the correct clothing and have thoroughly practiced their background/cover stories, so as to blend in, and not be questioned by Houdini's innocent neighbours, or kids playing on the street.

But if challenged they would be able to easily justify being there. Patrick Culliton (Houdini – The Key, 2010) quotes an article by Houdini's detective, Rose Mackenberg, in which she says, "We worked independently and together....we all had prearranged stories." You just have to look at Vacca and Kukol/Williamson in the 'WHO' section, to see what great lengths Houdini went to in hiding his secret army. He made Vacca train to be a barber, and opened a shop for him, just so they could talk together without anyone suspecting. Stationary people, like newspaper sellers and shoeshine boys, would have to remain at their posts so that on Doyle's return journey he would have no cause for suspicion.

The initial problem for those following Doyle on foot ['tailing'] would be having to wait until he came out of the house without drawing attention to themselves. As well as hiding in the basement of Houdini's house, if the sidewalk was being dug up outside the house, they could be the workmen going for a cup of coffee, or inspectors checking out the job. As a very minimum, a three man team would follow Doyle. Two would be spaced out, one behind the other, walking some way behind their 'target', while the third 'operative' would be across the street on foot, parallel but slightly behind him. The nearest one tailing Doyle would then walk past him if he temporarily stopped, for example to tie up a loose shoelace, or was recognised and asked for an autograph. 'Operatives' stationed ahead would replace all three at regular intervals. The far side of street corners would be ideal places for this hand over because those tailing could just go around the corner instead of following Doyle across the intersection. Back-up uniformed policemen would be on each corner to cover any hiccups. Every possible scenario would be repeatedly tested until everyone thoroughly knew the area, and could easily switch tactics if Doyle acted unexpectedly.

Just one of the many things the outdoor team had to be wary of was human pedestrian behaviour. They could not risk becoming distracted or lose their moving target if he did anything unforeseen. They had to continuously gauge how much lead to give Sir Arthur. They had to be near enough to act if he stopped to do his writing [a 'close tail'], but at the same time not close enough to be detected [a 'loose tail']. As well as being able to seamlessly hand on to replacement 'trackers' at regular intervals, they had to work under a wide range of varying conditions. Just one of the problems could be a sudden group of people pouring out of a building between themselves and Doyle. Another would be a disturbance like a fight or a mugging, or even an unexpected downpour of rain.

They needed a higher coverage in areas of greater pedestrian activity ['heavy traffic'], and a lower presence in the not too busy spots, to prevent giving the game away [be 'blown' or 'burnt'], or raising suspicion ['getting warm']. We will never be able to discover what exact procedure they deployed, but we can be absolutely sure that it was repeatedly tested until it was completely successful in every way, with no unnatural movements to give them away.

So, moving on to the second major problem, what did Houdini's outdoor team do to discover Doyle's message, without him being aware of it? Well, their main difficulty was that they had only one chance at it. They had to succeed; failure was not an option. The time available to accomplish it was very restricted, and, unfortunately, completely in Doyle's control. They either had to secretly observe his writing while he was doing it, or in the moment when he had finished and was about to put his paper and pencil away.

My educated guess, based on everything else Houdini did, is that they used two completely different approaches, and employed several techniques operating in tandem for each of them. The initial tactic would be to stealthily glimpse the message as he wrote it. If that failed, plan B would be a ruse to get him to show what he had written without him thinking too much about doing so.

Houdini would have used a standard magician's ploy to prolong the time Doyle took to write the message. It would also have prevented Sir Arthur producing it in a typical Doctor's unfathomable scrawl. Harry would have instructed Doyle to allow the spirits time to assimilate his message. As Doyle was well aware, those paranormal beings reside on another plane from ours, and to make their task of interfacing with us as easy as possible, we have to assist them. How do you do that? You print [not write] each letter clearly and distinctly, and while doing so you also concentrate on each one as you put it down. That would greatly help the spirits, which Sir Arthur completely believed in, to learn his message, AND, also greatly assist Houdini's clandestine assistants, which I believe in!

To help understand this phase of the quest, I made a thorough study of techniques for secretly detecting writing in progress. Ernst helped out greatly by explaining that Houdini had asked Doyle, "Have you a piece of paper in your pocket upon which you can write something?" Harry had obviously seen Sir Arthur scribble down story ideas from time to time, just as Harry himself did for his own magic musings. [Ernst eventually inherited Houdini's notes.] Houdini would also have realized that for Doyle to write on a piece of paper, while on the street, would require a support. His one hand would have to hold the paper while his other did the writing. Try doing that now, and you'll see that what you are writing is readily available to the view of others. The alternative is to rest the paper on a knee or a wall, which makes it even more exposed to view. That is why Houdini asked Doyle if he had a piece of paper. I'm quite sure that if he did not, Houdini would have provided a piece of paper for him to use.

The problem was to get close enough to Sir Arthur to see what he was writing without arousing suspicion. I discovered one method for glimpsing Doyle's writing in an article written by Houdini himself. As it was published around the time of the experiment (Popular Radio, Oct. 1922), it would definitely have been his current thinking at that time. In relating how fake mediums secretly obtained their information, Harry wrote, "Even at a considerable distance an opera glass, properly focused on the spot, serves the purpose of the peep-hole." The 'peep-hole' reminded me of something else I came across. Combining both the 'opera glass' and a 'peep-hole' would be even better.

Bob Gysel, Houdini's undercover/dirty tricks man [see "WHO" section] explained in his magazine (Psychic Fakery No. 2) a method for allowing a mindreader, imprisoned in a packing case, to describe people in the audience. Although Gysel's magazine was undated, I managed to date it to 1923, which was just after the period when the slate test took place. Gysel described using "an extra special German field glass" to see out of one of the air holes in the box. I envisaged someone in a packing case, on the back of a wagon pulled by a horse, slowly following Doyle. Sir Arthur would be under observation through a hole in the box all the while. But what if the angle was bad, preventing the writing from being seen? Well, the man in the box would only be one of a small team of covert observers. All their angles of observation would be greatly improved by 'pencil reading'. They would not have to see the actual written words at all – only the pencil itself during the writing.

Houdini would have taught his outside team the simple conjuring strategy of pencil reading, a technique often used to detect words being written. Do I have proof that Houdini was aware of the art of pencil reading? Yes. Harold Kellock (Houdini His Life Story, 1928) quotes from an autobiographical fragment Houdini left behind, which has a spectator warning another that: "He will read the question by the movements of the top of the pencil." If you watch the end of a pencil, with a bit of practice, you can learn to tell what the person is writing. [In our case printing.] Tony Corinda stated (13 Steps To Mentalism, 1958) that pencil reading could be done from as far away as twenty feet and from the side-on view as well as the front. Uriah Fuller asserted (Confessions of a Psychic, 1975) that it was also possible to become expert at reading just the action of the arm [which would take quite a bit of practice!].

I suspect several of Houdini's people pencil read Doyle's message, and each of their readings was sent to the waiting assistant in Houdini's library. I think it was the logical thing someone who never left anything to chance would do. Each of the pencil readers would try to outdo the others in being successful. They would all think of it as a message obtaining exercise, and would have no idea what Houdini was going to do with their knowledge.

Okay, so what would Houdini's outdoor team do if their furtive methods of glimpsing Doyle's message, while he wrote it, failed, i.e. what was plan B? I envisage a visual signal from each operative if he/she had succeeded. If it did not appear, then an audible signal, such a policeman blowing his whistle, would mean rapidly move into the second phase - direct confrontation. This would need to be done in the few seconds between Doyle finishing his writing and his returning the paper and pencil to his pocket. It would be very tricky as only a tiny window of opportunity would be available. The time would be slightly extended by Doyle looking up to see why the policeman was blowing his whistle. It would require multiple methods, or 'outs', to succeed. Each of those ruses would have to be quite logical, and thus instantly forgotten by Doyle as having no significance, just something that could happen to anyone at any time. In other words, they would employ a subterfuge to get him to reveal his message without him being aware that it was the sole purpose of the incident.

So, how do you do that? [Remember the 'convenient' accident Houdini explained to Oursler?] Well, there are several ways, and they would all need to be ready for instant operation. They would have to be carried out by someone Doyle would not remember later. A natural pretext had to be employed. Some of the possible candidates could be a little old lady needing assistance because she was feeling faint; a pretty girl asking directions; or, returning to our policeman on every street corner, he could intervene. The police officer would ask if he could assist, on the assumption that Doyle was a tourist seeking directions. It was quite normal for tourists to ask a policeman on the beat for information in those days. In fact a typical anecdote involved a lady asking a New York cop how to get to Carnegie Hall. His reply was, "Practice, lady, practice!" That is what Houdini's secret street surveillance team would have done until it was second nature.

The policeman could also question what Doyle was doing. This was definitely not out of the normal for Doyle. I say this because in the early 1960s I had a third floor flat in London's Paddington area. The landlord had promised to eventually repair the doorbell, but, because I couldn't hear the doorknocker, I was forced to make appointments, and then stand outside the front door waiting for my visitors. One day while waiting outside, a London bobby walking past stopped and asked what I was doing there. So, Doyle would not have found a policeman's interrogation unusual.

Another method would be for someone, like a homeless person, to accost Doyle, asking for money. This individual would grab Doyle's arm before he had time to put his piece of paper away. The nearby policeman would then step in and pull the unwanted person off Doyle. Then, if the first person missed the message, the policeman would ask Sir Arthur what he was writing. Would you refuse to tell a policeman?

Does that all sound like I'm stretching my imagination a little too far once more? Well, we all draw on our past, and Harry was no different. His 1906 book (The Right Way To Do Wrong) had a chapter on Beggars and Dead Beats. In it he told us: "There is probably not a reader of this book who has not frequently been accosted on the street corner by the poorly-dressed, shivering wretch who asks in a whining voice for a coin or two to get him a night's lodging." And if you couple that clue with another piece of evidence that I fortunately unearthed, the probability of an 'uncommon' beggar is rather high. So, what was that information?

It was in a letter from Houdini's undercover/dirty tricks man Bob Gysel to Henry Sara. His Aug. 1, 1930 letter [from David E. Price's wonderful magic collection] described how Gysel had made a lot of money while begging for 2 years. His secret was: "My dad made me a solution that I would put on my limb, and every night near a theater I would stand in ragged clothes partly showing the running sore. I would approach a young couple to get a couple of dollars, explaining that I wanted to get to Hot Springs for a cure." Based on what I've discovered about Gysel, I think his primary objective would be to get money out of Doyle - the message would be secondary! After a quick peek at Doyle's words, Gysel could have been immediately grabbed by a conveniently passing policeman and arrested for bothering a distinguished looking gentleman. Gysel would then be rushed off in a police car to get the message to Houdini's waiting assistants in the library.

By the way, the message itself would not have to be seen directly! This would help keep Doyle from becoming suspicious. Houdini revealed a method for secretly gaining sight of a written message in his 1924 book (A Magician Among the Spirits). He explained: "I had a mirror on a rubber elastic....kept it palmed in my hand, with it saw..." Gamblers have used 'shiners' for centuries to glimpse cards as they were being dealt. Yes, the words would be backward in the mirror, but remember we are not talking about writing – Doyle would have been asked by Houdini to print his message, concentrating on each letter as he wrote it.

A good mentalist [mind reading magician] trains himself to read upside down, as well as backward. As a freelance consultant, during my working life I attended many job interviews. The people questioning me usually had the questions they wanted to ask written down in front of them, not realizing I could read upside down! Yes, it was a tremendous advantage. Now can you see how Doyle would not have suspected his message had been read?

There is one other cheeky thing I suspect Houdini may have done. Doyle thought Harry used supernatural powers to accomplish his escapes. So, did Harry exploit that belief? Did he remind Doyle, at the bottom of the outside stairs, that we are surrounded by the invisible entities that mediums contact? Did Houdini then point out that those beings had to be able to see the message if they were to reproduce it on the slate Doyle had hung in the library? Since Conan Doyle would be well away from Houdini, why not suggest Sir Arthur hold the message up so the spirits could easily see it! No, I will never be able to prove he was that bold, but it would fit in very much with what I've learned about him.

Once the message was identified it would be sent back to the basement of Houdini's house to be electrically transmitted to the assistants in the library. I can't resist imagining a speeding police car, siren blaring, carrying the necessary phrase back. As well as the delivery men I mentioned, it would be inconceivable to think that he didn't have several other options working in parallel, such as convenient telephones available along the route, in case there was a problem. In his book (The Right Way To Do Wrong, 1906), Houdini says, "...some of our present day clairvoyants who are appearing before the public, and making use of radio, wireless, induction coils, etc." So, it's possible the information gleaned from Doyle was radioed back to speed up the operation, but it was early days for radio, so that could be subject to failure, which was not an option. Other radio receivers in the area could also pick a radio message and give the game away, so I tend to favour the police car. But, Houdini did write an article for Popular Radio around the time of the slate test, so he was obviously exploring that technique.

The outside scenario would be repeatedly gone over with stand-ins for Sir Arthur. I tend to think those filling in for him would be Houdini's friends who secretly helped him from time to time. They would be rotated in their use so they would still be fresh and not begin to act predictably. I'm inclined to think that he used the police detectives and his hired private detectives to do the shadowing. After all, that was part of their job. The long hours of practice and rehearsal would require complete dedication [or someone to pay for doing it]. They would, in turn, be reinforced with Houdini's more dedicated people, like Gysel, acting as fixed individuals along Doyle's route.

The whole shadowing system, from Doyle leaving the house until his return, would be repeatedly rehearsed because there was no room for error. Every feasible variation would be tried, until any option could be effortlessly switched in or out without the person doing the writing being any the wiser. The task was to get the message back to the library without ever being suspected. They only had one shot at it. As Houdini told Oursler, he would have taken into account everything that might happen.

Each participant had to master his/her part of the scheme. Each would have to have the 'back story' for their character down pat. Each would have to know their 'patch' of the street like the back of their hand. There would be a lot happening around them, but they had to do their work so no one on the street would be wise to them, and think they were up to no good. If all else failed, a flash of a badge and the mention of official business would be used. Each dry run would encounter a different street scene. It was an ongoing learning process because there was no way you could predict exactly what the people you would run into would do. [It was a learning process just like Houdini's private detectives that visited fake mediums went through - with each visit they found new ways to detect frauds.]

Initially, each segment of Doyle's journey would be gone over to devise the best plan for allocating a position for each stationary undercover individual. Then all the parts would be put together in a dress rehearsal that simulated the real thing. Houdini's team would assess what worked, what went wrong, and what unexpected things occurred. Any problems would be thoroughly analysed. The time for returning the message to the house would be recorded, and then they would attempt to beat it. The overall scheme would evolve through a process of constant development, polishing and refining. It could never be perfect because you could not foresee exactly what would happen. Accepting this would allow them to not worry too much, be able to improvise 'on the fly', and reduce the risk of failure.

After much hard work, eventually the whole set-up would reach the stage where it ran like a well-oiled machine, one that could handle any situation encountered without a hitch. The individuals involved were no longer worrying about being discovered by Doyle. They were relaxed and confident, and concentrating on how best to carry out their assignment. If anything unplanned happened they could meet the challenge by seamlessly switching to another method of attack. The team would have reached the point of becoming a cohesive, committed unit that was going to succeed if it was the last thing they ever did.

Their technique had to be perfect, as they would only get one attempt at it. If you blew it, you didn't get a second chance. Yes, it would take a tremendous amount of work to get to that point. As Harry explained, he had spent most of the winter preparing for it, BUT that's why no one would even begin to guess that Houdini had gone to all that trouble. His secret would be safe. My guesswork may not be completely correct in the exact type of surveillance system Harry used, but what he did create proved to be a masterpiece of coordination and planning that would continue to perplex people for nearly a century. The magic Houdini produced here was in making something extremely difficult appear invisible.

Chapter 8: FINAL THOUGHTS

"A conclusion is the place where you got tired of thinking."
- Steven Wright

"It always seems impossible until it's done."
- Nelson Mandela

THE CLEAN-UP

Once Houdini had produced the astonishing message for Ernst and Doyle the trick was not finished. Most people realize there is preparation in presenting a magic trick, but few appreciate that it is not completely over once the magic occurs. Often the magician is left 'dirty', i.e. he has to get rid of incriminating evidence. Again the method of 'clean-up' must be a natural integral part of the performance and pass unnoticed. In fact it must be so natural that if asked later the spectators would not remember anything beyond the magic happening.

So, what had to be cleaned-up after Houdini's slate test? Out on the street, any trace of the secret technique employed to obtain Doyle's words would have vanished once he had gone back into the house. Everyone involved would have dispersed to leave no sign of what had occurred. [I envisage a possible Thank You Party at a later date, with a reminder of the necessity to keep what had happened forever secret.] Restoring Houdini's library to its normal condition would not have been so easy. The apparatus was still 'dirty'. There was the gimmicked slate and special cork ball to eliminate, as well as the jumper connected to the wire in the book. I don't think 'believer' Doyle would have wanted to see

294

anything as he was convinced that what he saw was 'real'; but magician Ernst might wish to give the apparatus a once over. So, what did Houdini do?

I think Harry would have ushered his guests out of the library to more comfortable surroundings. If they were not too willing to move, then a ruse to get them out would be mounted. [Remember that Houdini had the house wired so that everything they said was being carefully monitored.] A typical ploy would be for Bess to arrive and announce that she had just brewed a real English cup of tea for Sir Arthur. Once the room was clear, there were two options. The easy one was to remove and hide everything, and then have a maid announce she had cleaned up the room while they were having tea. [Yes, I checked that the Houdinis had a live in maid.] But I think the other option would have appealed more to Houdini. What was it? It was adding a 'clincher'! If you are going to blow away a fellow magician, then go all the way - 'don't take any prisoners'!

I think that once the room was clear the hidden assistant came out again, and changed everything back to exactly the way it had previously been. Yes, it would mean writing the message on the original slate exactly as it was on the gimmicked slate, but miracles are made from little details like that. Of course, when it was done, Houdini would have found a way to allow Ernst to sneak off to investigate the library. So, what if Ernst did not take the bait, and remained with his two clients?

Houdini would then have made an excuse for them to return to the library. There he'd ask Ernst and Doyle to remove the slate while he tidied up the table that still had the container of ink on it. Can you imagine the look on Ernst's face when he examined the slate, and found it was just what Houdini had said it was – an ordinary everyday slate!

PERSUASION

Another final thought involves Houdini's powers of persuasion. My initial thinking was that Houdini was able to effortlessly show that he was completely mystified by the contents of the message because he did not know what Doyle had written until it appeared on the slate. Then I wondered if Houdini knew the meaning of the written message. He would certainly be familiar with the first part of the phrase (mene tekel) as that was the name of a special deck of cards. Typically, a magic experiment using the mene tekel cards appeared in 'The Sphinx' magic magazine around the time of the test (Nov. 1923). As a former "Kard King" Houdini would have been quite at home with that pack. But did he know the religious significance of the statement?

I found the answer to that question in a lecture Houdini gave in 1922, (printed in The Sphinx, Oct. 1936). He said, "We have records for five generations that my direct fore-fathers were students and teachers of the Bible and.... I recall when only a child, I used to devour the biblical tales of old." There is further indication that Houdini was aware of the meaning of Doyle's message. Henry Ridley Evans, a Baltimore journalist, magic historian, and Houdini friend, explained the meaning of that Biblical prophecy in 'The Sphinx' for November 1920. Kenneth Silverman's book (Houdini!!!, 1996) explains that Houdini worked with Evans on the latter's magic history book, proof reading and commenting on each page in great detail.

So, this leads me to ask, "Did Houdini subconsciously plant the phrase in Conan Doyle's mind beforehand?" He was an expert at subtly suggesting something that someone would think was his or her own idea. As the slate was being hung up Houdini may have hinted at the subject. Yes, it's a mere conjecture, which I'll leave you to ponder over.

REVEALING THE SECRET

It is just possible that Houdini was going to reveal to fellow magicians how he had accomplished the slate mystery. Why do I say that? Well, the magazine of The Society of American Magicians (M-U-M) for Jan. 1923 suggested it. Under the heading "Slate Writing", it explained that the Dec. 1922 meeting of The Society was to have been a discussion of slate writing. [If you accept my April/May 1922 date from the 'WHEN' section, then this was just a few months after the performance.] The program had been specifically planned by President Houdini, "but unfortunately his enforced absence interrupted its fulfilment." It seems that "his speedy departure for the West interfered with the delegation of his intent, so the entertainment was of necessity extemporaneous, and not as had been planned." So, would Houdini have explained all? [By the way, if you don't accept my 1922 date, but prefer the 1923 one, then was he going to discuss a work in progress and solicit input from fellow experts? – But then Ernst was a member....] Either way, again we'll never know.

THE RINN CONNECTION

After investigating several pieces of circumstantial evidence involving Joseph Rinn [Houdini's boyhood friend and sometime hidden assistant], I began to form the opinion that Rinn was involved in the slate test, or at the very least was aware of its details. Businessman, magician and psychic researcher Rinn [see WHO Section for details] had included two pieces of information in his 1950 book (Sixty Years of Psychical Research) that caught my eye. The first was the fact that Houdini had wired up every room in his house to overhear what was said while he was absent. Rinn's second interesting item concerned an article he had written for the New York Herald (Oct. 18, 1923). In it he talked of a medium producing a message by the use of a chemical preparation.

He said she could have used heat to bring out the chemical. That alerted me to look a bit further into Rinn's activities, and I unearthed Zeno!

The Sphinx for Dec. 1922 announced that a new crime mystery play written/produced by Joseph F. Rinn would open in December. It was to include revelations of how fraudulent mediums' tricks worked. The Jan. issue gave a short outline of the play's plot. It involved a gang of bandits guided by a master crook, the mysterious "Zeno", a murder, and a séance in a sealed room. But the part of the explanation that fascinated me read: "A wireless outfit is later discovered in a garret of the adjoining house wired so completely with electromagnets that tables could be turned, messages written on slates, etc." Yes, it sounded a lot like my theory of how Houdini's slate test was accomplished. I had to find out if Houdini was involved in the play in any way.

When Rinn's anti-spiritualistic mystery played Chicago, the local Assembly of the Society of American Magicians put on a banquet for the author and the actors. Among those attending was "our most illustrious Harry Houdini." So, Houdini was connected, but did he have any input to the play? I found my answer in eccentric illusion builder/designer/mechanic and stage manager Guy Jarrett's 1936 book (Magic and Stagecraft). Jarrett, who didn't usually have anything nice to say about magicians, called Rinn, "a great guy." Jarrett later described an argument he had with Rinn when Houdini had advised him that one of Jarrett's illusions for the play was dangerous. So, Houdini was definitely advising on a play that included wires, electromagnets, and messages on slates.

In the play, I think Houdini was recycling what he had already used. This was not the first time. Where else had he done it? William Kalush and Larry Sloman's 2006 book (The Secret Life of Houdini) revealed that Houdini had used the idea of his wired up house in one of his films. The opening scene of Houdini's film, 'The Master Mystery', has Department of Justice agent Quentin Locke [Houdini] eavesdropping on his corrupt boss via a hidden "Dictophone". So, it seems that Houdini couldn't resist using secret methods in different ways, and must have advised Rinn on how he had fooled Doyle. [For the record: a) Jim Steinmeyer's 1981 annotated reprint of Jarrett's book says Rinn's "show" had a respectable run of 89 performances; b) Houdini's film 'Master Mystery' was the first appearance of a robot in a film.]

JUSTIFICATION

Okay, it's finally time to defend my conjecture of how Houdini fooled his guests. Perhaps the first criticism would be, if my idea is correct, why didn't someone else come up with the premise before I did? Other investigators had many years to research the problem before I came along, but in creating their theories they became victims of their 'internal biases'. Just as Doyle did, they suffered from overconfidence. They believed their abilities were more than adequate to crack the mystery without doing a great amount of research. Once they formulated their hypotheses they accepted them as being correct, and stopped investigating. Many even deliberately distorted Ernst's description to fit their theories, stating that he was obviously wrong!

The other error people made was to assume that Houdini would not go to all the trouble he did for a single performance. They ignored the fact that Houdini had said that he had been working on it for many months. Do modern conjurors have the time and patience to do something similar? The answer is yes. Teller, the silent partner of the famous magic duo, Penn and Teller, gave his version of the principles magicians employ (in Smithsonian magazine, March 2012). One of them was to "Make the secret a lot more trouble than the trick seems worth." He added that, "you will be fooled by a trick if it involves more time, money, and practice than you [or any other sane onlooker] would be willing to invest." Teller than described a trick they had spent many weeks preparing for a single performance on a TV talk-show. He ended by saying, "More trouble than the trick was worth? To you, probably. But not to magicians."

As I've said, I initially ignored the solutions others had put forward for the slate test, so that I would not be biased in my approach. But once I had reached the point where I was reasonably sure I had discovered Houdini's secret I gave them a once over.

The method usually put forward by others as being the correct one, is the guesswork of Milbourne Christopher. I decided to go through his hypothesis one point at a time. Christopher wrote: "An assistant in the room adjacent to Houdini's library had opened a small panel in the wall and extended the rod with a magnet through it. The ball on the slate had an iron center, of course." Christopher's idea, unfortunately, is not very practical. In Silverman's book, between pages 308 and 309, is a section of pictures. One of these pictures shows Houdini in his library. The walls are all lined with shelves of books. Even if a panel of fake books could be opened, the rod would have had to be several yards long. This would have made it very unwieldy and too long to operate realistically. It also would have been seen by either Conan Doyle or Ernst as the slate was swinging in the middle of the room. Additionally, the writing would have had to be done in reverse letters. Christopher also did not explain how the ball on the slate had an iron core, after Conan Doyle had his choice of any one to cut in half, and another to put in the inkwell.

Christopher goes on to say: "Ernst had not remembered that when Doyle returned to the room, after writing words outdoors, Houdini had checked to make sure the slip of paper on which Doyle had written was folded, then immediately returned it to his friend. Before doing so, the magician had switched slips. While Doyle was busy retrieving the ball from the inkwell and taking it to the board, Houdini read the words. His conversation cued his hidden assistant...."

This also is highly suspect. Ernst remembered which hand Conan Doyle held the paper in when writing the message. Surely he would have recalled Houdini handling the paper especially when there did not seem to be a logical reason for doing so. As an expert magician, Ernst would also have been looking for a switch. Another point against Christopher's conjecture is that Houdini would not have known which way Conan Doyle had folded the paper, or had an exact duplicate of the type of paper on hand. Houdini's dummy piece of paper would have had to be folded in exactly the same way as Conan Doyle's paper or it would have given the game away. And finally, why wouldn't Ernst spot Houdini reading the message?

Christopher said: "His conversation cued his hidden assistant." Any code Houdini used would have had to spell out each letter of the message due to Conan Doyle's message not being an English sentence. This meant that a specific code word had to be used for each letter of the message [with a possible "repeat the previous word" cue.] This is not just a deduction, because I managed to locate Houdini's code. I did not really expect to find it, but after a substantial search I did. It was explained in Joseph Dunninger's book, "Inside The Medium's Cabinet." Dunninger said the code had appeared in Harold Kellock's biography of Houdini. It was the book Bess Houdini had commissioned soon after her husband's death. Kellock's book was dedicated to Houdini's dearest friend, Ernst.

Kellock wrote that the Houdini's had used the code for thirty-three years. Although Kellock explained the number transmission system he did not give the method for spelling words. Dunninger explained the technique. [I will not repeat it here to thwart possible allegations that I exposed magic techniques not having a direct bearing on my thesis.] I am quite confident that Ernst, a knowledgeable conjuror and Houdini's dearest friend, would have been very much aware if Harry had started using an artificial language. If you doubt my claim, please look up the code, and try to devise a few sentences [ones that you would normally use] to spell out Conan Doyle's Biblical message. For the above reasons I felt that I had to reject Christopher's account as a probable solution for Houdini's method.

I suspect Houdini eventually changed his mind, and decided to tell Doyle how he had accomplished his slate test, but it was too late. Doyle was already convinced Houdini had super powers and would not be dissuaded. What do I base that assumption on? Well, Ernst's book quotes a May 10, 1923 entry in Houdini's "Day-book": "I told Sir Arthur that I had a number of extraordinary spirit slates of a mechanical order and that I would allow him to examine the slate thoroughly, and that I thought it would be next to impossible to discover the method. He did not seem greatly interested in slate writing." This would seem to infer that during the experiment Houdini might have actually given Ernst and Doyle the mechanical slate to inspect, and not, as I've inferred, later have replaced the ordinary one with the special slate, as I've stated.

There is no way to know for sure whether the examined slate was the electric one. If the construction of the fake slate had been as near the real thing as possible, then Doyle and Ernst could have been allowed to see it. That would have cut down on the time needed to connect the hooks to the power supply, as well as writing the message with the chemical solution. After much deliberation, I'm inclined to think Houdini had the examined slate switched for the gimmicked one. My reasoning is that if Doyle or Ernst damaged the slate by dropping it during the examination, the trick would probably have been over at that point. This would also be why Doyle was sent so far away [3 blocks] so as to create time for the switch.

Although using the false slate initially would have solved any problems with hanging a duplicate slate, in exactly the same manner as the original; it would raise the problem of writing the hidden message on a hanging, swinging slate without the invisible ink running down the slate surface. One way around that problem would be to use a flap of thin slate, the size of the writing surface. This was a common method used by both pseudo-mediums, and magicians. It could be written on while being held horizontally, and then fitted into the frame of the hanging slate. In the end, I think the team would have experimented with using both a mechanical and a non-mechanical slate at the examination stage, and then chosen the best solution.

THE GREATEST SECRET

I have left the greatest magic secret of all until the end. So, what is it? It's the fact that magic secrets are unimportant. The concealed method is nothing. Faked apparatus, sleight of hand, and misdirection are all simply tools. There was nothing really new or outstanding about the methods Houdini used. In the main, his hidden assistants did all the physical work. The real secret of his experiment was his presentation – how he interacted with his two guests. By offloading the crucial, covert work to his assistants, much of the pressure was taken off Houdini. He could then subconsciously put all his conviction into stressing that his apparatus and actions were what they purported to be, i.e. his body language would be perfect. There would be no subliminal 'tells'.

Earlier I mentioned Robert-Houdin's edict that a magician was an actor playing the part of a wonderworker, and explained how magic differed from the legitimate stage. Well, I left out one thing at that time. It was the fact that in the theatre the actor's script was more important than the actor. The actor could be replaced. Here the magician was more important than his tricks. Would-be magicians present puzzles to show how clever they are. Top magicians can make reading the phone book entertaining. It was not Houdini's unusual mechanical devices, or his assistants' concealed input, that created a masterpiece of magic that completely astonished his illustrious visitors. What caused the real magic to happen in their minds was Houdini's dynamic personality and his artistry, coupled with his brilliant showmanship, nerve, and total belief that he was actually performing real magic. The secret all along was not the magic; it was Houdini.

So there you have it, my pursuit is over. Thank you for joining me on my quest. But I can't resist asking if you think I've provided adequately strong circumstantial evidence to establish my theory? Can I now say "Gotcha Houdini"? I'll leave it to you to decide. But if you agree that I've succeeded, then can I also say "Gotcha" as well to Sir Arthur, because Houdini wasn't his unconscious medium after all, merely a magical legend using 'normal' trickery. But, there's one interesting thing I realized along the way that I must end on. What is it?

Hopefully you'll recall how away back at the very beginning I talked of Juan Ponce de Leon's quest for the fountain of youth. Well, I believe that both Houdini and Conan Doyle's 'fountain of youth' was spiritualism. Sadly, because they were approaching it from different directions, it destroyed their friendship. Of course, they both were my fountain of youth. Now that my quest is over I need a new one. Hmm, let's see.....

BIBLIOGRAPHY

It would take a book the size of this one to catalogue all the thousands of items examined during the many years of research on this quest. So, to save a few trees, the following lists only the books, magazines and newspapers, that were specifically referred to in the text.

a) General newspapers and magazines. (Specific dates are given in the text.):

The American Electrician (U.S.A.)
American Mercury (U.S.A.)
Autograph Collector (U.S.A.)
The Billboard (U.S.A.)
Black And White Budget (U.S.A.)
Chicago Examiner (U.S.A.)
Daily Express (London, U.K.)
The Buffalo Times (U.S.A.)
Liberty Magazine (U.S.A.)
Light (U.K.)
The New York Times (U.S.A.)
The New York Herald Tribune (U.S.A.)
The Occult Review (U.K.)
Popular Radio (U.S.A.)
Proceedings of the Society for Psychical Research (U.K.)
The Readers Digest (U.S.A.)
Skeptical Inquirer (U.S.A.)
Smithsonian (U.S.A.)
The Strand Magazine (U.K.)
The World's Fair (U.S.A.)

b) Magazines published specifically for magicians. (Applicable dates appear in the text.):

Abracadabra (U.K.)
The Bat (U.S.A.)
The Conjurers' Monthly Magazine (U.S.A.) [Editor Houdini]
Conjuring Arts Bulletin (U.S.A.)
The Conjurors' Magazine (U.S.A.)
The Demon Telegraph (U.K.)
Genii (U.S.A.)
The Jinx (U.S.A.)
The Linking Ring (U.S.A.)
M-U-M (U.S.A.)
The Magazine of Magic (U.K.)
The Magic Circular (U.K.)
The Magic Key (U.S.A.)
Magic Magazine (U.S.A.)
The Magic Wand (U.K.)
The Magical Spectator (U.K.)
The Magician Monthly (U.K.)
Magicol (U.S.A.)
Magigram (U.K.)
Mahatma (U.S.A.)
The New Tops (U.S.A.)
The Osarian Magazine (U.S.A.)
The Pallbearers Review (U.S.A.)
Psychic Fakery (U.S.A.)
The Sphinx (U.S.A.)
The Wizard (U.K.)
The Yankee Magic Collector (U.S.A.)

c) Books published both exclusively for magicians, and for the general public, that were either mentioned in the text, or were a great help:

Abbott, David P. - Behind The Scenes With The Mediums, 1907.
Abrams, Max - Annemann, 1992.

Alfredson, J. & G. Daily - A Bibliography of Conjuring Periodicals in English, 1986.

Anon. - Revelations of a Spirit Medium, 1891 (see also Harry Price).

Bamberg, David - Illusion Show, 1988.

Bird, J. Malcolm - Margery the Medium, 1925.

Booth, John - Forging Ahead In Magic, 1939.

Booth, John - Psychic Paradoxes, 1984.

Boston, George L. & Robert Parrish - Inside Magic, 1947.

Bowyer, J. Barton [Bart Whaley] - Cheating, 1982.

Brandon, Ruth - The Life And Many Deaths Of Harry Houdini, 1993.

Burger, Eugene - Spirit Theater, 1986.

Burger, Eugene - The Experience Of Magic, 1989.

Burlingame, H. J. - Leaves From Conjurers' Scrap Books, 1891.

Cane, Melville - The First Firefly, 1974.

Carrington, Hereward - The Physical Phenomena of Spiritualism, 1920.

Cervon, Bruce & Keith Burns - Dai Vernon A Magical Life, Vol.4, 1992.

Chislett, T. H. - Spirits in the House, 1949.

Christopher, Milbourne - Houdini: The Untold Story, 1969.

Christopher, Milbourne - Houdini: A Pictorial Life, 1976.

Christopher, Milbourne - Seers, Psychics and ESP, 1970.

Christopher, Milbourne - The Illustrated History of Magic, 1973.

Cochran, Charles B. - The Secrets of a Showman, 1925.

Coleman, Earle J. - Magic: A Reference Guide, 1987.

Conan Doyle, Sir Arthur - Rodney Stone, 1896.

Conan Doyle, Sir Arthur - The Great Boer War, 1900.

Conan Doyle, Sir Arthur - The Lost World, 1912.

Conan Doyle, Sir Arthur - Our American Adventure, 1923.

Conan Doyle, Sir Arthur - Our Second American Adventure, 1923.

Conan Doyle, Sir Arthur - The History of Spiritualism, 1926.

Conan Doyle, Sir Arthur - The Edge of the Unknown, 1930.

Corinda - 13 Steps To Mentalism, 1958.

Culliton, Patrick – Houdini: The Key, 2010

Dawes, Edwin A. - Stanley Collins, 2002.

Dingwall, Eric J. - How to go to a Medium, 1927.

Dunn, Ricki - The Professional Stage Pickpocket, 2006.

Dunninger, Joseph - Houdini's Spirit Exposes, 1934.

Dunninger, Joseph - Inside The Medium's Cabinet, 1935.

Dunninger, Joseph - Magic and Mystery, 1967.

Erdnase, S. W. - Artifice Ruse and Subterfuge at the Card Table, 1902.

Ernst, Bernard M. L. & Hereward Carrington - Houdini and Conan Doyle, 1932.

Findlay, James B. - Second Collectors Annual, 1950.

Fitzkee, Dariel - The Trick Brain, 1944.

Fitzsimons, Raymond - Death and the Magician, 1980.

Frikell, Samri [Fulton Oursler] - Spirit Mediums Exposed, 1930.

Fuller, Uriah [Martin Gardner] - Confessions of a Psychic, 1975.

Fuller, Uriah [Martin Gardner] - Further Confessions of a Psychic, 1980.

Garcia, Frank & George Schindler - Amedeo's Continental Magic, 1974.

Gibson, Walter B. - Houdini's Escapes, 1930.

Gibson, Walter B. - Houdini's Magic, 1932.

Gibson, Walter B. - The Original Houdini Scrapbook, 1977.

Goldston, Will - Sensational Tales of Mystery Men, 1929.

Goldston, Will - Great Magicians' Tricks, 1931.

Goldston, Will - Secrets of Famous Illusionists, 1933.

Goldston, Will - Who's Who In Magic, 1934.

Goldston, Will - Great Tricks Revealed, 1935.

Gresham, William Lindsay - Monster Midway, 1954.

Gresham, William Lindsay - Houdini: The Man Who Walked Through Walls, 1959.

Hades, Micky - The Make-Up of Magic, 1962.

Hahne, Nelson C. & Joe Berg - Here's Magic, 1930.

Hibberd, David - Chronicle of Magic 1900 - 1999, 2003.

Hjortsberg, William - Nevermore, 1994.

Hoffmann, Professor - Modern Magic, 1876.

Hoffmann, Professor - Later Magic, 1904.

Hopkins, Albert A. - Magic: Stage Illusions and Scientific Diversions..., 1898.

Hopkins, Nevil Monroe - Twentieth Century Magic, 1898.

Houdini, Harry - The Right Way To Do Wrong, 1906.

Houdini, Harry - The Unmasking of Robert-Houdin, 1908.

Houdini, Harry - A Magician Among the Spirits, 1924.

Hull, Burling Gilbert Galt - Original Slate Secrets, 1929.

James, William - The Will To Believe...., 1896.

Jarrett, Guy - Magic and Stagecraft, 1936.

Jastrow, Joseph - Error And Eccentricity In Human Belief, 1935.

Jones, E. H. - The Road To En-Dor, 1920.

Jones, Kelvin - Conan Doyle and the Spirits, 1989.

Joseph, Eddie - How To Pick Pockets, 1940.

Kalush, William & Larry Sloman - The Secret Life of Houdini, 2006.

Keene, M. Lamar - The Psychic Mafia, 1997.

Kellock, Harold - Houdini: His Life Story, 1928.

Lett, Steve – Lett's Make Original Magic, 1989.

Lewis, Eric C. - Magical Mentality, 1934.

Lippy Jr., John D. and Edward L. Palder, Modern Chemical Magic, 1959.

Loomis, Bob - The Quest For The Ultimate Secret, 1993.

Marks, David & Richard Kammann - The Psychology of the Psychic, 1980.

Maskelyne, Nevil & David Devant - Our Magic, 1911.

Mulholland, John - Quicker Than the Eye, 1932.

Murchison, Carl - The Case For and Against Psychical Belief, 1927.

Nelms, Henning - Magic and Showmanship, 1969.

Orrin, J. F. - Put It Over, 1933.

Oursler, Fulton - The Greatest Story Ever Told, 1949.

Oursler, Fulton - Behold This Dreamer!, 1964.

Pavel - The Magic of Pavel, 1981.

Price, Harry - Leaves From a Psychist's Case-book, 1933.

Price, Harry - Fifty Years Of Psychical Research, 1939.

Price, Harry & Eric J. Dingwall - Revelations of a Spirit Medium, 1922 (reprint).

Proskauer, Julien - The Dead Do Not Talk, 1946.

Raffles, Mark - The Pickpocket Secrets of Mark Raffles, 1982.

Rapp, Augustus - The Life and Times of Augustus Rapp, 1959.

Rauscher, William V. - The Great Raymond, 1996.

Rauscher, William V. - The Houdini Code Mystery, 2000.

Rinn, Joseph F. - Sixty Years of Psychical Research, 1950.

Rinn, Joseph F. - Searchlight On Psychical Research, 1954.

Robinson, William E. - Spirit Slate Writing and Kindred Phenomena, 1898.

Scot, Reginald - The Discoverie of Witchcraft, 1584.

Severn, Bill - Bill Severn's Guide to Magic as a Hobby, 1979.

Sharpe, Sam - Neo-Magic, 1946.

Sharpe, Sam - The Magic Play, 1976.

Shimeld, Thomas J. - Walter B. Gibson and The Shadow, 2003.

Silverman, Kenneth - Houdini!!!, 1996.

Stashower, Daniel - Teller of Tales, 1999.

Tabori, Paul - Pioneers Of The Unseen, 1972.

Tarbell, Harlan - The Tarbell Course In Magic, 1978,

Van Ash, Cay & Elizabeth Sax Rohmer - Master of Villainy, 1972.

Waldron, Daniel - Blackstone: A Magician's Life, 1999.

Walker, Mark - Key Bending, no date (1979?)

Walker, Barbi & Robert Seaver - The P & L Book, 1992.

Wass, Verrall - Astound Your Audience, 1936.

Whaley, Bart - The Encyclopedic Dictionary of Magic, 2000.

Whaley, Bart - Who's Who In Magic, 1990, 1991.

Wilker, Peter - The Creation of Magic, 1991.

Wilson, Edmund - The Shores of Light, 1952.

Wissner, Wayne - Houdini & Gysel, 2013.

Richard Wiseman - Deception and Self-Deception, 1997.

Wiseman, Richard & Robert Morris - Guidelines For Testing Psychic Claimants, 1995.

Wonder, Tommy & Stephen Minch - The Books of Wonder [2 vols.], 1996.

ACKNOWLEDGEMENTS

Instead of declaring that I was out of my tiny little mind, many very kind people helped me with my quest. It would certainly not have been completed without them. Those "magic nuts" mentioned in the text are David Hibberd, Peter Lane, Max Maven, the late David E. Price, Daniel Stashower and the late Alan Wesencraft. An especial thank you goes to Richard Wiseman for the foreword, and both Chris Brinson and Brian Lead for their encouragement. All the others not specifically mentioned are also thanked very, very much, especially the members of the Association of International Magical Spectators.

APPENDIX

FURTHER READING

Nothing stays the same. Ideas and findings continuously evolve, so I've tended to list the following items in published date order. The purpose was to enable you to select a period and discover the thoughts on the subject that existed at that time.

1) HARRY HOUDINI:

a) Books, Pamphlets & Magazines Written and Edited by Houdini:

These are just a very few of the more than 200 items Houdini authored [along with his various secretaries and ghost writers].

[i] Magazines Edited by Houdini [in date order]:

The Conjurers' Monthly Magazine, 1906-08.
M-U-M, 1917-26 [Journal of the Society of American Magicians].

[ii] Just some of The Many Books and Pamphlets Written by Houdini [in date order]:

Magic Made Easy, 1898.
The Right Way to Do Wrong, 1906.
The Unmasking of Robert-Houdin, 1908.
Handcuff Secrets, 1909.
Miracle Mongers and Their Methods, 1920.
Magical Rope Ties and Escapes, 1921.
Houdini Exposes the Tricks used by the Boston Medium
        "Margery", 1924.
A Magician Among the Spirits, 1924.

b) Biographical Works on Houdini [in date order]:

Below are just a very, very small sample of the many, many books written on Houdini and his exploits. [Those I've listed are usually considered to be the major works on him, and again are in date order]:

Kellock, Harold - Houdini: His Life Story, 1928.
Cannell, J. C. - The Secrets of Houdini, 1931.
Ernst, Bernard M. L. & Hereward Carrington - Houdini and Conan Doyle, 1932.
Sardina, Maurice - Where Houdini Was Wrong, 1950.
Williams, Berly & Samuel Epstein - The Great Houdini, 1950.
Gibson, Walter B. & Morris Young - Houdini on Magic, 1953.
Gresham, William Lindsay - Houdini: The Man Who Walked Through Walls, 1959.
Kendall, Lace - Houdini: Master of Escape, 1960.
Christopher, Milbourne - Houdini: The Untold Story, 1969.
Christopher, Milbourne - Houdini: A Pictorial Life, 1976.
Gibson, Walter B. - The Original Houdini Scrapbook, 1976.
Meyer, Bernard C. - Houdini: A Mind in Chains, 1976.
Randi, James & Bert Sugar - Houdini: His Life and Art, 1976.
Henning, Doug & Charles Reynolds - Houdini: His Legend and His Magic, 1977.
Fitzsimons, Raymund - Death and the Magician, 1980.
Lead, Brian & Roger Woods - Houdini: The Myth Maker, 1987.
Brandon, Ruth - The Life and Many Deaths of Harry Houdini, 1993.
Weltman, Manny - Houdini: Escape into Legend, 1993.
Silverman, Kenneth - Houdini!!!: The Career of Ehrich Weiss, 1996.
Bell, Don - The Man Who Killed Houdini, 2005.
Kalush, William & Larry Sloman - The Secret Life of Houdini, 2006.
Culliton, Patrick - Houdini: The Key, 2010

c) Bibliographies of items on and by Houdini:

For much more information than given above see [in date order]:

* The "Opinionated Bibliography" in Gresham's 1959 above book.
* Manuel Weltman's articles in the Oct., Nov., and Dec. 1967 issues of 'Genii' magazine.
* Arthur Moses's unique grouping of books, and magazine articles, containing such categories as fiction, poetry, and cookbooks(!), in the Oct. 1990 issue of 'The Linking Ring' magazine.
* Stephen Forrester's seven page article, "Houdini In Popular Magazine and Contemporary Newspapers", in 'The Yankee Magic Collector #5', 1992.
* Arthur Moses's, Houdini Periodical Bibliography, 2006, which includes articles by or about Houdini in magic magazines and for the general public, from 1898 to 2005, but does not include newspaper articles.
* The incredible Ask Alexander database of The Conjuring Arts Research Center, containing searchable material assembled for Kalush & Sloman's 2006 book. The database is now being constantly updated. Available online at www.conjuringarts.org.

2) SIR ARTHUR CONAN DOYLE:

'Conan Doyle' is a double or compound surname. Not all authors realize that. So, when seeking information on him, look in indexes under both 'Conan' and 'Doyle'. I have often used 'Doyle' alone in the book to save on paper and rescue a few trees from the woodsman's axe.

a) Books, Pamphlets & Magazine Articles Written by Conan Doyle:

[i] Some of the Many Magazine Articles:

The Adventures of Sherlock Holmes, The Strand Magazine, 1891-3.

[ii] Just Some of the Many Books Written by Conan Doyle [in date order]:

A Study in Scarlet, 1887.
Rodney Stone, 1896.
Micah Clarke, 1889.
The Sign of the Four, 1890.
The White Company, 1890.
The Exploits of Brigadier Gerard, 1895.
The Great Boer War, 1900.
The Hound of the Baskervilles, 1902.
Sir Nigel, 1906.
The Lost World, 1912.
The Poison Belt, 1913.
Wanderings of a Spiritualist, 1921.
Memories and Adventures, 1924.
The History of Spiritualism, 1926.
The Edge of The Unknown, 1930.

b) Some of the Biographical Works on Conan Doyle [in date order]:

Lamond, J. - Arthur Conan Doyle, 1931.
Pearson, Hesketh - Life of Arthur Conan Doyle, 1943.
Carr, John Dickson - The Life of Sir Arthur Conan Doyle, 1949.
Nordon, Pierre - Conan Doyle, 1967.
Jones, Kelvin I. - Conan Doyle and the Spirits, 1989.
Booth, Martin - The Doctor and The Detective, 1997.
Stashower, Daniel - Teller of Tales: The Life of Arthur Conan Doyle, 1999.
Lycett, Andrew - Conan Doyle: the Man Who Created Sherlock Holmes, 2007.
Lellenberg, Jon & Daniel Stashower, Charles Foley – Arthur Conan Doyle: a Life in Letters, 2007.

3) BOTH HOUDINI AND CONAN DOYLE:

Three major books written on the "strange friendship" between Houdini and Doyle are:

Ernst, Bernard M. L. & Carrington, Hereward - Houdini and Conan
    Doyle, 1932.
Polidoro, Massimo – Final Séance, 2001.
Sandford, Christopher – Masters of Mystery, 2011.

4) SPIRITUALISM:

If you wish to undertake a more detailed search for information, for and against modern spiritualism, then this section is a good place to start.

a) Books [in date order]:

Maskelyne, John Nevil - Modern Spiritualism, 1876.
Anon. - Confessions of a Medium, 1882.
Seybert Commission - Preliminary Report....to Investigate Modern
    Spiritualism, 1887.
Davenport, Reuben Briggs - The Death Blow to Spiritualism,
    1888.
Anon. - Revelations of a Spirit Medium, 1891.
Truesdell, John W. - The Bottom Facts Concerning the Science of
    Spiritualism, 1892.
Evans, Henry Ridgely - The Spirit World Unmasked, 1897.
Podmore, Frank - Modern Spiritualism, 1902.
Carrington, Hereward - The Physical Phenomena of Spiritualism,
    1907.
Abbott, David P. - Behind the Scenes With the Mediums, 1907.
Hill, Arthur J. - Spiritualism: Its History, Phenomena, and
    Doctrine, 1919.
McCabe, Joseph - Spiritualism: A Popular History From 1847,
    1920.
Houdini, Harry - A Magician Among the Spirits, 1924.

Conan Doyle, Arthur - The History of Spiritualism, 1926.
Frikell, Samri [Fulton Oursler] - Spirit Mediums Exposed, 1930.
Lawton, George - The Drama of Life After Death, 1932.
Dunninger, Joseph - Inside the Medium's Cabinet, 1935.
Mulholland, John - Beware Familiar Spirits, 1938.
Knight, Marcus - Spiritualism, Reincarnation, and Immortality, 1950.
Rinn, Joseph F. - Sixty Years of Psychical Research, 1950.
Hall, Trevor - The Spiritualists, 1962.
Brown, Slater - The Heyday of Spiritualism, 1970.
Christopher, Milbourne - ESP, Seers, and Psychics, 1970.
Hardinge, Emma - Modern American Spiritualism, 1970.
Jackson, Herbert G. - The Spirit Rappers, 1972.
McHargue, Georgess - Facts, Frauds, and Phantasm, 1972
Pearsall, Ronald - The Table Rappers, 1972
Price, Harry - The Confessions of a Ghost Hunter, 1974.
Christopher, Milbourne - Mediums, Mystics, and the Occult, 1975.
Stemman, Roy - Sprits and Spirit Worlds, 1975
Keene, M. Lamar - The Psychic Mafia, 1976.

b) Bibliographies of items on Spiritualism:

For far more information than I've given above see [in date order]:

* A cornucopia of material is Harry Price's Short-Title Catalogue of Works on Psychical Research, Spiritualism, Magic...., 1929, and the 1935 Supplement. It lists over 500 pages of books and other material. Price continued adding to his collection until his death in 1948. It is now part of The University of London Library. The up-to-date index is available on-line. You can spend a lifetime investigating Price's library and only scratch the surface of methods of deception. [Yes, I'm talking from experience.]
* M. Lamar Keene's 1976 book, The Psychic Mafia, includes an annotated bibliography of over 100 books.
* Part Four of Eugene Burger's Spirit Theater, 1986, lists 19 pages of annotated books under headings of History, Investigation, Manifestations, and Performance.

5) SLATE WRITING:

These references explain the trickery involved in pseudo-slate writing, and are just some of the many books I looked at while researching this one:

a) Books [in date order]:

Robinson, William E. - Spirit Slate Writing and Kindred
      Phenomena, 1898.
Hull, Burling - Original Slate Secrets, 1929.
Hull, Burling - The Invisible Hand Writes, 1929.
Warlock, Peter - Slates – a Learner's Course, 1941.
Warlock, Peter - The Best Tricks With Slates, 1942.
Corinda, Tony - Mini-Slate Magic, 1958.
Ganson, Lewis - Mini-Slate Magic, 1973.

b) Other sources of information [in date order]:

*Professor Hoffmann wrote How and What to Observe in Relation to Slate Writing Phenomena in The Journal of the Society for Psychical Research for August 1886.
* Hereward Carrington's 1907 book, The Physical Phenomena of Spiritualism, has a large section devoted to spirit writing on slates.

6) JUST SOME OF THE MANY MAJOR RESEARCH SOURCES UTILIZED:

- Harry Price Library in the University of London Library.
- Houdini's letters to Harry Price in the Harry Price Library.
- Magic Circle Library in the Centre for the Magic Arts (London).
- Conjuring Arts Research Center's online Ask Alexander
      Database (New York).
- Houdini's own personal scrapbooks on Ask Alexander. [The
      clippings are mainly unreferenced, but usually dated.]
- Various internet search and Houdini web sites.

TABLE OF CONTENTS

16501705R00177

Printed in Great Britain
by Amazon